URBAN PLANNING IN TRANSITION

URBAN PLANNING

EDITED BY Ernest Erber AIP

IN TRANSITION

Grossman Publishers NEW YORK 1970

Contents

PART 2 THE STATE OF THE ART

P A R T 3 THE PROFESSIONAL PLANNER'S ROLE

Foreword

With the publication of this volume, the American Institute of Planners makes available to a larger public a discussion of vital questions that will have to be answered if this nation is to develop the capability of mastering those problems associated with its rapid and continuing urbanization. The nature of these problems was explored by AIP on the occasion of its fiftieth anniversary, observed at its 1966 conference in Portland, Oregon, and its 1967 consultation in Washington, D.C. These meetings were devoted to taking a long look ahead—especially the 1967 consultation which assembled many of the world's foremost authorities on the future of man and his environment—to advise with the planning profession on what it might expect during the next fifty years. The volumes[1] which ensued from these conferences convey the insights and imaginative speculations of those exploring the frontiers of philosophy, science, the arts, and the evolution of the institutions that shape man's environment.

In 1968, the professional planners assembled in Pittsburgh to take stock of the implications of the look ahead toward 2017, and to decide on how they would respond as the discipline and the profession directly concerned with altering the future. In keeping with the 1968 conference theme, "The Planning Profession's Response to Now Challenges," the papers which follow reflect the urgency of that challenge as the authors address themselves to the urban scene of the 1970's.

The American Institute of Planners is indebted to those who contributed to make this timely volume possible; my predecessor, Irving Hand, who led AIP during the two years that marked the completion of its first half century and the entrance into its second; Ernest Erber, who as Program Chairman, commissioned the papers presented at the Pittsburgh conference

[1] Ewald, William R., Jr., Editor, *Environment for Man—The Next Fifty Years*, Bloomington, Ind., Indiana University Press, 1967. *Environment and Change—The Next Fifty Years*, 1968. *Environment and Policy—The Next Fifty Years*, 1968.

and edited this volume, and last, but not least, the more than thirty authors who contributed to the pages that follow.

July 1969
Washington, D.C.

Alan M. Voorhees
President
American Institute of Planners

ERNEST ERBER

Urban Planning in Transition

AN INTRODUCTORY ESSAY

The rattle of gunfire in the streets of Harlem in 1964 and the incendiary conflagrations that lit the night sky over Watts in the following year heralded the detonation of the social dynamite that had accumulated in American cities, especially in the decades since World War II. The urban problem, no longer confined to the esoteric pages of academic journals, became a daily topic for the press and air waves. The words "Urban Crisis," now capitalized, became part of the common currency of the public affairs dialogue.

The public reacted with renewed surprise and shock at each successive revelation of the extent of inter-group hostility, social dislocation, and institutional malfunction. Even those millions of postwar relocatees who had moved from the cities—in part in flight from a worsening environment, in part in attraction to suburban amenities—had not suspected the extremity of the cities' plight until the events of the Sixties laid bare ever deeper layers of diseased urban tissue—social, economic, and physical.

Though the public had not been well served with an early warning system on the urban scene, they *could* have known from the studies of the city and regional planners that American cities were headed for deep trouble. Its form, however, had remained somewhat obscure, if not misread, in the planners' warnings, and the turbulent events caught planners hardly less by surprise than the rest of the nation. As the planning profession adapted to the rapidly moving urban developments, it began to undergo a transition in role, function, and methodology. The urban crisis, in triggering programs that greatly enlarged the role of government in the social and economic affairs of society, increased the planners' awareness of the more subtle, but yet deep, on-going changes that have for some decades been affecting the governmental and cultural context within which planning takes place. The awareness grew, if for no other reason than because of the changes in the roles planners were being called upon to play. The fiftieth anniversary of the American Institute of Planners in 1967 helped measure the extent of urban planning's transition from its origins in civic design. It caused planners to realize also that the transition of their profession continues into an as yet unclear future role in a rapidly changing American society already vastly different from that served by city planning's pioneers in the early decades of the century.

The effort to comprehend the dynamic of planning's transition and its implications for the future compose the theme of the papers that constitute this volume. Initially prepared for the 1968 conference of the American Institute of Planners, the papers represent the most comprehensive effort to date to analyze planning's new and expanded role in American society and *who* should do *what* kind of planning. These questions come under three major headings: the changing societal context within which planning is carried on; the changing methods by which it is done; and the changing roles in which planners are cast and their capability to function in them. Each of these questions is the basis for one of the three parts into which this volume is divided. The three parts of the theme are, of course, inseparable if one seeks to comprehend fully the nature of the transition now under way. It is necessary to recognize their linkages. Since each paper is written within the purview of its own specific subject matter, however, this essay seeks to provide the reader with a framework designed to relate the separate pieces to the whole and to each other.

The future of America's cities has always been, of necessity, the focal point of the planner's professional concern. Consequently, planners were fully cognizant of the economic, technological, and demographic trends that were undermining the cities' stability in the period before World War II. If the planners' preoccupation with densities, land-use compatibility, and traffic movement (abetted by a limited sensitivity to social tensions resulting from their middle-class backgrounds) blinded them to the rapidity with which the unsolved ills of race and poverty were rising to the flash point, they *did* know and publicly declare that America's cities were headed toward deep crises. The literature of the planning profession for the postwar decades, and even as far back as the between-the-wars Twenties and Thirties, is replete with a concern for the future workability of America's cities that amounted to a preoccupation with the subject of impending breakdown. The breakdown was described by planners in terms of declining economic function, housing obsolesence, traffic congestion, and the deterioration of municipal services. The planners' failure to perceive the breakdown also in its social and political forms, specifically in terms of race and poverty, is significant to the profession for purposes of its own self-analysis. It is hardly significant to the nation as a whole, however, in examining its failure to respond to the planners' ample warnings of serious trouble ahead.

Today it is customary for many latter-day urban experts to seek to enhance their own stature by making snide references to the planners' long preoccupation with "brick and mortar" planning when it is people who should matter. To know that this is not the whole truth one need only read the planning literature of the decades before the social scientists discovered "maximum feasible participation." Henry S. Churchill's *The City is the People* is a good place to begin. Though it is untrue to charge that planners engaged in land use and transportation planning were ignorant of social conditions in cities, it is true that the *practice* of planning was confined almost entirely to the physical environment. A criticism of this shortcoming should not be directed at the planning profession, however, but rather to those who determined the sphere and limits of planning in American society. If the planning profession is to blame for the absence of social planning in the past, it is only in the same vein that the social work profession is to blame for the existence of the now discredited welfare system and the absence of a guaranteed annual income, or the political scientists for the absence of "participatory democracy" or a workable system of inter-governmental relations in metropolitan areas.

Since the papers that ensue are largely self-critical analyses by the planning profession (additional barbs are supplied by critics from other fields), it is useful to introduce some balance at this point by dwelling on the perceptions of planners in the past in diagnosing the fatal trends in central cities and calling for timely remedies. The nation did stand forewarned by planning studies that its urban timbers were rotting and that severe storms were brewing. The inaction of the nation in the face of these storm warnings is unrelated to the warning's lack of specificity as to wind direction or velocity. It should have been enough to have been told that the urban structure was coming apart at the seams without being informed as to which seams would give way first. Or enough to have been told that the end was in sight, even if misinformed that it would be with a whimper rather than a bang.

Typical of planners' doomsday literature on the urban future is J. L. Sert's *Can Our Cities Survive?*, based on a decade of studies by an international group of town planners and architects and published by Harvard Press in 1942. "Up to recent times," wrote Sert, "city planners have disregarded the fact that, when a certain degree of maturity is reached in the cities of today, they universally exhibit the same alarming symptoms. *These endanger their very existence."*

After describing increasing congestion, spreading blight, and intensifying chaos, Sert notes that the city dweller observes "this process going on— from his home, on his way to work, or in the vicinity of his office, shop, or factory. Throughout the whole daily cycle, his life is in some way affected by the city's ills, and he is aware that something is wrong." Noting that the modern city is a product of modern technology, Sert observes that, as applied to the city, "it carries within itself the elements capable of destroying the concentrated metropolis it has helped to create." The failure to make the city livable, Sert declared twenty-seven years ago, causes people "to abandon their over-crowding neighborhoods for 'a quiet home' in remote suburbs, undeterred by hours of uncomfortable travel back and forth. Industry, too, moves out—to cheaper land, to regions of lower taxes, to convenient sites on rail sidings or side roads. *The city is breaking up.* Such dispersion of great cities knows neither control nor planning. It is provoked by urban chaos itself, and is facilitated by modern means of transportation."

Showing an awareness of public ignorance and apathy, Sert challenged his contemporaries: "It has not even occurred to most people to question the condition of our cities. A conscious minority, however, familiar with the gravity of the situation and recognizing its eventualities in the near future, might well ask themselves the question: Can—and should—our cities survive?"

Writing only a few months after V-Day (December 1945), Charles S. Ascher, then director of the Urban Development Division of the Federal National Housing Agency, stated the case for *Land Assembly for Urban Redevelopment,* one of the agency's publications that set forth the basis for Title One of the Housing Act of 1949. It was written to warn against the consequences of supplying all new housing on vacant land at the metropolitan fringe.

Citing the need for 12,600,000 new nonfarm homes in the decade ahead, Ascher asked, "Where will these millions of new homes be built?" He then described the deceptive ease of spreading out over the distant landscape: "There is no dearth of land on the fringes of most cities. Land appears to be available in large tracts, easily assembled, at reasonable prices. There is no cost for tearing down old structures. There are often fewer controls in the outlying townships, no building code, no zoning regulation. These factors attract the builder to the fringe land.

"The families who are to live in these new houses are also attracted to the fringe in search of human values for themselves and their children; openness, greenery, play space, community feeling. Low taxes are accepted happily, without too much thought for the inadequacy of services that go with them.

"This search is sometimes an illusion. If too few neighbors arrive, services remain inadequate. Streets remain unpaved, there is no good high school within easy reach. If the fringe land becomes more intensely developed, the demand for urban services—police protection, better schools —drives up the cost of government. The empty lots are no longer open for softball games. The commuting grind may become wearing after a while.

"Meanwhile, slums and blighted areas in the centers of cities rot."

No one argued with the planners' warning that building housing only on the open land on the metropolitan fringe would cause the cities to rot away; nor with the planners' broader question, "can our cities survive?" It was not as if the planners' voice struck the solid wall of a canyon and bounced back—it was simply spoken into a vacuum. No one answered the planners because no one was called upon to defend a national urban policy, since none existed. FHA continued to underwrite wholesale the subdivision of land for tract housing, and the Bureau of Public Roads continued to underwrite extensions of the highway system to service new land development. Each did what came naturally, given their programs and their constituencies. Urban sprawl was not a national policy; it was the by-product of specific programs that were, so to speak, policy-neutral.

"Policy-neutral"; this traditional stance of government in the United States vis-à-vis social and economic development must be understood as the essential starting point in constructing a framework within which this volume's separate papers can form a comprehensible whole. "Policy-neutral" is the other side of the coin of what Alan Altshuler speaks of as "the tremendous vitality of American pluralism" (p. 183). The latter would be described by the current undergraduate generation as "everyone doing his own thing" and "working out of their own bag." Policy neutralism and pluralism are the the the two complementary sides of the coin of anti-planning; at least, as the negation of overall or comprehensive planning.

The history of planning in the United States is its genesis in confinement to the minimum feasible role by a nation dedicated to maximum private initiative, and the efforts of planners, allied from time to time with the more farsighted political currents (as under both Presidents Roosevelt), to bring the "dynamism of pluralism" into balance with national purpose in terms of the conservation and national allocation of resources and the maximum opportunity for social mobility made possible by freedom of choice, enabled, to the extent necessary, by public provision for health, education, welfare, housing, transportation, and recreation.

America's historical dedication to unfettered freedom in private exploration of resources made it anti-planning in its basic philosophy, both as institutionalized dogma and as popular mores. We hero-worshipped the "rugged individualist." The entrepreneur was at the top of the status index; the civil servant way down the list. Teachers were rated by the quip that "those who can—do; those who can't—teach." Private enterprise was cloaked with a sanctity given no other secular institution, and government was viewed as a necessary evil with that government governing best that governed least. This hardly constituted favorable soil for the growth of a profession based on the concept that the utilization and allocation of our resources would benefit from establishment of deliberate goals by public authority to be achieved through systematic control of development by governmental agencies.

If the rationality of the planners' proposition could not be refuted in principle, it could be utilized if confined to functions that caused no appreciable interference with the free play of pluralist market forces. One such function was the regulation of land use and the planning of public facilities by local government. Industrialization and rapid urbanization had caused unplanned land use to become a threat to another American value as powerful as pluralism and as essential to it as its material base—private property in land and buildings. The unplanned growth of municipal public improvements made property values uncertain and local tax rates chaotic. The municipality, a public corporation, was also engaged in pluralistic enterprise in competition with its neighbors. The ability of a municipality that planned its development to be a more effective competitor for desirable additions to the local economic base therefore became another reason for planning. Thus was born in this sternly individualistic nation a profession based on planning.

Planning was accorded a very small corner of the action in the vast, powerful, expanding interaction of economy, social forces, and government that shaped industrial and urban America in the twentieth century. The planners' corner, the severely limited authority of municipal planning, was subjected to the impact of the powerful pluralist forces operating through the market, facilitated by government programs adapted to their needs. The municipality was caught up in the economic and social forces of development and shaped by it. The city planner's role was to mitigate the worst effects of industrialism and urbanism upon his limited territory. America had made comprehensive planning the tail to the pluralist dog. Planning was assigned the task of *counteracting* the effects of industrialization and urbanization upon the environment but was never assigned the redirecting of these basic forces to make their effects beneficial rather than harmful.

City planners occupied themselves with design for improved civic appearance, with traffic movement, parks and boulevards, subdivision of land and zoning, location of schools and town halls. To the extent that their efforts collided with political machines that made development subject to political needs rather than a master plan, planning became identified with municipal reform, usually a business- and taxpayer-based movement. Within the pluralist spectrum, therefore, planners became aligned with middle-class, business, home-owning, largely suburban forces, because this was the only segment of American society that had need for planning, if only in a severely restricted role. For the rest of the nation, the planner was the "girl with a big bust when Twiggy is in style" as Henry Cohen aptly puts it (p. 174).

Despite the limitations placed on planning at the local level by too little authority and territorial limitations, and perhaps in part because of these constraints, planners applied themselves assiduously to devising a methodology that would make the practice of planning subject to the recognized principles, standards, and techniques common to a profession. How else could they master the knowledge for planning in a basically anti-planning culture other than by self-development? Their efforts resulted in techniques for research, codification, analysis, synthesis, projection, and plan formulation that have become uniquely identified with the planning profession. Since the early planners came from architecture, landscape architecture, and engineering, soon to be joined by those from the legal profession via zoning, aspects of planning methodology can be traced to these other professions. In later decades planning borrowed from the social sciences, especially economics. The methodology of planning, however, is *sui generis* and quite alien to the average practitioner of these ancestral disciplines.

City planning was the only area of American life and letters concerned with the systematic examination of the techniques of purposeful and systematic change of the natural and man-made environment. Business administration and military logistics also emphasized planning. But their objectives were within "closed systems" with high degrees of predictability and control. This led to methodologies designed to affect relatively few phenomena which were, consequently, far less complex than planning methodology. After all, business and the military are institutions *within* society; the city, on the other hand, is a slice of society itself and, depending upon size, contains to a lesser or greater degree combinations of all the factors found in society as a whole.

It is this aspect of city planning that forced planners to be comprehensive. They could not be content with "problem solving," that rediscovered panacea of a recent crop of urban experts. Planners learned early in their experience that the solving of a problem without a comprehensive plan usually results in worsening other problems or simply shifting it to another location. Comprehensive planning *is* problem solving, but within a knowledge of all interrelated factors and within a time perspective of changes affecting them.

During the 1920's and into the 1930's, planners became increasingly aware of the uniqueness of their function. They began to inquire whether the basis of their profession was a special knowledge of how cities develop or a special methodology for predicting and controlling purposeful change that had application to all forms of developmental phenomena. This question is inherent in the sharp exchange between Lewis Mumford and Thomas Adams in 1932,[1] upon the publication of the *Plan for New York and its Environs,* prepared under Adams' direction. Mumford saw the plan as superficial because it failed to encompass basic social and economic objectives. Adams defended the plan as a metropolitan application of the tested techniques of city planning.

The Mumford–Adams polemic highlighted the differences between the two schools of thought that had begun to crystallize in the 1920's.[2] Each drew, in large part upon different international, largely British, planning theory and practice. Mumford was a disciple of Patrick Geddes, the proponent of a unitary planning concept which viewed the natural environment, man's artifacts, and his social and economic functions as an integral whole. Adams was a disciple of Ebenezar Howard and Raymond Unwin, whose model garden suburbs had a profound influence on city-planning theory.

[1] *New Republic,* June 15 and July 6, 1932.
[2] Roy Lubove's *Community Planning in the 1920's* contains an excellent analysis of these trends. (University of Pittsburgh Press, Pittsburgh, 1963, p. 155.)

The Geddes tradition and the Howard-Unwin tradition started from a common rejection of the urban environment created by industrialism, especially the overcrowding of central cities and planless engulfment of their surrounding countrysides, including once pleasant towns and villages. They also shared in seeking to design residential environments that emphasized lower densities, open space, and land-use and circulation arrangements that emphasized community purpose and convenience. But Geddes was basically a social critic who saw the slag heaps and slums as manifestations of shortcomings in industrial society that went far deeper than errors in city building. He consequently sought solutions that embraced national and regional reallocation of resources and regroupment of population to provide an economic basis for a different social, as well as physical, environment.

Mumford, and the talented group with whom he was associated in the Regional Planning Association of America, came in time to view model garden suburbs as interesting experiments that had only passing significance for the major challenges faced by planners.

Adams and the Regional Plan Association, formed to implement and extend his plan, accepted the basic social arrangements and the metropolitan concentration of resources and population as "givens" and sought to create a more rational and livable environment by specific improvements that would bend trends within the major thrust of urban development.

From the vantage point of historical retrospection, we can conclude that Mumford and Adams were both right within their respective roles—Mumford as social critic and Adams as practicing planner. Mumford knew that Adams' regional plan would not touch the lives of those city residents who were underpaid or unemployed, insecure, ill-housed, and helplessly adrift in shifting, purposeless urban change. Nor would it offset the imperious concentration of people and wealth in a dozen metropolitan centers that sucked the rest of the country dry of resources and talent and returned to it packaged foodstuffs and packaged culture, including packaged architecture.

Adams, on the other hand, knew that he was preparing plans for action. They could be the basis for action only if confined to the existing limits imposed by society's value system and the political reality of the given distribution and balance of power. Adams' rationale was that of the workaday planning profession. It could not be otherwise, because, as Henry Cohen postulates in his perceptive analysis of planning and decision-making (p. 174), "The placement of the planning function in the decision-making system is determined largely by forces outside of the planning field." These forces have changed considerably in their needs for planning in the almost four decades between the Mumford-Adams exchange and the publication of this volume. The planning profession has repeatedly re-adapted its function in response to the changing role of government in social, economic, and environmental affairs.

As noted by Louis B. Wetmore (p. 227), the planners debated their function in 1936–38 and decided to change the name of their professional organization from American City Planning Institute to American Institute of Planners and to enlarge their area of concern to encompass city, state, region, and nation. Though challenged by some who sought to have planners also encompass planning of nonphysical change, AIP decided to let well enough alone and reaffirmed its function as primarily land-use planning. It remained thus until the impact of the urban crisis in the 1960's raised the question anew and initiated the current transition in planning.

It was not coincidental that the planning profession redefined its role in the late 1930's and again in the late 1960's. Each decade was marked by major enlargements of government's roles in social and economic affairs; the first under the rubric of the New Deal and the second under that of the Great Society. In each case planning's role was considerably enlarged as government assumed responsibility for social and economic well-being in areas where private enterprise had failed, requiring planners in previously unplanned fields.

Franklin Delano Roosevelt proclaimed at his inaugural that Americans have a right to look to their government for social and economic action when other institutions in the pluralist spectrum fail them. Roosevelt, making good his promise of federal initiative, moved on many fronts, temporarily curbed only by a conservative Supreme Court.

Price regulation in manufacturing and agriculture, collective bargaining, minimum wages, public housing, reforestation, public works on a massive scale, stimulation of county and state planning, TVA, and planned green-belt towns characterized the New Deal's programs to counteract the Depression and move the nation forward once more. "Rugged individualism" became the subject of cartoonists' grim humor and a pluralist competition ensued for federal intervention in each segment of society—farmers, home owners, bankers, labor, oil producers, and the unemployed, all looked to federal programs to rescue them.

It became apparent that government required a knowledge of the resources of the nation, such as it had never needed before, to guide its efforts in putting the country back together again. This need gave rise to the National Resources Planning Board—the nation's first and only peace-time effort to plan comprehensively at the national level. NRPB gathered a staff which included outstanding social scientists, lawyers, architects, engi-neers, and city planners. The latter served as a conduit for planning methodology, developed at the local and regional levels, to flower into new perspectives on national planning of such physical resources as minerals and such social resources as manpower.

This pioneer work in national-resource planning served the nation well in expediting mobilization of resources for World War II. Its concept of federal monitoring of the economy was carried into the Full Employment Act of 1946 and the establishment of the Council of Economic Advisors.

The Housing Act of 1949 gave rise in 1954 to Section 701 which provided federal funds for local, regional, and state planning. In pace with the vast expansion of the suburbs, 701 funds fueled a proliferation of local planning. The need for professional planners became insatiable. The pro-fession doubled in size every few years. But there was no progress during the 1950's toward a renewal of the steps toward national planning begun in the 1930's. The only major national planning during the Eisenhower hiatus was the execution of the previously planned National Highway Project—the construction of over 40,000 miles of expressway, called the largest public works project in history. It proved to be devoid of comprehensive planning when its urban sections became battlegrounds as municipalities tried to relate the expressway alignments to comprehensive city plans and the continued integrity of neighborhoods. In this phase of pluralist compe-tition, highway engineers triumphed over comprehensive planners. One of the victims was public transportation, again coming to the fore in the 1970's as the urban expressways fail to solve journey-to-work congestion.

The Gross National Product, specifically its size and growth rate, emerged as a critical issue in the 1960 presidential election campaign. John F. Kennedy contended that the national economic growth rate was a re-sponsibility of government. The issue ushered in a decade of renewed penetration of social and economic affairs by governmental action. More so than in the past, it became a conscious practice to use the federal budget, tax policy, and credit control as tools for regulation of the national economy, based on relatively short range planning by the Bureau of the Budget, the Council of Economic Advisors, and the Federal Reserve Board.

Congress enacted the Area Development Legislation, based on the con-cept that regional economic retardation is unhealthy for the nation, and launched a major project designed to raise the level of economic activity and living standards in Appalachia; this was regional planning on the scale and functional inclusiveness first set forth by the Regional Planning Association of America in the 1920's. (Alas, there is no evidence that its execution encompasses their dimensions of social invention.)

The Sixties also saw a resurgence of the federal government's efforts to conserve natural resources and protect the nation from the alarming increase in air and water pollution. Under the energetic direction of Secretary of the Interior Stewart L. Udall, the federal program, which he called conservation's "Third Wave," took on new dimensions. The program was increasingly based on new concepts of ecological balance, resulting in firmer resistance to short-range economic gains made at the expense of long-range damage to nature's restorative capability. The program was also increasingly urban-oriented. It made the existence of an urban America and a projected population in excess of 300 million the basis for proposals on pollution control and open space conservation.

Conservation programs in the past had been based either on the need to conserve timber, mineral and other natural resources for long-range economic needs or on the values of wilderness and wildlife protection. In its "Third Wave," federal conservation concepts began to merge with those of regional planners on the relation of urbanization to natural resource management, based on a common recognition that a highly urban nation would be livable only if it paid the price to assure itself a quality environment. An increasing number of planners found that employment on federal conservation programs was compatible with their professional standards and social ideals, though they remain frustrated by the unsolved policy questions debated in this volume by Ralph M. Field (p. 56). Lynton K. Caldwell (p. 71), and Malcolm D. Rivkin (p. 83). The latter address themselves to an aspect of national resource planning that comes increasingly into focus in the annual battle over the national budget allocations as, specifically, questions of priorities for pure water vs. housing for the poor; open space conservation vs. education; underground power lines vs. public transportation, and so forth.

Metropolitan disparities, administrative fragmentation, and functional chaos created by planless sprawl around central cities received an increasing amount of attention from the federal establishment in the Sixties, especially with the creation of the Department of Housing and Urban Affairs and the widely distributed studies of the Advisory Committee on Intergovernmental Relations, echoed in Congress by Senator Edmund Muskie.

Planners were active participants in the ensuing efforts aimed at the creation of metropolitan mechanisms for planning and limited governance.

Metropolitan regional studies, adequately financed with federal funds, were initiated in the largest Standard Metropolitan Statistical Areas, initially focused on transportation but eventually included land use, employment, population, and open space. Housing remained significantly omitted. These studies made extensive use of electronic data processing and simulation models. Regional planning reviews, as a prerequisite for a wide range of federal aid grants, began to establish planning on an official and all but mandatory basis. Planning was being interrelated across levels of government, and local planning was being rescued from its insulation, a condition that had rendered it ineffective in coping with the major forces of urbanization and, at the same time, permitted its misuse for antisocial purposes, such as the exclusion of lower income groups.

The emergence of official regional planning agencies with review powers and the establishment of metropolitan councils of governments began to create a new political and administrative framework for planning on the urban scene. Countless new questions were raised for planners as to the most effective roles of the different levels of government, the relationship of land-use control to tax policy, and the apparent contradiction of efforts to curtail suburban home rule at a time when central city neighborhoods were asserting their demands for community control. The possible solutions are reviewed in Hans Blumenfeld's paper on national policy for urban land-use planning (p. 88) and Rita D. Kaunitz's paper on the role of state government in urban affairs (p. 102).

For the vast public, urban problems came to mean the black upsurge, the war on poverty, and the government's expanded programs for health, education, and welfare. As indicated at the beginning of this essay, no new public issues had the dramatic impact on the planning profession as did those related to race and poverty. In measure, this was due to the proliferation of governmental programs triggered by urban unrest. Planners found it necessary to adapt and readapt their programs and procedures to the rapidly changing urban scene. Planners also found a need for their services in new programs where "software" planning was involved. Since these programs dealt with measures to enhance the earning ability of the poor, planners became engaged in long-range manpower planning and its related field of skill escalation. Planners found their methodology useful in areas distantly removed from site planning or zoning or traffic flows; as distant as the subject matter of the papers by Bernard J. Frieden (p. 281), E. David

Stoloff (p. 295) or Jerome W. Lubin (p. 299) from the writings of Daniel Burnham, Frederick Law Olmstead or Edward M. Bassett.

Increasingly questions were raised as to the nature of "software" planning: exactly what is social planning? And what does a social planner do? Bertram M. Gross, with a distinguished record of scholarship in the field, refers to social planning as "currently one of the great 'blah ideas' in America and the western world." Gross reacts to the confusion which surrounds most discussions of social planning, the confusion caused largely by those who exude great enthusiasm for the idea but little clarity as to what they mean (p. 52). John W. Dyckman's paper is a major contribution to clarification, especially in his distinction between social planning and societal planning (p. 27). Francis Fox Piven's rejoinder puts the issue within its political context by arguing that it is not the lack of social planning that causes a problem, but the kind of social planning we are getting (p. 45).

The impact of problems of race and poverty upon the planning profession cannot, however, be explained only by the new roles it has opened for planners, nor the enthusiasm and confusion over social planning it has generated. Its impact stems rather from the emergence of the organized participation of the poor, largely racial minorities in the planning process with the concomitant appearance of professional planners as their advocates.

Advocacy planning is not a new role for planners. In the past, business-based groups often had professional planners on their staffs, or as consultants, to review official proposals and, if they differed, to challenge them. Middle-class reform groups also availed themselves of planner advocates. So did suburban home-owner groups when engaged in opposing a highway alignment. "Citizen participation" in the planning process had long-standing and respectable status among planners. Somehow it was different with the emergence of the poor—perhaps because their challenge did not proceed from the same set of values and was not garbed in espousal of noble civic purposes. The poor wanted an advocate able to get a "bigger piece of the action" for them or to resist urban renewal "simply" because it meant relocation from their homes and often from their neighborhoods. No planner denied the right of the poor to seek planning advice on behalf of their own naked self-interest. But the impact of doing this cast a cloud over a concept that served planning as a bedrock principle—the public interest.

Professional planners had always noted that their services were *pro bono publico*. The planners' code of ethics differs from that of the design professions from which it stemmed because its point of departure is the public interest, while the ethics of other professions stress fidelity to the client's interests, usually in the private domain.

Planners were trained in the tradition that their client was the public. However, if one planner represents city hall, another a downtown business group and the third a community organization of the poor, who represents the public interest?

The effort to answer this question raised the further question: *is* there a public interest? For planners, this question takes on the dimensions of the "God is dead" controversy in theological circles. Its implications, already quite plain for most planners, are spelled out in Altshuler's advice that planners seek clients from the wide pluralist spectrum of interest groups in American society. The exchange between William and Margaret Wheaton (p. 152) and C. David Loeks (p. 165), with observations by Charles R. Ross (p. 171), constitutes a penetrating exploration of the existence of a public interest above and beyond the claims of contending groups, or as a common bond of interest between them.

The implications of the challenge to the public interest doctrine are clear, direct and serious—and, if true, shattering. If there is no unifying public interest to be served, if the science and art of planning is to be placed in the service of each special interest group in a pluralist society, what happens to the concept of comprehensiveness? Can there be a profession and a discipline of planning without its unique and unifying concept that parts should be designed only in relation to wholes if balanced development is to result? Or is balanced development only another way of saying "social equilibrium," a state of affairs far more attractive to the haves than to the have-nots? Is this, perhaps, the clue to the unsettling train of events unloosed for the planning profession by Harlem and Watts? It would seem that this consequence of America's concern with race and poverty in the Sixties had far greater impact upon the planning profession than did the discovery that planning methodology was applicable to the "software" programs of HEW and OEO.

The Federal Government's increasing concern with urban affairs and the natural environment took the form of a proliferation of separate, largely unrelated programs revolving around grants and/or loans. Their rapid escalation and bewildering variety rendered useless the usual techniques by which the bureaucracy monitored programs and recorded results. This state of affairs hastened the introduction of a management tool rooted in the methodology of planning—the Plan-Program-Budget-System (PBBS)—

perfected in corporate business planning and introduced into the Federal Government via the military.

The rudiments of PPBS are to be found in such basic and early texts of city planning as Ladislas Segoe's *Local Planning Administration*[3] and Robert A. Walker's *The Planning Function in Urban Government*.[4] Planners had always sought to make the budget a servant of plans via programs, but they were rarely successful at the municipal level, except in capital budgeting. Though old-line fiscal officers were confounded by this new device, planners were definitely riding the tide when President Johnson's edict made PPBS the gospel for the entire federal establishment.

Thus at a time when comprehensiveness was being challenged in the name of pluralist advocacy and functionalist planning, government, confronted by myriad, unrelated, problem-solving programs, adopted as an essential working tool a management device, based on comprehensiveness and taken from the planners' methodology, for systematic, controlled application of resources to guide phenomena toward predetermined goals. In short, federal bureaucracy was told by presidential order to introduce planning into on-going administration. But if program administrators become planners, does this not place in question the role of a separate profession of planners? Or is each administrator to have a planner at his elbow to exercise the planning functions of administration? Would not the latter seem to be the trend in the corporate world, with the growing recognition of planning functions, evidenced by the increasing number of Vice Presidents in Charge of Planning, of Planning Departments within the corporate structure, and the growing emphasis upon planning services in the field of management consultation?

The new roles of planners in the "software" field, the emergence of PPBS, and the growing prominence of planning in nongovernmental institutions (business, hospitals, higher education) would seem to strengthen the thesis advanced by Henry Fagin (p. 125) and Herbert J. Gans (p. 239) that planning is basically a methodology that is transferable to all efforts to achieve selected goals by the systematic application of resources in programmed quantities and time sequences designed to alter projected trends and redirect them toward established objectives. This approach argues that what makes planning a discipline and its practice a profession is *what* it does and *how* it does it—not where or to what it is done. It would follow from this that planners have the capability of planning a

---

[3] The International City Managers' Association, Chicago, 1941, first edition.
[4] University of Chicago Press, Chicago, 1950.

city's future, not because they are experts on the city, but because they are experts on the realization of a chosen future. It follows then that the methodology by which this is done would be transferable to the future development of manpower, open space, mental health services, higher education, plant location, and the elimination of illiteracy.

Peter A. Lewis and Theodore E. Hollander challenge this thesis from the vantage points of other disciplines (pp. 142, 147). It is also challenged from within the planning profession by those planners who hold that the methodology of planning is uniquely related to land-use regulation. They contend that the effort to transfer planning from its traditional land-use base to a methodological base will diffuse the planning discipline into an unrecognizable amorphousness.

The test of planning's capability to exist as a universally applicable methodology would appear to begin with the ability of the discipline to train its practitioners to a competence in planning without regard to *what* they are planning, equally adept in planning the rehabilitation of neighborhoods or of unemployables. H. Wentworth Eldredge sees the training of competent planning staff as one of the most formidable obstacles to comprehensive planning at the national level (p. 3). It is Lawrence Mann's considered judgment that the future of planning education is "fuzzy" (p. 249). Despite the sharpness of Leo Jakobson's brilliant rejoinder, he gives little reason to believe that his various types of planning-school graduates will be universal methodologists (p. 266). Peter Lewis suggests that if Fagin's test for planning ability is valid, then the best planners should be turned out by the Harvard School of Business. But it should also be noted that Lewis prefers the Bureau of the Budget to a national planning organization.

Britton Harris offers some solace to the profession in prescribing data processing and model simulation made possible by the computer as operational tools to help master the complexity and fluidity of the phenomena the planner attempts to codify and analyze (p. 192). George M. Raymond does not see all this as resolving the really difficult problems (p. 203).

Archibald C. Rogers' paper (p. 302) serves to remind the profession of its traditional role in urban design. Perhaps the profession should consciously keep one foot planted on this terra firma before it shifts too much of its weight onto the foot that is exploring untested ground. As Isadore Candeub (p. 216) points out, there is little in traditional planning techniques that remains unchallenged.

How can the planning profession meet these many challenges—"software" roles, advocacy, ecological balance vs. economic development, universally applicable methodolgy? Louis Wetmore renders sober, practical advice to counteract the many heady brews being offered the profession. But is his advice usable within the rapidly changing current trends? With society in flux, with the public and private sectors threatening to swap roles in many spheres, with the discovery that the planner's skills provide a competitive advantage to his clients, who can tell in what way the profession will be called on to serve society in the future? Reminiscent of the ancient mockery of "physician cure thyself," the planning profession, which aims to plan the future of cities, states, and nations, is not able to plan its own future. In the end, the planner is the servant and society is the master.

That urban planning is in transition is abundantly clear from the papers which follow. It is left to the reader to interpret them, to conclude which, of several directions, it will, or should, take. The fact that the papers are all provocative, and a few downright brilliant, makes for stimulating reader involvement. It also makes for a cautious, deliberate formation of conclusions based on all the evidence and all the arguments.

This volume was made possible by the authorization and sponsorship of the American Institute of Planners. My designation as editor by the Board of Governors is deeply appreciated. I am indebted to many for their assistance and patience in the preparation of this volume, especially Robert L. Williams, Executive Director of AIP at the time this work was undertaken.

PART 1

THE SOCIETAL FRAMEWORK

H. WENTWORTH ELDREDGE

Professor of Sociology, Dartmouth College. Previously a
consultant on the White House Staff for International Se-
curity Affairs and a member of the President's Citizens
Committee for International Development. Lecturer at the
London School of Economics, Dartmouth College, and
NATO Defense College. "Visiting Scholar" guest of the
West German Republic and at the University of Ljubijana
in Yugoslavia. A.B., Dartmouth; Ph.D., Yale. Co-author:
Culture and Society. Editor: *Taming Megalopolis: An In-
troduction to Urban Planning and Urbanism.*

Toward a National Policy for Planning the Environment

The massive deterioration of the American environment, physically and
socio-psychologically, especially in the great cities of our overwhelmingly
urban nation, is serving as a clarion call to action by both the concerned
and those directly affected. A threat to the American dream of a civilization of style and quality is perceived by a sizable minority including
sophisticated intellectuals, governmental and business power holders,
questing young, and the alienated poor—especially the vociferous black
ghetto dwellers. The correction of the "long laundry" list of these ills could
be "the moral equivalent of war," enlisting the energies and enthusiasms of
the entire population for the rest of the century. A war for peace and
fruition, not death and destruction.

The three significant volumes resulting from the 1966 and 1967 American Institute of Planners' conferences on "The Next Fifty Years," edited
by William R. Ewald, Jr., and entitled *Environment for Man, Environment
and Change, Environment and Policy,* are an impressive start for a major
effort to develop a national policy for upgrading the environment. The
sheer bombardment of complex ideas contained therein is both stimulating
and bewildering. An Isaac Newton is called for to bring it all into perspective, with a "software" Leonardo to devise workable socio-politico-eco-

3

nomic gadgetry, along with a Machiavelli to put the resultant schemes into operation.

Predictably, the pragmatic upholders of segmental or incremental planning schemes emphasize that governments must cope with the overwhelming rush of events and "do something." It should be noted that "doing something" about slums by means of urban renewal actually exacerbated the slum housing picture and most certainly has played a part in the Negro revolt as another sign of "class oriented," incomplete, short-range remedial action. It should also be noted that the Interstate Highway System has further upset the housing balance as well as broken the back of passenger railroad traffic at a time when our air transportation system is cracking at the seams. No one disputes that immediate remedial action is needed, but it should be obvious to even the most "gung-ho" administrator that coping with visible ills on an *ad hoc* basis is not remotely connected with the planning ethos of strategic as well as tactical schemes for clearly delineated goals, based on the careful selection of options and a recognition of realistic, actual, and potential resource allocation possibilities.

It is important that the basic intellectual position represented here be clarified. *Standort* is the correct philosophical term for these seven tenets of belief and concern, not uncommon today among generalist, problem-oriented social scientists:

1. Total environmental planning is the only way to cope with today's challenge to our survival as a civilized society. Such planning must deal with the natural environment; population; national territory; social-political-economic-cultural functions; and extended time. This has been called holistic planning; it deals with macro-scale systems.

2. Rapid socio-cultural change is clearly accelerating; problems seem to come faster than solutions. The leading independent variable in this rush of change is *not* technology, as is usually naively stated, but new (often scientific) knowledge which results in physical technology and, more important, in managerial or societal technology (the design and management of human institutions and, increasingly, of persons). Planners are basically concerned with "monkeying" in institutional design; they are engaged in exploration into this crucial area of societal technology—the redesigning of our societal institutions and how they work. That physical technology is bound up in this process is patent.

3. Postive planning with goals of style and quality for life (however defined) rather than remedial/contingency/adaptive/negative planning should be the planner's aim. We choose the mirage of optimum environ-

ment. Planners are engaged, to modify Herman Kahn's phase, in searching for *alternate possible futures* of merit.

4. "Planning means Freedom" which is not *newspeak* but the conclusion as well of philosopher Charles Frankel in his 1963 paper before AIP. A complex society, with a complex culture and a huge population, in a rapidly shifting world, needs large-scale systems of management or everything will go out the window despite the ignorant youngsters of the New Left. Planning can both save and enlarge our cherished values.

5. Options must not be closed out. The old planning phrase was "make flexible plans"; it is now embodied in the new cybernetics approach to planning-as-a-process with continuous feedback into revised goals, into revised plans, programs, and administrative devices and processes. With predictable shifts in values, this generation's Utopia may be the next generation's hades. Open-ended options are the watchword.

6. Professional administration (rule by experts) versus participatory democracy ("planning-with-people") is the dilemma of the late twentieth century. Robert Wood agrees with the Center for the Study of Democratic Institutions that postindustrial society must arrive at some sort of Hegelian synthesis of these two polar positions, which is much easier to posit than to accomplish. The Model City program is a major experiment in this direction—although on a micro-scale in each city—and we could learn much from it. Can alienated little people, in a world they never made and do not really understand, play a meaningful part in running a society which is seemingly becoming daily less understandable in its chaotic complexity—even to the so-called experts?

7. A mixed polity is a fact. We freely discuss the advantages of a mixed economy in outperforming both wooden communism and an anchronistic laissez faire. But we fail to recognize in our pluralistic society that not only do three-tiered governments govern, but also that in addition government corporations, government bureaus, private foundations, quasi-private corporations, quasi-public corporations, foundations, universities, labor unions, private corporations, free associations including even SDS—all play a part in governance. This is certainly a mixed polity, perhaps a mixed-up polity. It pains my ordered bourgeois soul (long nurtured on sound structure-function analysis) to agree that perhaps in this untidy process of our moving, muddled society we can get more lift than through an orderly pattern—inadequately perceived. Do we really get more horsepower out of this phantasmagoric mess? The answer seems optimistically to be "yes." In any case, no one is going to order the American political process in the

foreseeable future. In some circles this is deemed to be a "behavioral political science approach"—operationally oriented.

The United States is most certainly experiencing today a weird period in its history; we have never had it so good, or been so powerful, as the Frenchman Servan-Schreiber has told us, and yet we have seldom been nearer to the rending of the delicate fabric of community that tenuously unites our multi-groups! It would be quite useless to catalog our well-publicized bundle of national problems; but one wonders whether there is any genuine urgency felt by our middle-class majority of solid citizenry to grow up and actually face our problems in adult fashion.

According to Tom Wicker in *The New York Times* of September 10, 1968, that sturdy middle-class majority, "The Forgotten American" of Richard Nixon, could not care less about America's multiplex dilemmas, ". . . and he is the fellow whose massed voice tells the rest of us that we will not have gun-control laws, we will not have better cities at the expense of higher taxes, we will not have racial equality in jobs, housing and unions, and that our lives will remain blighted with all the ills and ugliness that cost tax money or business profits to remove."

Can our citizenry be made to see that the monumental task of preparing our society for the twenty-first century is "the moral equivalent of war"?—with all its excitement, challenge, and danger? The first stage in the development of a national environmental policy would seem to be massive public education. As Gunnar Myrdal pointed out to the AIP conference of 1967, American affluence is heavily mortgaged by our miserable cities and our miserable poor. While man can adjust to almost anything, states René Dubos, it would seem that American man is presently adjusting to a woefully inadequate *internal environment,* himself. Unless the level of human sophistication can be raised markedly, our population will be prepared to do little about the external environment, as has been evident.

No modern socio-politico-economic planning system on a national scale can hope to be accepted—much less operate in any way successfully—with the human behavioral and societal norms of the contemporary United States. We are simply anachronistic in terms of modern attitudes, even more so in institutional forms and administrative practice. Even India has a putative five-year plan; admittedly our communal riots have been far exceeded there in viciousness, even though our black outcasts, too, rebel in the streets and on the roofs. The public education job before us in the land of juvenile attitudes and the land of the governmentally timid is immense. We have appeared to feel capable of organizing the world, but not ourselves. If today as planners whose constituency is both the future and the present, we engage in trend-bending, we most certainly have an imposing task ahead to prepare the USA for the twenty-first century, and perhaps even to survive the twentieth without internal system explosion. This excludes the always possible outside-the-system catastrophic intervention. Planners make revolution without blood in the gutters; they, too, deliberately foster change and hope to manage societal evolution for the "good of mankind."

Consideration must next be given to the dimensions of the total system that national planners must attempt to manage, not necessarily in totality, but at least by both tactical and strategic intervention hand-in-hand with governments per se and with their clients: the people of today and tomorrow. It hardly needs to be reiterated that America is not yet ready to accept a national plan, although quite possibly within a few years a national policy for planning the environment might be stomached. Our history and ethos are against it. But history has a way of being rushed by events such as the Civil War—not to mention Pearl Harbor—even the 1929 Depression launched the New Deal. It might just be possible in the 1970's to make a quantum jump in our societal management, by rational choice rather than as answer to catastrophic prod. If the useful, merely informatory, National Resources Planning Board disappeared in four years, some twenty-five year ago, let us not yet anticipate an immediate GOSPLAN for the USA, whether it be four, five, or six years in duration (although at least fifty developed and developing nations have such a societal device of more or less efficacy). There is, however, much preliminary work toward a national planning policy that can be undertaken immediately.

In the societal milieu of an alienated America, guilty and shocked about the first war in glorious color to enter the family dining room, with Black Power rumbling offstage as an earnest of missed promises, with dissident youth violently questioning the conventional values, here is a brief run-down on the parameters of the task for planning (or at least making preliminary policy for) a total national system for managing the total environment—all this under the rule of law. The scale of that task is awe inspiring in its dimensions and presently beyond our competence—which merely points up the question of how fast can we become competent. To repeat, to face this massive challenge is for our hopefully civilized society "the moral equivalent of war."

*

A micro-system plan is subject to continuous upset by variables outside the system: witness highway construction in the USA without a macro-system of total transportation planning—much less a national land-use plan—or local school development without a solid national education plan (fiscal and otherwise). The "real world" macro-system for effective planning purposes with which we are concerned and for which we are considering a national environmental policy, is the United States. No one disagrees with the reality of linkages with our territorial neighbors (and who isn't) and with the reality of multiple functional linkages outside our borders, and that both these connections are vital in the present and even more vital for the future. It is, of course, obvious that this macro-system of the USA can be upset by external variables. But the initial worthwhile exercise is the immediate exploration of the whys and hows of a total national environmental plan for the nation-state USA. It is methodologically handy to order the enormous press of phenomena to be managed into five major rubrics. They are as stated above the natural environment; people; territory; function; and time. Let us briefly explore each facet of this schema:

1. The natural environment. The term "natural" has already become a misnomer; man's works touch everything on earth (not to mention portions of space), but there is a residual physical, biological, generally ecological *place* in which man exists. That man is doing odd things to this place is evident. A widespread recognition of this "rape of the continent" has rightfully stirred up considerable ecological interest within recent years, sparked by such great environmentalists as William Vogt, reinforced by land economists such as Marion Clawson and conservationists such as William H. Whyte. The total ecological environment is being pushed back to a world system with man, the most rambunctious organism, inside as a major actor, as *The Territorial Imperative* and *The Naked Ape* indicate. The US national ecological environment with surface, sub-surface, and above-surface material elements; climate and geological environment states and changes; all plant and animal life with resources separated out of this matrix; these are the basic facets of this study of elemental importance. To plan America, it is necessary first to plan an on-going relationship with the natural environment. This is a truism which Hans H. Landsberg summed up nicely in a terse article published by *Daedalus* in 1967. His conclusion about our resource base is that while it is clearly possible to do without it, it seems more civilized to do with it in a planful fashion. Even the chemical industry's clever disaggregation of the flow of simple raw materials does not disprove the fact that resources are finite.

2. People: (a) population quantity. The key to any reasonable coping with the "revolution of rising expectations" in developing countries is a population limitation policy. Too little for too many is the hurdle in planning from scarcity—especially if the too many increase more rapidly than productivity, which appears to be the normal story. In the quasi-privately-affluent USA, bogged down by a strange war draining the public sector, we are seemingly losing ground in meeting the expectations of the slum-disadvantaged 20 to 30 per cent of the population, at least in their eyes. A drive for a rationalized increase in productivity initiated through the public and mixed sectors (including full use of under-used human resources) is clearly indicated immediately, as well as an altered distribution pattern—to be accomplished in large part through the partial transfer of the results of productivity by some such device as the guaranteed annual income or negative income tax. But above, beyond, outside, and fundamental to all this is an ordered birth-control policy in a massive program to match our haphazard, humanistic, death control. As is all too well-known, population management proposals here run head on into various forms and degrees of primitive superstition and the fact that the population-age structure of the USA precludes the possibility of having major results much before thirty years—even with an accepted, fully launched program. It is most assuredly time to start since, clearly, population densities and distribution will be much more awkward before they are much better. There is undoubtedly ample unused land, but it is in the shortest supply where needed most and cannot be reallocated under present public powers.

Thus, crude *quantity,* coupled with the trained *quality* of the population, is a key variable and perhaps the most powerful tool for planning intervention in a total environmental policy.

People: (b) population quality. "Modern man," as defined by Alex Inkeles, is a fragile creation possessed of semi-rationalism; he should exhibit these nine personality traits to qualify as modern:

(1) a readiness for new experience and an openness to innovation and change;

(2) a disposition to form or hold opinions about a large number of problems and issues that arise, not only in his immediate environment, but also outside of it, including a more democratic set toward opinion;

(3) an orientation to the present or the future rather than to the past;

(4) an orientation toward and involvement in planning and organizing as well as belief in it as a way of handling life;

(5) a belief that man can dominate his environment in order to advance his own purposes and goals;

(6) a certain confidence that his world is calculable and that other peoples and institutions can be relied upon to meet their obligations and responsibilities;

(7) an awareness of personal dignity in oneself and others, as clearly evidenced by attitudes toward women and children;

(8) more faith in science and technology;

(9) a great believer in "distributive justice"—rewards according to contribution not based on whim or qualities unrelated to this contribution.

Inkeles claims that the personalities of backward peoples must be altered to fit these nine characteristics in order to participate fully in modern society as modern men. It is patent that a sizable portion of the present United States does not qualify as modern men according to Inkeles' definition: training hardcore unemployed is much more difficult than first imagined:

> "It can involve teaching a man how to catch the correct bus, or how to get up in the morning, or getting him glasses so he may learn enough reading for simple jobs," Virgil E. Boyd, the president of Chrysler Corporation, said.
>
> "These people can't read simple words such as 'in' and 'out' signs on a door."
>
> "They have to be taught the letters that spell common colors, so they can read the instruction card that tells them to put a blue or green steering wheel on a car as it comes down the assembly line. And, they must learn simple addition so that they can count boxes of parts they take off a supplier's truck."
>
> "If you can't read, how do you know what it says on the destination signs of the many buses that go by on a given busy street. And a grown man isn't going to get on—and be sent off—the wrong bus very many times before he stops getting on buses any more. So we showed these people, one by one, how to recognize the right bus to take, and in some cases how and when to transfer to another necessary route."
>
> When Chrysler checked on why many were regularly late the company discovered that "only one in five owned an alarm clock. Why? Because they'd never had to be any particular place at any particular time before."

Unless the *internal environment* of man, himself, redevelops, neither institutional jockeying nor surface manipulation of the external physical environment (natural and man-made) will much effect the style or quality of life. It seems reasonable to assume that the full potential, in human terms, of the population's average level of intelligence has never been remotely approached, here or elsewhere. An effort to realize it calls for a massive reordering of national priorities and resources in order to upgrade the internal environment of human beings for the postindustrial "learning-society"—which after all is the putative purpose of the entire planning operation. This means earlier education, more intensive education, a larger education establishment, never-ending "public education," ceaseless re-treading education, more facilities, more teachers, better teachers, and so forth.

3. Macro-scale territory. It could be argued with reason that land use actually belongs under rubric 1 as part of the natural environment and an ecological fact. Obviously, this entire five-part treatment is an artificial method of dealing with a *Gestalt* or total pattern. Territorial scale, how-ever, is of such significant import that it merits a separate heading. To design a city block, a "neighborhood," to locate a single building—be it a factory, shop, movie, or home—without taking into consideration the total territory of a functional city is simply a form of intellectual and operational naïveté—from which many suffer. The system design of such mini-ex-amples is too small to lead to anything important in and of itself; outside variables weigh far more heavily than internal variables. Even the design of a single functional city or metropolis will suffer from the lack of a mean-ingful regional (including that megalopolitan urban region) scheme as part of a meaningful national land-use policy. This national territorial policy for urban, rural, and "raw" land must include decisions as to where to develop urbanization, industrialization, and the transport that links it, where to leave free space, and some decision on the optimum population/settlement grain (fine or coarse) of the varied parts of the total territory. These are key considerations basic to the management of a national system. In passing, mention should be made of Melvin Webber's non-territorial com-munity and a bow made to the communication-as-extension-of-transporta-tion continuum.

4. Function. It would take the poundage of numerous Ph.D. disserta-tions to begin to cover adequately this central bundle of planning param-eters. It includes the development of social, political, economic, cultural/aesthetic life. It is composed of both the societal structures and the physical forms; it is in common parlance social (better societal) planning on a macro-scale. In order merely to sketch the dimensions of the task and clarify the ideas here presented, there follows some slight amplification

and elucidation; gaps will be readily glimpsed in this too brief treatment:

   (a) social (end values)

      (1) the family and community inter-group relations are the cru-
      cibles of human personality and the arena of most human living
      (connected with housing and local community physical design);
      (2) positive health (mental and physical); (3) religious internal
      and external forms and meanings.

   (b) economic (instrumental values)

      (1) primary tier: raw material production, etc.; (2) secondary tier:
      production, etc.; (3) tertiary tier: service—transportation/com-
      munication of goods, people, and ideas (as a special case); (4)
      quarternary tier: education, etc., for postindustrial society.

It seems pointless here even to attempt to rip apart the complex interrelated facets of productivity, distribution, and consumption; to consider
varied forms of public and private enterprise; and to discuss at length the
workings of the system of labor, capital, and resources, however "owned."
While man does not live by bread alone, he can't live without it or its
equivalent. The structuring of the economic system gives the power to
produce the things and services to accomplish society's goals. Without the
increasing production, which gives the muscle to manipulate, there can be
little societal change; this by no means implies that the GNP is an end in
itself. Increasing productivity is only a means, but the fashion in which the
basic economic function is carried out quite correctly is recognized as
strongly conditioning ends.

   (c) political (instrumental values)

      The American political structure and process are both ready for
      redesign. It is far better for reasonable men to change our govern-
      ment by orderly processes, responsive to the altering societal milieu,
      than to have the fabric of life and the Constitution ripped apart by
      chaotic riot of violent minorities in the face of a leaden apathy on
      the part of the majority. The replanning of governmental structure
      and function is thus on the agenda as a major operation. Or must
      it be like birth control a decade ago—can't we even talk about
      major alteration in our form of government in public as respon-
      sible people? Specifically the forms and process of local govern-
      ment in relation to the metropolis; state government in relation to
      the regions; the form of the national government including the
      sacred Constitution itself, as well as the troika system of legislature,
      the courts, and the executive plus bureaucracy.

All of this structure in the late twentieth century is up for grabs; albeit orderly grabs to stave off, as the very minimal goal, disorderly ones!

  (d) recreational/higher cultural (end values)

      If postindustrial society is to be a learning and leisure society, we are as prepared to use "free time" in a positive fashion as the Congo and Nigeria/Biafra are to exercise responsible democracy. Sebastian de Grazia has gracefully informed us in *Of Time, Work and Leisure* that "free time" can be merely killed time and that leisure (the cultivation of one's potential) can, and must of necessity, be hard work. With increased time per day, per week, per year, per lifetime, "free," the organization of structure/form to meet function is as enthralling as necessary. "After abundance then what?" as Eric Larabee queries.

Kevin Lynch and others have sketched the aesthetic qualities which the environment may offer, although the relationship of physical form to behavior remains one of the great research challenges despite a growing bibliography of varied merit. It is a truism that the whole gamut of public, community, and private (profit and near profit) recreation, from the highly intellectualized to the most simple physical, or even to mindless loafing, must be increasingly thought through and resources assigned. The spectrum of optional recreational needs is endless and is connected with education and close to the end values of human life, except for those happy few whose rewarding work serves itself as leisure. But they are a small minority.

    5. Time. In remedial planning, the time span is immediate. In our federal budget, we manage to look ahead for one year in muddling capital accounting with current income and expenses. In our urban capital budgets with ordered priorities, we stretch out to five, ten, even fifteen years, in our schemes "to better" the urban lot—on a physical level with hoped for societal spin-offs. The benighted Marxists claim they plan for all eternity. Two years of offering an exploratory seminar in Futurism (in the varied environments of Berkeley and Hanover) have convinced me that it is not only possible but obligatory to operate plans and certainly form policies for macro-time spans. Despite the recognizable and well-publicized pitfalls of inadequate projection techniques, complexity of the system, value changes, unknowable variables inside and outside the system, there is a considerable pay-off in reaching out to 1980, 2000, and 2020 as did the contributors to the AIP commissioned articles for *Environment and Policy*. They were asked to contribute *realistic* plans, programs, and policies for up to fifty

years ahead. Elsewhere in a different connection I have listed six pay-offs
from Futurism studies for operational planning:

(a) Social change projection. Guide lines may here be glimpsed as to
what "surprise-free projections" and the "standard world" of the
future will be like.

(b) Alternate possible futures. This forces creativity and can be coupled
with hardheaded Plan-Program-Budget Systems (PPBS). It most
certainly upsets the trite acceptance of a given value system and a
unilinear evolutionary process. It reaffirms the faith that all planners
have in potential trend-bending and in building "desired states."

(c) Process. Futurism consists of what will be, what might be, why and
how to bend the trend. Process, as stated above, is implicit in this
form of intellectual/operationally-oriented exercise.

(d) Value shifts (possible ones) are forced to a high level of attention.
This is the most sensitive part of all macro-time-scale planning and
perhaps the most thought provoking.

(e) National economic and social accounting. The whole question of
monitoring change and the sophisticating of our present inadequate
and too shrewd monetary accounting, so ably presented by Bertram
M. Gross and by Sheldon and Moore is brought to the fore. Mention
should be made here of immediate possibilities for the combination
of information systems and sampling to amplify our hard data on
"soft" (socal, aesthetic, etc.) questions.

(f) People planning. The best of macro-time planning programs can
founder on shoals of babies—not to mention nonmodern adults. One
hardly dares to mention human genetic quality control—just around
the corner—a skill which no one is yet remotely prepared to exercise.

My schema for total environmental planning could be resliced or
combined into fewer or more components, but the key idea is to delimit a
meaningful macro-system. For purposes of both analysis and operation, the
system can be—must be—broken apart and dealt with in sub-systems, be
they space-, time-, or function-oriented. But again, each sub-system is not
an end in itself; it is a portion of a whole. All thought and action must be
holistic to work in the real world leading toward a national policy for
planning the environment.

As planners, we had better start planning the planners, who will make the
national plans. There are few such people readily available today in the
United States or anywhere else, although various planning types have been

retreaded in that direction. For this challenging task, we shall have to make preliminary judgments of what these future expert philosopher-kings will need to know. How to plan several decades hence the ever more complex United States, rumbling about at an even more rapid pace in an ever more complex world, is an awesome assignment.

Quite frankly many are somewhat pessimistic as to whether the United States in its present form is capable, given its history and social values, of succeeding in coping with the imposing societal problems of the not-too-distant future.

To begin with, the research professional schools must be set up to train the planners; hopefully cybernetic feedbacks will modify schools, curricula, and practice as more is learned. As professionals plan to plan on a national scale, the three tiers of our government will actually be at work continuously piecing together fragmental, incremental, pragmatic, segmental efforts toward national planning. In the long run, a new administrative structure must be designed and grow into being at the national level; this structure will quite obviously be redesigned continuously with operational experience. We shall hopefully increase in wisdom both in the governmental administrative process and in the public political process. All this will take much longer than one thinks despite that awful rush of events. The lead time is undoubtedly decades. But if man has any faith in human rationality and long-range positive planning, as well as short-range remedial planning, a preparatory start in professional education must be initiated very soon indeed.

The key to the entire program in professional education, as an interim strategy, would be the formation of four or five major National Planning Institutes. Each would be a consortium of great universities and research centers and would have three basic functions: The creation of an evolving system of a Ph.D. in National Planning Programs; the granting of a Ph.D. in National Planning based on a nationally agreed-on set of criteria and as a nationally granted degree, perhaps by the National Science Foundation in conjunction with participating universities; research in an increasing scale on all facets of a national environmental policy. Necessary postdoctoral training and degree revalidating would take place here.

The Nixon-created Cabinet-level Council for Urban Affairs could take the lead in inaugurating such a program. Although its parameters are technically limited to "urban," the inclusion of the Department of Agriculture in the seven-department group suggests larger considerations—only Interior seems to have been left out. There is no question that the federal

National Urban Institute and the Urban Coalition with Urban America could all prove of great value in this total scheme. Could not the AIP serve as the relevant professional group, aided no doubt by Planners for Equal Opportunity (PEO) and American Society of Planning Officials (ASPO)?

The robust training program would consist of a solid required core of high-level substantive seminars, always intellectually exploratory in nature, as well as some rigorous training in social science and planning methodologies, both quantitative and qualitative (where hard data is unknown or unknowable). Four years of course work on reasonable stipends as young professionals (up to $10,000 per year plus fringes) would be the minimum requirement to lure outstanding candidates into the field. Unquestionably a goodly number of courses would be community/people-oriented and based (whatever the scale) to give a solid gut-feeling for "planning with people." As Chester W. Hartmann of Harvard's Department of City and Regional Planning has described their Urban Field Service, it would seem to fit the bill! This would meet the complaints of the present generation of graduate school students who decry the "uninvolved," "removed," "meaninglessness" of present urban/regional planning curricula. The actual Ph.D. dissertation itself would be cross read by a national committee of the National Planning Institutes; a serious effort would be made to have subjects researched of genuine importance with a view to publication rather than the carrying out of a hackneyed exercise merely to earn a degree. There are few resources and little time to waste. If the candidate bits off more than anyone can chew in a reasonable time and sets up a problem for eventual possible solution, this would be considered a satisfactory effort. A national Ph.D. preliminary exam might be administered to all degree candidates possibly in an "assembled form." Credits could easily be transferred from one university in the program to another and from one institute to another.

It would be presumptuous for me to detail the precise curriculum for a Ph.D. in National Planning; everyone from government official, to student, to citizen must get into this act; but some indication of its possible dimensions is in order. Such a research curriculum should have as one of its primary responsibilities the task of finding out precisely what such a curriculum should entail. It might well cover eight main facets of training:

1. Intellectual depth and sophistication as well as training in creativity. Background seminars in philosophy and the humanities in the exploration of values and goals.

2. Analytical techniques for discovering and managing large amounts of

data. Very sophisticated research and operational methodologies including theory construction. This would include operation research, game theory, mathematical models, etc., and would lead to complete familiarity with modern research hardware.

3. Substantive training and information on a macro-scale. All of this study will have an operational as well as an analytical dimension in ecology (largely natural science) and ethology; demography; geography (land use to regionalism); economics; political science (behavioral and public administration); sociology and anthropology (descriptive, quantitative as well as socio-cultural change theories for multi-group society); futurism (both on the national and international scale).

4. Substantive traditional physical planning concerns (again on a macro-scale) interpreted as well from a socio-politico-economic point of view (holistic total environmental approach): basic services; work; transport/communication; recreation/high culture; housing/community; urban design.

5. Operational planning in our society: plan-program-budget system; budgeting and fiscal policy; local and national government practices; cooperative national planning (multi-tiered); law (and how to alter it creatively faced as a *sine qua non*).

6. Field experiences in local and national agencies during summer terms and also connected with regular course work or in lieu of traditional studio training. Work abroad on a national planning level would be a welcome substitute.

7. A major publishable research paper for the Ph.D. degree (operationally oriented) to commence after the fourth year of courses and to be the result of at least part-time employment in a macro-scale planning office. It should be a creative effort to plan nationally (or quite possibly regionally) in one of the methodological, operational or major substantive areas, generally with a long-range point of view. It could be policy making rather than precise program planning—especially if the time span goes beyond meaningful planning capability (say further than ten years).

8. Postdoctoral training. A Ph.D. in National Planning is naturally only the beginning. Since we are attempting to move into the future with this project, two new and advanced conditions must be built into such an operation so crucial for our national existence. (a) The degree must be revalidated every five years by passing a national examination developed by the National Planning Institutes. (b) Postdoctoral training is expected of each degree holder with a sabbatical year every fifth year at federal

expense in order to qualify for and hold an operational speciality, i.e., macro-scale economic, macro-scale transportation systems, national physical ecology, etc. Thus each career professional will be expected to have an up-to-date precise macro-scale operationally-oriented skill, in addition to his up-to-date holistic grasp.

Such a career entrance and potential course would tend to draw exceptional individuals. Especially if the true import could be dramatized to the American people continuously by its top leadership—specifically the President of the United States—and publicized by the various national planning groups as well as the powerful urban-oriented, nongovernmental institutes now viewing their task as being on a national environmental scale, as it most certainly is.

These National Planning Institutes would constitute the Staff College for "the moral equivalent of war," as could the Cabinet-level *expanded* Council on Urban Affairs serve as a counterpart to the National Security Council for United States internal affairs.

A start must be made at once in developing governmental structure and process, as it will be at least a quarter century before there is a reasonably adequate federal National Plan Commission operational. Here are four concrete proposals in an approximately programmed order:

1. A massive public education drive. The federal Council for Urban Affairs along with the private Urban Coalition should serve as spearhead, sparked by the AIP and aided and abetted by ASPO, the US Chamber of Commerce, Urban America, National Association of Housing and Redevelopment Officials (NAHRO), American Institute of Architects (AIA), Committee for Economic Development, Resources for the Future, the National Science Foundation, the Federal Urban Institute, the Planning Foundation of America, National Planning Association, National Industrial Conference Board, etc. This could be initiated by the President; the Seventies might be named a National Planning Decade, although such an idea may be both optimistic and premature. Parenthetically, the powerful American business community may, within measurable time, be ready to see and to encourage a transference of its managerial skills, including systems analysis and long-range planning, into large-scale government—a transfer already initiated dramatically by PPBS missionary Robert Mac-Namara, former Secretary of Defense.

This public education program would be aimed at two specific targets: local and national officialdom, both elected and appointed; and the general public (with numerous tactical variations for different sub-groups). The general theme will be the insistence on a major concerted national effort to engage in some very hard preliminary thinking about a national plan. This could be defined as planning with people and could be instrumented through various regional conferences. The National Planning Institutes would be explained and pushed as the next step. Especial linkages would be maintained with these consortia of American universities/research institutes discussed above and in the following proposal. It is necessary that public monies, as well as private, be devoted to this public educational effort as well as to the National Planning Institutes. Suggested public resources would be the NSF, HEW, HUD, Departments of Commerce, Labor, Agriculture, Interior and Defense, Bureau of the Budget, Council of Economic Advisors, etc. State and city money would be both needed and welcomed, especially for the preliminary public educational effort and in the local institutes. It is assumed that a number of the major foundations would be prepared to support an effort of this order.

2. National Planning Institutes granting the Ph.D. in National Planning would be set up as part of or adjacent to existent intellectual resources. Geography plays a part in these concrete suggestions for a program consisting of five centers: (a) at Cambridge (Boston), based on MIT/Harvard resources; (b) at the University of Chicago/University of Wisconsin/University of Michigan/University of Minnesota complex; (c) a University of California (Berkeley) and Stanford (Palo Alto) Institute; (d) a Pennsylvania/Pittsburgh Institute; (e) a Washington, D.C. Institute, in due course as a must.

Each of these institutes could be clearly connected with relevant university planning schools, as the nucleus on which to build, as well as leaning heavily on the physical science, social science, and planning research centers already in existence at or near these named locations in their multitude of forms and aims. It would not be an easy task for the existing planning schools to move even farther away from their original city-oriented physical planning and land-use concern. But they already have gone up in territorial scale beyond the city to the region; the next obvious step in scale indicated would be the national level. When American planners serve abroad, they seem to feel no great hesitation at working on a national planning level. Why not at home? That the planning schools are increasingly social-science oriented is clear; undoubtedly there are in the university resource centers mentioned operationally-oriented social science bodies which could be included as co-equals. Research toward creative legal forms would be emphasized. It is more than likely that the local graduate student population would be enthusiastic and critical participants in developing the institutes.

3. A central information/statistical center. It would appear natural to develop the functions of the Census Bureau and, separating it from the Department of Commerce, add it directly to the President's office and staff. It could be combined readily with the many other fact-gathering centers in our society which, through computer linkages, could store and make retrievable on a minute's call relevant macro-scale data and correlations. Gaps in our statistical information could be identified and, over time, filled. Specifically four major functions are in the long run envisaged: (a) automatic data collection of all human transactions in the USA from births to checks; (b) sampling techniques to obtain needed data, rather than the laborious use of census, "hand labor" techniques of the past; social indicators as well as monetary indicators; (c) attitudinal studies (public opinion polls centralized); (d) the monitoring function of on-going planning programs as well as "standard world projection" of unplanned action. Here would be the raw material and testing ground for a national socio-politico-economic accounting yearly produced for and by the President.

4. A National Planning Cabinet as aid to the President to coordinate the internal moral equivalent of war. The Russians use a formalistic GOSPLAN and the British, in World War II, developed a special War Cabinet composed of relevant major ministry heads, plus concerned chiefs of other government activities. We are between these two possibilities, it seems, in our governmental style. Why not have a selected group of persons, the chiefs (in effect) of Defense, Treasury, HUD, HEW, Labor/Commerce, Interior, Agriculture, with a tight secretariat of professionals meeting regularly to devise the strategy (policy) and assign the tactics (planning) for our movement into the twenty-first century? The Eisenhower Administration actively used the National Security Council for planning our external affairs with an Operations Coordinating Board to follow up the decisions made for foreign affairs. Similarly, a National Planning Monitoring Group could call on the information listed in proposal 2 above and see that assigned tasks were carried out by operational bodies to which they were assigned. Similarly, the National Planning Cabinet would prepare the yearly Presidential State of the Nation Summary, the Fiscal Year Budget, and the Five-and-Ten-year Plan Projections and Programs (solidly PPBS based). Mr. Nixon seems disposed to use the National Security Council for foreign affairs regularly; his creation of the

Cabinet-level Council on Urban Affairs gives evidence of faith in such a strategy for internal problems. The latter needs only a slight amount of rethinking and retooling to be a National Planning Cabinet (for internal affairs) in being.

The magnitude of the alteration in American thinking required to accept such a sophistication of our governmental structure is all too obvious; the eventual costs would only be exceeded by the staggering costs—both human and monetary—of not doing. Hundreds of billions of dollars invested in the public sector will be called for, multiplied manifold by private sector decision and allocation. Without elaboration here, it is assumed that Harvard psychologist Burrhus Skinner's advocacy of continuing, sure, positive rewards far exceed punishments in speeding learning and causing desired action. John Reps has explored this manipulative technique cogently in "Requiem for Zoning"; it now is clear that "cookies" are generally more efficacious motivators than "whips" in getting positive actions. Need it be said that the basic managerial technique is federal policy leadership coupled to local administration and feedback, with federal resources serving as splendid "cookies."

The United States must finally grow up as a people in the twentieth century to survive with distinction into the twenty-first and beyond. This means a revision of our fundamental values as well as our societal structure and process. Planners must grow up faster than their charges, the people, whether the planners perceive themselves as a professional elite or a portion of the involved leadership of a participatory democracy.

WILLIAM R. EWALD, JR.

Development Consultant, Washington, D.C. Previously Senior Vice President and Treasurer of the American Affiliate of Doxiadis Associates; development consultant to the President's Appalachian Institute Committee. Directed AIP's three-year consultation on "The Next Fifty Years," a multidisciplinary examination into the future environment of the United States on the occasion of AIP's fiftieth anniversary. Civil Engineering degree from Brown University and graduate work at the University of Michigan.

National Planning Cannot Wait for an Elite

A COMMENT ON THE ELDREDGE PAPER

The long-range future has no facts. Some people are intimidated by this.

Justice Holmes once observed that "There are one-story intellects, two-story intellects, and three-story intellects with skylights. All fact collectors with no aims beyond their facts are one-story men. Two-story men compare reason and generalize using the labors of the fact collectors as well as their own. Three-story men idealize, imagine, and predict. Their best illumination comes from above through the skylight."

We need all of these intellects. There is *always* going to be more emphasis on the here and now. What needs to be done now, should be done now. But not to take account of the meaning of what we do for the future seems to me to be a great mistake.

What happened to Lake Erie happened bit by bit over the years. Probably it was practical during those years not to enforce the pollution laws that could have been enforced. What was happening at the time was well-known by the few. But it was not acceptable as public information. It was not practical to talk out loud of the ultimate future consequences of this pollution or what to do about it. That is what we are talking about when we discuss national policy. As H. Wentworth Eldredge has pointed out,

22

there is a need to know more. There are things that have to be done and things that have to be learned.

As a nation we are going to have $55 trillion (GNP) to spend in the next thirty-three years, and we are going at it with two-year plans. Probably all professionals could readily agree that they want the rate of the growth of the GNP to go up and the population rate to go down, and that the benefits to the nation from that sort of combination would also provide enough surplus energy to benefit the world. That would be a basis for national policy. But you cannot even think about things like that in two-year increments.

Eldredge proposes to begin work on the foundations of a national plan by putting all emphasis on training the minds that will be needed to create such a plan. In his view there is really not much we are going to be able to do for the next ten or twenty years about national planning or policy directly. Meanwhile, he seems to say, we ought to become educated to the policy for the nation's development.

I think this approach is wrong. The occupants of the White House for the next ten or twenty years are not going to have such control over where this country is going that we will survive without *some* deliberate national policy for the nation's development.

The problem with decentralization is that typically the very people who call for decentralizing the power of the federal government are just plain against *all* government power. They are against strong City Halls. They are against strong state governments. They are against a strong federal government. This is the danger to watch for—the decentralization that is really dismantling.

What is our practice now? Do we really understand democracy? We have legislative, executive, and judicial arms of government at all levels in this federal system. But then we proceed to decimate the executive. We are afraid of the executive branch. Most mayors have very restricted powers. And the governor, after he is elected, cannot really do what he said he was going to do. We do not even trust our legislative representatives enough to provide them the time and the staff to perform. There are similar problems at the federal level. Our philosophy appears to be that a sure way of defending ourselves from our democracy is to *weaken* it. The system is there to be implemented, but we are frightened by it.

The executive branch needs to take long-range as well as short-range looks. Things that can be managed inch by inch, should be. But there are other long-distance matters that call for long-range and national policy. The greatest number of man hours will, and should, go into the short-term efforts. It takes careful fitting to have things work. Theorizing about a door is one thing. Designing a door is another. But if it is going to be hung, it has got to work.

Japan has the longest-range national plan in the world. It looks twenty-five years ahead. In 1963 and 1964 I worked to convert a static twenty-year physical plan for New York State into a dynamic sixty-year development policy that took into account the process of planning and development. General Motors looks seven years ahead. These are exceptions. By and large, government agencies and business operate on two-year looks into the future.

In short, we are trying to face the future with short-term thinking and short-term institutions. We are trying to force the future with specialized skills, not holistic ones.

When we really understand what is facing us—when it is made real to us as a nation—we will do what we need to do. When we understand the two great forces of concentrations of people and their expectations, we will do something about it. We will understand how technology is changing human understanding of geographic space, time, the industry, and society. I do not believe there is any national policy or national institute of training to be put ahead of this general understanding by people in general.

Maybe there is reason to say that we are an irrational people, incapable of national plans; that we have obvious things to do and that we are not doing them. Perhaps we had better work on the here and now because that is what we understand. As for national policy, perhaps we had better restrict ourselves to training the experts who are going to run the nation twenty years from now, as Eldredge proposes. I am not prepared to settle for this approach.

I agree with Eldredge's recognition that macro-planning at the national scale is not being taught, and should be. I agree with his statement of the systems planning as necessary to national planning; that before we are through everyone must be involved; and that we need a focus at the national level. Most of all I agree with his use of William James' statement on "the moral equivalent of war," which I've often paraphrased—that peace *must be* as exciting as war.

But if I read correctly his emphasis on a special national planning elite that is trained and recertified every five years and by implication is the *one* group that *alone* is allowed to plan the nation—I disagree wholeheartedly.

I disagree if we are being asked to wait patiently for twenty years before we move on with the deliberate development of this nation. If we are going to wait to plan this country from the top down, then we are not going to plan it.

Eldredge calls for a "nationally recertified elite" trained in a national academy of planning and running a great campaign for education of the people. I'd like to know "to what?" What will the elite know to "educate" the people to? Perhaps, instead, we simply need the means *now* to point out to the people the experience they are living in *now* and moving into the future. They may be capable of educating themselves once the choices ahead are made clear.

While great skills for national planning must be developed, I think it is a grave mistake to take that as the first step toward national policy development. It has a fetid air of paternalism about it.

There are factors at work that give hope for the early emergence of national policies for development: (1) the cost of poor performance to this nation in creating the environment has become obvious to everybody; (2) markets for environment as an industry have been identified in a way that they never have been before, to the point where industry is starting to find ways to be subsidized into this new market by the federal government; (3) political priorities have shifted toward making environment something that can elect politicians; and (4) there is a new professional competence as a result of a growing convergence of the professions based on a widespread realization by all that they are inadequate for what they need to do next.

There are some things which should not be calculated on a cost-benefit ratio. There are times in program-planning-budgeting when the computer should be turned off. The computer is probably just the mental discipline we need to help define our best choices. But there are some choices that are not going to be made—should not be made—strictly on a cost-benefit ratio. There is a mixture of rational and irrational that makes us human. In making these choices between the ant hill, the very strictly disciplined ant hill, and anarchy, I predict that we will reject both extremes.

This business of planning for the statistical man is the wooden kind of plan that we do not want here. It is the reason we need Eldredge's National Institute for Planning—to learn more. But it is also the reason we have to change the entire planning procedure and open the whole process up in a way that will be disturbing to the current style of "public hearing." But it will make it possible to take us where the *people* want to go. Planning *with* people is our national policy of highest priority. It can begin now. We cannot wait for "the elite" to come twenty years from now to tell us what to do.

Planning *with* people taken seriously, we will have to recognize that the majority of Americans are middle class. Gunnar Myrdal, at the AIP's fiftieth year conference in Washington, stated that the US mortgage to its poor had come due. He stressed that the United States could not have a program for only the black poor and not the white poor. I would go further and say this country cannot have successful national policies for the benefit of only the poor.

In order to develop major, truly nationwide policies, there must be the support of the majority—the middle class. They must see how they and their children will benefit. If they do, it is not too much to expect that they would be willing to see the poor benefit more than themselves and advance faster. Without this understanding by the middle class it is doubtful if national policies that handle the total environmental problems of the poor—social, economic, and physical—can be devised in scale with the need.

JOHN W. DYCKMAN

Professor of City Planning and Chairman of the Department of City and Regional Planning at the University of
California, Berkeley. Currently director of a study of the
history of city planning for the Twentieth Century Fund,
and a member of the Research Advisory Committee to the
Task Force on Economic Growth and Opportunity of the
US Chamber of Commerce. Served on the President's Task
Force on Natural Beauty and the Committee on Public Expenditures of the Committee on Urban Economics. M.A.
and Ph.D., University of Chicago. Author: *The Control of
Land Development and Urbanization in California; Capital
Requirements for Urban Development and Renewal; Ex-
plorations into Urban Structure* (summary chapter); *Alternatives in Water Management.*

Social Planning in
the American Democracy

An advanced (or "post-") industrial society characteristically makes wide
use of planning techniques and institutionalizes large numbers of social
services. In such a society, social planning may be either planning for
social services or planning, whether economic or physical, which is sensitive to the social outcomes of its plans and which places differential value
on these outcomes. Put differently, American planning that qualifies for the
designation "social" is either that kind of planning, whatever its perspective, that deals with social services, or is planning for environmental or
economic goals that takes into account the social consequences of its
effectuation.

In our society there is very little of what might be called "societal"
planning. That is, there is very little planning that seeks to directly restructure the society so as to alter its social relationships. This activity, to the
extent that it takes place, exists outside of government. It is the province of
utopians and traditional revolutionaries (contemporary radicals, I will
argue, have less taste for utopian schemes). The absence of such informing
societal perspectives protects US social planning from certain dogmatisms,

27

but also robs it of coherence and of an essential taste for large-scale change. Without this somewhat more global perspective, social planning is largely remedial and patchwork. There is a consequent emphasis on social services as ends in themselves without regard for the social changes that such services might be expected to work or for the long-run behavior that they would encourage. Social planning is not only pragmatic and piecemeal, but is bound strictly to the short-run effects.

The ideal of comprehensive planning which until recently was widely cherished by US city planners was in no sense contradictory of the proposition that democracy American style is inimical to societal planning. We have had "holistic" physical planning that has remained so aloof from social planning, let alone societal planning, that social and even economic "plans" have not been included in our "comprehensive plans." In economic planning, social changes—which have been presumed to take place more slowly than economic changes and in any event, to be less regular and manageable—have been ignored or treated as random shocks on the system. And there is little properly "social" planning.

City planning in the US, along with economic planning, has attached itself to the strong style of incremental reform. At the same time, we have a tradition comparable to that of the British in organizing social services in caretaker style. In this tradition, we have favored service strategies, rather than income strategies, to use the terminology of Marris and Rein. We have opted for the direct, rather than the indirect, consequences of social programs and have established large service bureaucracies that do only the most limited, partial, and short-run planning within the confines of their accepted missions. The most indirect and long-run of our social programs has been universal public education. But after a century's experience with a highly developed system of common schools, we are arriving at the realization that a single institution operating on a social situation is not a social plan. The "ladder" climbing which was so confidently asserted as the social goal of the American people to be achieved by the public schools remains blocked for a substantial segment of the population. Belatedly we realize that if education is necessary for social mobility, it is not sufficient. The certification of common school graduation has been cheapened as a social advancement coin. The social and economic demand for common school graduates has shifted, and we have done nothing to manage the demand that could complete the plan.

I cannot propose to recount the whole drift of social planning in the US or even to list the elements of an ideal social planning program. For obvious reasons, I am concerned most seriously with the development of social planning at the urban, or metropolitan level. More ambitious societal planning will concern me only to the extent that its absence hampers or forecloses effective local social planning. To a considerable extent, too, there will be a bias in the direction of selecting examples with which the traditional city planning movement has been concerned.

Accordingly, I will deal with the drift of social service planning toward a management perspective and management planning devices, with the residual issues unresolved by these techniques, and with a case—that of metropolitan planning—which dramatizes the present situation of social planning in America. The course of the analysis will hopefully cast up some elements from which a program for more significant social planning can be made.

The functional assignments for social planning in an advanced industrial society might be divided broadly as follows: (1) defining and providing an adequate level of social goods—the task of locating social needs and specifying quantities needed; (2) organizing the distribution of social goods, providing for redistribution of resources, and securing "equity" in distribution; (3) managing certain environmental, economic, and social externalities resulting from individual or group actions; (4) planning for social change.

The first of these functional tasks is strictly speaking an economic planning job. It has emerged as a social planning issue slowly, and only after the dereliction of our market economic system. Before the Depression of the 1930's, social planning and economic planning barely touched hands. The location of social needs was the work of the century of reformers who struggled to amend the workings of the market system and repair its casualties. The market left these tasks to the workings of direct "poor relief" or to the education in consumption and savings mores practices by the settlement houses. In the Depression of the Thirties, John Maynard Keynes made a case for public expenditure to maintain aggregate demand. The shift in perspective which this argument required was dramatized by the well-publicized dispute between Harold Ickes, representing the older, more-superiority school of dispensing public services, and Harry Hopkins, representing the newer, "give 'em the money even if they spend it on the races" view.

By the 1950's when Keynesian principles of aggregate economic management were well accepted, John Kenneth Galbraith proposed an argument of countervailing public consumption need. His well-known position is that the concentration on aggregate demand and other "aggregates" obscured the unequal growth of private and public consumption and the appearance of grave deficiencies in the public package, particularly deficiencies in the public environment. From one standpoint, he was thereby echoing an old refrain in American reform ranks, that of the vulgarity of market tastes and styles, and the neglect of social—meaning public service —concerns. Thus he bridged two of my functional categories, the provision of public goods and the management of certain externalities. But by avoiding the reality of differences in public tastes and issues of social change, Galbraith side-stepped the tensions lurking in the remaining social planning tasks.

Organizing the distribution of certain social goods early took the form of establishing service institutions and bureaucracies. Poor relief became public welfare, German refugees in the 1850's led the drive to institutionalize park and playground services, public housing grew from small beginnings in World War I housing to the 1949 Act and so on. (Wilensky and Lebaux have described the process very well.) The plans of the social service agencies are sometimes included in the comprehensive planning schemes of the urban planners, but rarely enter into the process in an integral way. Their budgets are won by hard lobbying, usually on the part of the members of the supplying bureaucracy. Funds are secured from the tax dollar or from pooled Community Chest funds in an elaborate system of intergovernmental transfers and negotiations.

This system of social service provision is presently beleagured from many sides. Social critics and managers alike find present methods wasteful and irrational. The criticisms fall into two compartments. First, there is the attack on bureaucracy in its particular social service form, with its related issue of the demand for decentralization of government services generally. Second, there is a set of arguments that challenge the ability of present social planning to be equitable, as well as its inability to produce lasting effects leading to social change. In the jargon of the planners, the first set of criticisms goes to the "delivery system," and to the very choices of social goods made by the service agencies. The second set of arguments is more fuzzy, if ultimately more profound. It argues that present service systems are conservative in their effects, and outmoded in their style.

The latter criticism falls equally heavily on almost all the "Progressive" reform achievements of the early twentieth century. The tradition of city planning is closely woven in with that of the reformers of slum clearance and settlement house agitation. But the style of these early reformers and their successors is uncomfortable to present planners. Their crusading zeal rested on a Transcendentalism that is no longer easily worn by intellectuals. Their belief in fundamental values is distrusted by the positivistic managers who have inherited their social charge. Nevertheless, the caretaker mentality of the early social workers survives in aggravated form in many contemporary social service institutions, particularly in welfare and public housing, and the most stylish city planning is not free from it.

We might summarize the first set of challenges, the case against the handling of social programs, in these points:

1. There is too much leakage of funds, thereby reducing the effectiveness and impact of the programs, i.e., too much money is needed to get the service to the eventual users.

2. Present programs smell of colonialism—with supply agencies developing their own "markets" of users of the services, and developing service empires.

3. Programs encourage the growth of dependence and trap users in a positive feed-back relationship.

4. Standards set by social service planners bear little relationship either to the functional performance or outcome desired or, especially, to the desires and tastes of their clients.

5. Once set up, programs persist long after they have ceased to be functional and, because they are insensitive to social conditions, may become dysfunctional.

The spirit of many of these criticisms emanates from the New Management movement sparked by the application of economic ideas to defense and latterly to "softer" areas of government. But some of the criticism comes as well from reformers who are frustrated that two generations of application of programs fought for by earlier reformers have produced little social change and much confirmed dependency on public bureaucracies that are increasingly intolerant of their clients. Both groups feel that elimination of the undesired effects of present programs may be possible only with restructuring the whole relationship between government and its agents on one hand and the clients of the service agencies on the other. Neither of these groups, however, would proceed according to any societal blueprint, unless it be the implicit one of the ideal "open" market model.

Both the market-solution critics of social delivery systems have hit upon a demonstrable weakness in the machinery of the social service apparatus. It delivers products that are too often unwanted. But social planning is not geared to consumer response. Traditionally, the dispensers of social services have considered themselves as "taste makers" leading the untutored under classes to higher levels of appreciation. As taste-making, social planning has not been successful. No more successful, in fact, than city planning, which has not been able to sell the majority of Americans on high-density, multi-family housing, mass transit or organized playgrounds. The life style and class biases of the service suppliers are soundly in the American reform tradition. After all, the very people who denounce commercial advertising taste-making as cynical deception can be counted as strict adherents to rigid standards of public taste-making. Now they find the radical right and radical left, allied with the new rationalists of management and the academy, joining hands against them in a challenge which strikes not only at the tastes but the right of the agencies to impose them.

The tactics of the new rationalizers of social planning are built around conceptions of consumer sovereignty and market feedback so dear to advocates of "the open society is a market society" proposition. Naturally, market choice is the keystone of many of their proposals. But no effective markets exist in the public sector outside of the practice of selecting one's market basket of public goods by moving to the suburb or small town that has the favored package. And that option is denied to many, particularly to the low-income or ethnic groups who are clients of so many established services. So the alternatives to established social services systems are often imperfect approximations of the market ideal.

Reinforcing the market orientation is the management device of "planning, programming, and budgeting." The essential insights of this approach are (1) that measures of effectiveness should be applied to the *system* effects of outputs, and that these are more relevant than efficiency measures which deal narrowly with input-output ratios; (2) that indirect effects of actions may at times outweigh direct effects, and unanticipated consequences may be more "consequential" than expected ones; (3) that costs of effectuating programs may exceed the benefits of the programs; and (4) that programming overtime requires the anticipation of various feedbacks and the development of "strategies" of action. All of these considerations must be incorporated in the planning process which, as the above points demonstrate, must be applied to the total relevant *system*. (Hence the designation "PPBS.") In social planning, the viewpoints of PPBS are frequently internalized in the process of inventing new social programs which will be more "effective" than those now in use. This approach has found much current favor in the high offices of HEW under the direction of Wilbur Cohen.

Some of the devices favored by planners of these persuasions might be briefly described as follows:

1. First and foremost, the use of income strategies rather than service strategies. In general it is aimed at the circumvention of allocation by bureaucratic standards and on reliance upon the ability of the recipients of income subsidies to know their own self-interest better than bureaucratic interpreters. The negative income tax is the vehicle invented by economists (notably the conservative Milton Friedman) to "deliver" the income. In general, this strategy favors the direct delivery of services, products, and especially money. And it favors giving money over giving services on the grounds that money enhances choice while services reduce choice (ultimately they must be paid for by taxes which reduce the choices of the payers) of individuals by transferring them to government.

2. Where income strategies are not feasible, similarly direct methods are favored. There are many ways in which government can give people claims on products or resources which it wishes to have used. For example, instead of supporting public schools directly, the government might give educational vouchers payable to school suppliers and allow recipients to choose the school which suits them best. These measures have the advantage of bypassing supplier bureaucracies but they run into system-wide management disadvantages, too. Vouchers and other such payments have the advantage of supporting the consumption of certain public goods, but if the system effects are not controlled they might have the effect of inflating demand in a particular area to the distress of other desirable public demand. And, of course, the supported demand, as with negative income tax methods, in the absence of broad social planning, might redistribute current income without causing the income to "stick" to the recipients, or without affecting permanent income.

3. Development of reward and incentive systems which stimulate clients to change their status are favored by many social planners. Much has been written about the need to set up systems that encourage the dependents to break out of their condition. In public housing, steps have finally been taken to allow tenants to increase their incomes above the arbitrary limits and even to gradually purchase their houses. But these steps are still halting. Rules and regulations are promulgated which foster new dependency relations against the spirit of this principle. These effects have not been built into the proposals above. The incentive for dependency, for

example, is built into the negative income tax. The economic and social dynamics of compensatory programs must be well understood before they can be undertaken. At present, the potentially dynamic element of inter-personal comparison and competition is constrained by the administrative need for "equal treatment" which penalizes the unequally endowed. At their worst, such administrative rules become instruments of the *status quo*.

4. The more radical social planners have advocated creation of user bureaucracies to offset or neutralize the supplier bureaucracies. This is a form of consumer protectionism in the public sector that has been given force by the example of the Welfare Rights organizations, the Public Housing Tenant associations and similar groups. So far it has been of limited effectiveness because the tenants, clients, and other "users" have limited real power to bargain. Their real power would be enchanced if there were alternative sources of supply of the services in question, and if particu-lar agencies did not hold a monopoly on the services. The market choice might come into play in a situation of competition between public agencies providing the same or similar public goods. This possibility has in the past been limited by various restrictions of eligibility (e.g., by residence), by the ecology of revenue sources and capacities, and by legal and constitutional provisions. As a result, the present expression of public sector competition is that between cities and suburbs which offer different packages of public services.

5. Closely related to the last mentioned is the tactic of surrendering the initiative in program formulation to the users. Strictly speaking this may appear as the abdication of social planning if one is to anticipate the results. Though viewed as a radical proposal, it is being tried in a halting way in the poverty and Model Cities programs of the federal government. (There is division among the official planners as to the intent of the pro-grams to include this feature.) Community organization money has been used, indirectly or directly, to organize rent strikes and demonstrations. Poverty program money, directed to indigeneous leadership, has allowed these leaders to organize for their own causes. The danger that money may be diverted from the official or public purposes to special ends of the impacted groups is one which must be accepted if the notion of user control is to have any meaning. In fact, the objective of effecting social change leads directly to the issue of power, specifically the power of the poor and disorganized to change their status.

*

None of the above-mentioned tactical proposals is inconsistent with classical conceptions of the "open society." None requires Utopian social engineering. Perhaps the negative income tax plan is most demanding of social engineering, but those implications have not been worked out. Left unanswered, however, is the question of contributions to social change. Open societies foster piecemeal planning and shrink from planning societal changes. But are there major structural changes in the society that might be produced by the present drift in social planning?

To answer that question we should examine social programs for evidence of the transfer of power. The social program arsenal assembled by the Great Society designer was to be deployed, according to the Model Cities directives, against poverty and its indicators. But poverty, in the considered opinion of social scientists like Martin Deutsch, is a condition of powerlessness even more than a condition of income deprivation. Measures of income are relatively straightforward. But measures of power involve not only the dreaded inter-personal comparisons shunned by economists, but also indices of mobility, shift in economic and social status, measures of command over assets, and elusive indices of "opportunity."

Income is an aspect of power, but it would be a mistake to conclude that enhanced consumer choice at a generally low level of consumption is an important aspect of power in the community. Social planners should be alert to the social shift implications of the income strategies. The income strategies proposed will not automatically induce change and mobility. They do not extend to the transfer of assets and power. Plans for guaranteed annual income, for example, do not give low-income recipients immediate prospects of ownership, or of command over jobs which carry with them prospects for advancement. If nothing but the amount of income paid to each member of the society is altered, and if the guarantee takes the form of an absolute amount or floor under income rather than a share of income, the relative position of the beneficiaries of the guarantee may decline over time. Given the incentives of the plan, the lowest income people would tend not only to remain the lowest, but to be immobilized there. With higher income for nonwork, and with the job situation unaltered or worsened, avenues for upward mobility would be reduced. Thus it is necessary to accompany income strategies as well as service strategies with structural adjustments, and to open opportunities for change that are more difficult to program than the transfer of modest amounts of the national income.

The transfer of program power to the poor is one of the more interesting social planning devices of the poverty program, however tentative and nervous the application. At one stroke this tactic promised to both enhance consumer choice and extend that choice to "production" decisions. Despite the prospect of what the caretakers would see as abuses, this step appears as necessary if one wishes to avoid an extreme manifestation of the client dependence and bureaucratic imperialism rejected above. In the words of Harvey Cox, "Without such new points of countervailing power, the poverty program will turn out to be nothing but a government-sponsored union, providing anesthetizing trifles but leaving the unjust distribution of power untouched." In fact, even with the superficial transfer of power over the program promised by "maximum feasible participation," the distribution of real power would remain "largely untouched," but social participation in program-making and program allocations goes far to reduce the feeling of dependence and the burden of accommodation to bureaucratic values. The need to create political power which resides outside the normal system of power is a concern born of the desire to get close to the real preferences of the clients as well as of the disdain which many feel for the handouts of the Establishment. The representatives of the under classes want to feel that they have *won* these benefits, not that they are freely given. This feeling is itself material for a system of incentives.

The drive for participation in the program decisions is not empty and vainglorious. Public sector goods have their prices for their users, as do those of the private sector. The recipients of social services are commonly viewed as unqualified beneficiaries (sometimes resented as such, as in the case of nonwhite welfare recipients). But they, too, incur costs, and the indirect costs to them of the system of taxation plus categorical service supply is often perilously close to the benefit. The mix of goods and services which the disadvantaged would choose, and the methods of delivering the services, are frequently very different from those chosen for them by the more affluent members of the community. This reality should be clear to the city planners, proponents of school bond issues, and other promoters of liberal causes who have been repeatedly dismayed by the indifference or opposition of minorities and the poor to their loftily held proposals. If middle-class whites go to great trouble to move to suburbs which have their approved mix of public goods, we should not be surprised to find that poor blacks, who do not have the opportunity to indulge them, also have preferences for certain public offerings.

Of course, part of the problem of local equity results from the bag of tax options left to local government. Local government is largely stuck with the real estate tax, which is meeting stiff resistance and is the source of much right-wing political counterattack against social services, and with the sales tax, which is opposed by trade unions and the traditional left as regressive. Income taxation when used by the states or cities has a low ceiling and little progressiveness because the schedule has been effectively pre-empted by the federal government since the early 1930's. As a result, local governments must appeal to federal agencies. The federal agencies, in turn, must fight for the scarce funds on a program basis. So the federal agencies set up categories, matching requirements, standards for compliance, and eligibility conditions that tie local hands. By the time the money reaches local sources, few options remain for matching local consumer tastes and needs.

So it is apparent that changes in the provision and planning of social services must be accompanied by some changes in the methods of financing services. Those changes, in turn, are matters for some reorganization of the inter-governmental relations. Block grants and tax-sharing proposals now abound, and these are helpful in getting out of the bind. Until tax sharing is relatively thorough, however, local governments will be hard pressed to set up delivery of social goods which does not depend upon higher governments, and moves to decentralize administration and share planning with users of the goods and services will be hampered.

The challenge of these activists who wish to democratize the apparatus of social services strikes directly at the planning style of public agencies. At a time when planners are proud of their achievement in moving from narrow efficiency to systematic effectiveness measures, they are challenged with requirements of equity and power sharing. If the planners fall back on efficiency criteria, they are accused of accommodating the "power structure." Administrative rationality is not appealing to the have-nots if it merely makes the best of a bad situation. To make decisions on presumably scientific grounds without consultation of the clients has become synonymous with deception.

The gap between the traditional concerns of the planners and the latent preferences of the minorities is nowhere sharper than in the proposals of planners' metropolitanizing planning and programming. The effort to put social planning into a scheme for metropolitan organization, or to put metropolitan organization in the perspective of social planning, demonstrates this conflict.

*

The planners' case for metropolitan organization rests upon traditional conceptions of efficiency in transportation and similar services and upon the desire to improve the public provision of environmental amenities. There is usually also a strong conservationist sentiment. As yet, the metropolitan planning focus has not been turned to the rationalization of welfare programs and the design of social policies. The following remarks, nonetheless, are directed to the social planning issues in metropolitan organization.

The first social planning problem is that metropolitan organization is not attractive to those who presumably have the most to gain from change. Both the blacks and right-wing whites have declared their opposition to the principle of metropolitan regional organization. Proponents of metropolitan regionalism see in it an opportunity for central city minorities to break out of the "white noose of the suburban ring" which limits the housing, job, and social opportunities of those minorities. But the minorities, at least the civil rights sector, distrust this proposal. Having smelled the blood of city power in recent northern elections, they feel that metropolitan government is a plot to keep them from the chance at misrule of the cities which white ethnic groups, such as the Irish and Italians, have enjoyed in the past. The social benefits of metropolitan organization is a counterattack against the ideals of transfer of power which they feel have been implicit in the poverty and Model Cities programs.

In truth, metropolitan organization proposals do not meet the social planning tests I set up earlier. First, it stresses efficiency considerations at the expense of equity. Second, it opts for a product-mix different from that which would be chosen by the poor or by minority groups. It is an upper-white consumer package offered to the whole population. Third, it gives low priority to the social programs favored by the poor. And fourth, it potentially diffuses the power of militant minorities. These issues might be restated as questions of program priorities, representation and power, and equity in the sharing of costs and benefits. Let's consider these in turn.

The particular package of services that the poor expect from government is very different from that proposed by advocates of regional government. Affluent whites, who have all essentials needed in their private lives, have understandably turned to that frontier of consumption, the environmental amenities which can be controlled only by public action. Metropolitan government means, for these people, air and water quality, parks and open space, conservation of scenic assets, good suburban mass transit, and regional planning. Blacks, as well as whites, enjoy clean air, pure water, clean up of trash and garbage, parks and open spaces for recreation. (They would also enjoy having their streets and alleys free of rats and vermin.) But the poor know that their ability to enjoy recreation areas depends on their ability to hold down a job five days a week; that their ability to enjoy the beauties of the outdoor environment depends upon their ability to go home to a decent house. So their priorities are different from the priorities of many metropolitan proposals. In their scheme of things, a regional government which concentrates solely on environmental issues distorts the social priorities, and so should not be supported.

The representational and power questions are equally divisive. It is feared that in the present regional government proposals, the suburbs are bound to have more influence than the poorer central city areas. It is plain that supporters of regional government must woo suburban interests. And the suburbs are in a position to set a high price for joining metropolitan organizations. In this perspective, the principle of one-man, one-vote, hailed as a progressive and democratic ruling, is already out-of-date. Resorting to simple majority rule under the rubric of one-man, one-vote would throw metropolitan organizations firmly into the control of the consolidated white populations against the reduced weight of the minorities. What is needed is an amalgam of metropolitan centralism with community decentralism in order to protect the rights of minority communities to a degree of self-management as well as to a degree of representation on metropolitan issues. The minorities certainly have no stake in metropolitan organization that takes the form of "one big government."

Along with representation, minorities want some management control. This could take the form of local community control of certain activities, or might entail minority representation on management boards. Police control is a sensitive case of the former. Black communities want some home rule over the police who patrol their areas, but who usually live far from the areas. In this case, producer and consumer interests must be weighed. There are advantages of informational economies and other efficiencies in having a regional police force, but such a force might be even farther from the people it is supposed to protect than the present city police forces. If regional government wants to achieve efficiencies in policing by merging or combining forces, it should take care that the local communities, including the ethnic communities, are represented on that combined force, and that they retain local control over some services, such as policing of neighborhoods.

Representation on management boards is a distant prospect for the poor. But much of the existing and proposed metropolitan organization takes corporate form, as in the many special districts and authorities. The poor and minorities do not sit on these boards. And, as the Port of New York Authority record shows, these relatively autonomous bodies are not highly responsive to the social needs of the city minorities. The poor must hope that new kinds of corporate instruments will be developed which they will help to control and which will be more responsive to their demands. If the presently mentioned ideas of creating regional development authorities and regional development banks should take shape, the poor should have their representatives on the boards of these public institutions. Such authorities could support new enterprises in the metropolitan area, new locations of branches of national firms, loans for the expansion of existing enterprises and especially for the growth of businesses started by blacks, Mexican-Americans, Puerto Ricans, and other minorities. The Bedford-Stuyvesant model is a step in this direction, but it is too private, too remote, and too lacking in genuine local participation.

Even now, a contribution to the participation goal can be made by the existing authorities and districts simply by according the poor and the minorities a greater share in jobs, in management, and in direction. Our survey of about twenty such agencies and districts in the San Francisco Bay Area showed only one minority member, a recent appointee, on all the board memberships. The half dozen "regional" transportation agency boards do not have a single nonwhite member, despite the national attention to transportation as a key issue for the "ghettos." The poor neighborhoods are drastically affected, in construction and clearance, by the Bay Area Rapid Transit District (BARTD) developments without compensating benefits of improved service. The poor get the tracks, and the suburbs get the stations. If these communities had a fraction of the representation of the downtown interests this would not be possible.

The impact of regional improvements leads us directly to the equity question. If even rough equity is to be realized, there must be institutionalized safeguards in matters of planning, budgeting, pricing, taxation, and actual expenditure of funds to insure a "fair share" for the minority communities. The suburbs and small towns of the region will insist on these safeguards for themselves. Under federal principles, it will be more convenient to see that each nameplace is taken care of than to secure equal treatment for communities or neighborhoods within cities. Black and brown communities must have a planning voice, perhaps even advocate representation, so that they are not unduly "impacted" by improvement actions. And at the same time, they will not want to be saddled with inequitable burdens in paying for the regional package of services. This means that regional agencies must be committed to progressive tax and revenue policies in financing developments and operations. In short, the poor do not want funds withdrawn from social services highly valued by them in order to pay for environmental improvements valued by the well-to-do; they want prices they can pay for transit, parks, and regional services; they want the tax base and revenue policies of the regional agencies to result in progressive taxation incidence for these services and improvements. This may mean funding the environmental package out of income taxes, user charges on the industries and other deleterious users of air and water, and suitable transfers from surplus operations to deficit ones.

Realizing these objectives will require both functional and formal protection of the minority and local interest. Functionally, it may mean strict regulation of the minority share in jobs, training and education, and housing. The standard social planning prescription for the attainment of these ends has been the convenient one of improving transportation from the minority neighborhoods to the jobs and housing areas. This was the position of the McCone Report on Watts, for example. And the above-mentioned example of BARTD in San Francisco shows that it cannot be taken for granted. But it is surely not program enough. By itself, transportation is not a sufficient condition for increasing the minority share, however necessary it may be. Perhaps it may need to be supplemented by Metropolitan Regional Planning which uses its review and evaluation powers to screen federal grant applications for their applicability to the social planning goals. Such metropolitan planning is already mandatory under the 1966 Metropolitan Development and Demonstration Cities Act, and it is rumored that the Los Angeles first-round Model Cities application was turned down by the federal agency because it failed to attend to the obvious social priority.

But as yet the metropolitan agencies, notably the councils of government, have not taken the lead in asserting these priorities. At present, metropolitan planning agencies do not have such explicit goals, and do not seem to have the incentive to announce them. If these screening devices are employed and seriously enforced, the metropolitan funding forthcoming from the federal and state governments cannot be used simply to reward the growing political power of white suburbs. One way to compel such outcomes is to insist on a representative minority staffing of the planning and developing agencies. If these steps are not taken there is a strong possibility that decentralization of federal decision-making through block grants to the states and earmarked grants to the metropolitan agencies will become the vehicle for the enrichment of the haves at the expense of the have-nots.

Achievement of equity in program incidence of costs and benefits does not necessarily alter the distribution of power. But groups currently deprived of power will need an even break in these matters if their condition is not to be worsened. Metropolitan governmental activities will probably lead to increased expenditures. There is a corresponding need to finance these expenditures and the increasing role for local discretionary spending under new applications of fiscal federalism.

The instruments of taxation and user charges will be important supplements to federal grants in paying for regional improvements. Local metropolitan agencies may have considerable discretion in choice of methods of finance. Accordingly, it will be important for management to have social as well as revenue goals. It is one thing to put transit, parks and other regional services on a pay-as-you-go basis so as to reduce the burden on income and property taxes. But such charges have the distributional characteristics of sales taxes. The poor need access to the services at prices they can pay, or they will not share in the consumption. Social planning would dictate that the price structure of regional services be geared to improving the basket of goods consumed by the low-income groups. If this aim is in conflict with sound business practice and the solvency of the agencies, transfer payments must be found. It is this reality that the system of general governmental support, federal, state or local, must face. Facilities such as mass transit have been defended on the equity grounds that many people are unable or cannot afford to drive autos. Once built, they cannot proceed to price-out the very people who are their putative clients.

Though the equity issues in social planning are important, they do not constitute a full social planning program. When the negative implications of social planning have been dramatized, as in the case of metropolitan governmental planning, the task remains to construct the machinery for effective social planning. When this is faced, it is clear that a major ingredient of social planning is economic planning. Income maintenance, governmental fiscal and tax source reorganization, employment, job training, social security, and a host of other economic measures are the means for direct and indirect social improvement. If these are not sufficient, they are certainly necessary.

The Full Employment Act of 1946 was a first step toward national social planning, but its application has taken the form of rather restricted aggregate economic planning. I part company with the belief of the liberal Establishment that our economic planning problems are of minor order. Our present economic planning is a blend of fiscal planning and counter-cyclical measures for over-all income and employment maintenance. We have no planning directly addressed to the characteristics of employment and unemployment, to redistribution, to job or economic mobility, or even to the maintenance or improvement of consumption. Our subsidies to consumption are rationalized in terms of their indirect contribution to productivity.

We need a rational manpower policy. If the political obstacles to a policy of manpower distribution are insuperable, can we not have a policy on the *types* of manpower use which the government will encourage, and those it will attempt to dampen? Our full employment planning focuses on aggregates. Aggregate measures are less and less meaningful as we move from the Keynesian problem to the contemporary ones of "hardcore" unemployment, and to facilitating the transition of minorities from inferior to equal economic status. Some part of these problems is inescapably regional, but there is no national Regional Resource Development Plan.

At the metropolitan regional level, human resource development agencies must tackle the problems of relocation due to private and public programs, employment and residential mobility—especially of minorities—job training programs, coordination of health planning with housing and job planning, coordination of welfare and poverty programs, and the monitoring of economic opportunity, among other tasks. These agencies do not yet exist. The one area in which there are uncontestable economies of scale is in information gathering, handling, processing. We can afford to bureaucratize and institutionalize information and intelligence services in a period when the need is for decentralization and debureaucratization. Metropolitan information services can help social planning by setting up a system of government accounts which will show the real functional expenditures; expose the interchanges between levels of government that lead to double counting and overstatement of our social programs; show the actual objects as well as the sources of the programs; reveal the revenue and disbursement flows in the inter-governmental transfers. All of this information would be essential in the reorganization of programs and in the ultimate decentralization of the delivery system.

In addition to the data on the employment mobility and characteristics of job opportunities, some of which is gathered by federal and state agencies today, we will need longer-range forecasts of local employment prospects. Our concepts of "need" and "impact" are fuzzy and sometimes misleading. Large-scale exploratory studies of demand for public and other social services are overdue, studies which could substitute estimates of real wants for the current, arbitrary "unmet needs." Federal funding of the information and intelligence functions could permit local areas to develop measures of output, based on new accounting procedures, which would illumine the vague notions of "impact."

In the last analysis, however, the intractable problems of social planning will be those of division of interest and power. It may be Polyannaish to think that a society which is divided on regional, race, and class lines, as is ours, can voluntarily embark on societal planning which entails the wholesale transfer of benefits and even modest transfer of power. Great Society rhetoric cannot obscure these hard divisions, which reach into every metropolitan area in the country. Accordingly, the progress we make on this front may have to be measured in terms of our ability to push limited and partial planning programs.

If this is the case, I would hope that we might find our way to
1. attend to the *mix,* rather than the amount of public spending;
2. freely alter the *modes* of social service spending, to reduce present line losses and improve the effectiveness of delivery;
3. organize social planning so as to assure "client" representation in the actual planning phases;
4. press for the decentralization of major governmental revenue sources and redress the present fiscal federalist arrangements;
5. organize social information and intelligence for planning purposes;
6. give equity criteria equal footing with efficiency in the planning;
7. put the national Council of Social Advisors on an equal *de facto* footing with the Council of Economic Advisors;
8. reform present "comprehensive planning" so that economic and particularly social plans of cities, regions, and states are fully integrated with physical and resource plans.

With these steps, a beginning would be made on effective social planning of our "open" society. Perhaps then there would be less need for the Utopian social blueprints, though the need for social changes advocated by reformers and revolutionaries will always be with us.

FRANCES FOX PIVEN

Assistant Professor, Columbia University School of Social
Work. Lecturer, Urban Planning Program, Hunter College,
1966–67. Previously associated with the National Welfare
Rights Movement, Architects Renewal Committee for Harlem, Mobilization for Youth, Office of Economic Opportunity and the Ford Foundation. B.A., M.A., Ph.D.,
University of Chicago. "Organizational, Professional and
Citizen Collaboration in Social Policy," in Erwin Smigel,
Editor, *Handbook on the Study of Social Problems;* Co-
author, with Richard A. Cloward, of numerous articles on
poverty and race.

Social Planning or Politics

A COMMENT ON THE DYCKMAN PAPER

Professor Dyckman is very knowledgeable about a wide range of issues
involved in social planning. But he has also overlaid and obscured what is,
I believe, the most important issue and should be the starting point in any
discussion of social planning.

The activities we call social planning—whether, according to Dyckman's definition, "planning for social services or planning . . . which is
sensitive to the social outcomes"—are activities of government, and the
activities of government are formed by political considerations. Or, to put
it another way, social planning, while it involves professionals, is not
formed by the inspirations or vagaries of professional doctrine. Social
planning is shaped by politics, and what is wrong with our social planning
is also shaped by politics.

There are, according to Dyckman, four main tasks of social planning:
defining and meeting social needs; organizing the distribution of social
goods; managing certain environmental externalities; and planning for
social change. But clearly, all societies have some institutional arrangements for filling these functions, whether or not they are called "social
planning." And clearly, our society performs these functions as well. What
is amiss is not a lack of social planning.

What *is* wrong in my view, and I think in Dyckman's view also, is that

45

there are very grave inequities resulting from the way we perform our "social planning": the social needs of some groups go unmet; social goods are inequitably distributed; and even our arrangements for managing certain environmental externalities benefit some and hurt others. Are these inequities the result of a deficiency in our social planning techniques, i.e., the absence of a management perspective that would bring to bear on problems of equity expert analyses and solutions? Indeed, are the techniques of social planning of any help at all in redressing social inequities? Martin Luther King once spoke to this point when he countered the criticism that the Poor People's March had not formulated any specific programmatic demands by saying, "Underneath the invitation to prepare programs is the premise that the government is inherently benevolent—it only awaits presentation of imaginative ideas." And that also seems to be the premise of social planners.

Let me illustrate with some observations about the public welfare system in the United States. It is surely one of our major "social planning" programs, virtually determining the lives of many millions of poor people in the United States. Nine million people depend on it for the meager aid they do get; many millions more are kept miserably poor because they get no aid at all. The average grant for a family of four in the United States is $1900 a year; in Mississippi the same family gets $388 a year. In return for the pittance they receive, these millions of Americans live under the constant surveillance of welfare officials and under the constant threat that their benefits will be arbitrarily terminated. The system defines few legal rights for its clients, and, in any case being entirely dependent on a welfare check for their survival, clients have little of the wherewithal to demand that officials observe what few rights they do have. Perhaps the worst failure of the welfare system is that through its tangle of restrictive laws and practices it manages to avoid giving any help at all to the vast majority of the American poor.

What is wrong with public welfare? Is the trouble that it is a patchwork system, lacking in any societal perspective, or bungled by piecemeal mismanagement? I think not. I think, in fact, that if the political underpinnings of the welfare system are taken into account, it turns out to be a comprehensive and adaptive social planning *system*.

The complex arrangements through which public welfare is administered are, in fact, very responsive to local political realities in America. Most Americans regard every dollar spent for public relief with suspicion and resentment. Underlying these attitudes are the twin tenets of American social ideology: the economic system is open, and economic success is a matter of individual merit (and sometimes luck). Those who fail—the very poor—are therefore in some way defective as individuals. Reflecting this ideology, even leaders of the poor seem embarrassed to fight for "hand-outs" for those who should not or cannot work, or for those who cannot get a decent job at a decent wage. The middle class, for its part, wants to alleviate poverty but thinks that it should be done by "rehabilitating" the poor rather than by redistributing income. The working class is especially hostile, feeling that the welfare recipient is enjoying a free ride on their hard-earned tax dollars, and meanwhile scorning the value of work and the self-esteem of workers.

The Social Security Act of 1935 which first established a federal public assistance allowed states and localities substantial discretion in administering the program. Through the exercise of that discretion, the states and localities have evolved a complex mesh of laws, regulations, and practices which work to keep many people very poor.

Restrictive state welfare laws bar the poor from benefits: by imposing lengthy residence requirements as a condition of aid;[1] by imposing "unsuitable homes" regulations; by "employable mothers" rules (which make it legal for an official to strike a mother from the rolls on the *presumption* that employment is available). Such laws which make large numbers of the poor ineligible are designed in deference to popular American sentiment about the value of work and the immorality of the poor. Administrators of public welfare agencies reinforce restrictive laws with policies and procedures designed to appease public opinion by keeping people off the rolls, and by keeping budgets low. They achieve this objective by allowing the poor to remain ignorant of their eligibility (whoever heard of an information campaign by a Welfare Department?), by erecting a tangle of bureaucratic barriers against those who do apply, by arbitrarily and illegally rejecting many applicants, and by refusing to allot the full benefits provided by law to those who do get on the rolls. Meanwhile, the middle-class liberal ethos is also indulged: by legislative proclamations about eliminating poverty, and by a host of loudly advertised "rehabilitative" programs. It is doubtful that any social planner, contending with the same political realities, could contrive a more politically comprehensive and sensitive scheme —comprehensive and sensitive, that is, to the political forces with which a social planning system for the poor must contend.

[1] Declared to be unconstitutional by the Supreme Court in an opinion handed down on April 21, 1969.

What then of the possibilities for reform of the public welfare "delivery system" outlined by Dyckman? Public welfare is guilty on all counts: of leakage of funds to professionals, of imposing a colonial status upon the poor, of cultivation of dependence, of unresponsiveness to client taste, and of bureaucratic entrenchment. But all of these so-called flaws in the delivery system of public welfare are also functional for that system. New delivery devices, designs to achieve "systematic effectiveness" such as the use of PPBS, of direct income strategies, or the introduction of "user bureaucracies," are either unlikely to come about at all, or will be shaped to meet the political imperatives of the public welfare system. For its flaws are not the result of lapses in technique; rather its profound social failures are the result of elaborate political adaptations natural to a system designed for the poor by government in keeping with the dominant view that poverty is brought upon its victims by their own conduct.

In fact, public welfare is changing. But it is changing because a political force for reform is growing. That force is not being generated by social planning experts, or by social planning solutions. Rather it is the result of the vast movement of black people from the South to the northern cities where their numbers are beginning to count in national and municipal elections. The black poor were driven out of the South where they were trapped in a feudal economic and social system without the vote. With the mechanization of agriculture, they were driven to the cities of the North where blacks acquired two key political resources: the vote, and the threat of disruption. And government began to respond. Beginning in the early 1960's, a series of federal programs were launched which were designed to conciliate and integrate the new black voters. Federal health programs, the anti-poverty program, even urban renewal, all began to seek out and serve ghetto populations. And as the numbers of black voters in the cities grew, municipal government also became more responsive. One result was that the vast reservoir of eligible poor who were building up in the cities throughout the 1940's and 1950's began to get help from welfare. In city after city anti-poverty agencies, hospitals, and relocation agencies began to refer people for aid. And local welfare departments became more lenient. Overall, the number of people on aid to dependent children has increased by 1.6 million since 1960—and half of that increase is concentrated in sixteen major urban centers. The welfare rolls in cities like Baltimore, New York, and Newark have tripled since 1960. In other words, the poor and especially the black poor began to acquire some power in the cities. A welfare system that had always been attuned to conciliating other groups began to take some account of the poor as well. Indeed, one sign of the growing political power of the poor in the cities is the flurry of interest in "social planning," in new delivery systems, in "user" bureaucracies, and in direct income programs. For when political forces change, then so do our social planning schemes.

If political considerations are important in public welfare policy, they are of even larger significance in considering metropolitan planning. Although Dyckman expresses some worry about the politics of metropolitan planning, he answers these by insisting that planners *must* be committed to certain specifics in metropolitan development. For example, they must insist on progressive tax and revenue schemes, on programs that include social services as well as environmental considerations, and on programs that provide income, jobs, and a share in the control of programs for the poor. The main question, however, is whether metropolitan planning is likely to produce these worthwhile developments.

The politics of metropolitan planning is likely, I think, to work in precisely the opposite direction. What gains the poor have made so far, especially the black poor, is a result of their concentrations in the cities where their voting numbers, and their disruptive force, are beginning to secure policy concessions, both from national and city government. But with the establishment of metropolitan-wide jurisdictions with substantial authority over social planning, an entirely new political constituency will be carved out, a constituency dominated by inner-city whites and suburban whites. The poor and minorities in the central city will be swallowed up by this vast majority. What force will then exist to back up Dyckman's programmatic recommendations?

The mode of decision-making associated with metropolitan planning will also work to undercut the power of the unorganized and the poor. Metropolitan planning gives substantial decision-making authority to experts who sit in the upper reaches of metropolitan-wide bureaucracies, connected by a network of plans and programs to lesser functional bureaucracies. The style of decision is enormously complicated by technicism, and the actual process of decision-making is obscured in labyrinthian bureaucracies. How can the unorganized poor contend with such a government? How compelling will our good intentions as social planners be when we are not accountable to the people whose welfare we presumably have in mind?

What does our experience tell us? To whom do we experts defer? I think the answer is that good intentions of themselves are weak and malleable; we defer instead to those who can interfere, to the well-organized groups who have the money, the staff, the competence to pay attention to what we are doing, to watch over our operations, and who can threaten to impede our plans and programs.

Dyckman tries to answer some of these difficulties with proposals for citizen participation in metropolitan decision-making bodies. For example, the boards and staffs of various agencies should include representatives of the black minorities. I have little confidence in such schemes when they are not backed up by political capability. It is not Columbia University's appointment of a black trustee but its vulnerability to the trouble that students and the Harlem community can make for the University that will lead to changes in Columbia's policies in the ghetto. The black trustee by himself will do little, except perhaps to disguise the image of the interests that dominate Columbia. Metropolitan agencies are likely to give blacks a comparable "representation." Similarly, what will "local community control" mean under a metropolitan auspice? Just what is it that "the community" will control? Very likely, the administration of programs formed elsewhere, and formed in the interests of dominant groups. To say it *should* be otherwise is not to deal with the question of what political force is likely to make it otherwise.

It is important each time we speak of what we *should* do to take into account what we in fact have been doing, and why we have been doing it. Otherwise, our prescriptions will embellish the planning profession, but they are not likely to much effect what it does. Far worse than merely being impractical, we will cloud the air with deception—deceiving ourselves, and the groups whom we profess to serve.

Systematic planning, the use of management expertise, the introduction of service innovations—all of these developments can be used to reduce the inequities in our society. But they can also be used to conceal and increase those inequities. Metropolitan reorganization may bring with it comprehensiveness, expertise, and innovation. But if it also diminishes the power of the minority poor crowded into the central cities, our good intentions are not likely to count for much in the design of those comprehensive programs. And if the process of decision-making associated with comprehensiveness, expertise, and the cultivation of innovations means that a paraphernalia of technicism and bureaucracy are erected which render the planners' actions impenetrable except by those with comparable expertise and organization, the planners' good intentions will also count for little. For much as planners would like to think of themselves as an independent moral force, all our experience shows us that we work for government, and in the end our plans filter and reflect the dominant political forces which shape government action.

BERTRAM M. GROSS

Director, Center for Urban Studies, Wayne State University. Previously Professor of Political Science and Director
of the National Planning Studies Program, Maxwell Graduate School, Syracuse University. Former consultant on "social indicators" to the Secretary and Undersecretary of
Health, Education and Welfare and the US Public Administration Division. Former consultant to the Ford Foundation in India and Economic Advisor to the Israeli Ministry
of Finance. Chairman, National Capitol Regional Planning
Council, 1952–53; Executive Secretary to Council of Economic Advisers to the President, 1946–52; chief draftsman
of Employment Act of 1946; Information Division, United
States Housing Authority, 1938–41. Editor: *A Great Society; Action Under Planning: The Guidance of Economic
Development; Social Goals and Indicators for American
Society*. Author: *The Legislative Struggle: A Study in Social
Combat*.

The Challenge to Describe and Measure Social Change

A COMMENT ON THE DYCKMAN PAPER

I am interested in a word which trips lightly off the Dyckman-Piven pen
occasionally, and then is backed away from—power. I submit that Plan-Program-Budget System (PPBS) is an instrument of power. It was started
that way in the Department of Defense, and wherever it operates successfully, it is such. For a person who is validly concerned with the mobilization of power to change social systems and improve the quality of life for
all the people, this kind of thing cannot go unrecognized. Ideas, above all,
are instruments of power.

The concept of social planning is currently one of the great "blah ideas"
in America and the Western world. Dyckman's very sophisticated paper
helps draw the line between the residual concept of social planning and a
concept that would be oriented toward dealing with society or social institutions in terms of societal planning.

I am often asked to define social planning, and my first answer is, "Well, that refers to whatever economists are not doing this week." Of course, this residual concept includes a little more: something directed to dealing with black people or something done with a larger opportunity for participation by women as the second category of second-grade citizens in America. I have not yet made a head count of social planners, but I will wager that the sex ratio is quite different than it is in hard goods physical planning or economic analysis.

What economists do when they are planning is quite different from what they say they are doing. I had the privilege of writing the first, second, third, and fifth drafts of the Employment Act of 1946. When the Council of Economic Advisors was established by President Truman, our first job was planning to mobilize enough power to keep the Budget Bureau from killing us. We were successful. We also staved off the House Appropriations Committee for six long years. Economists are interested or—when you look at it behaviorally, which in government means politically—are involved in societal planning from top to bottom. It is ridiculous to talk about social (in the sense of societal) planning as though it is somehow divorced from dealing with economic facts: the allocation of economic resources based on the mobilization and use of political power.

The decisive question is: Are we interested in planning for changes in social institutions? Dyckman did speak of planning for social change. But if *social* means payments to the needy and other Bismarckian ways of preventing progress, then you can spend all your time manipulating formulae on how Milton Friedman should have devised his proposed Income Maintenance Policy, or how you would adjust it. But are we seriously interested in the planning of fundamental improvements in social institutions? If so, I think that we need desperately the kind of constructively negative criticism that Frances Piven has been making. We need still more, people who will take it seriously enough to try to define the nature of the political and social system and try to analyze what the power structure is. What is the value of social scientists who talk about the power structure and are not able to answer the question, "What *is* the power structure really?" or "*how* will you change it?" "When?" "What is needed to change it?" It is an evasion to say, "Before we can do this, before we can do that, we must change the whole system." How do you do that? Systems are not changed that way. Not at the present moment, in my judgment.

At the present moment, we have sort of the reverse of the Russian Revolution of the second decade of this century. Russia experienced a political revolution, and the people who found themselves in seats of political power, after realizing they were in the wrong country (it had been planned for Germany), decided they had better put into effect a social revolution. Somehow or other, they did it, mainly by improvisation and force. Planning was rationalized improvisation. Today, the highly industrialized nations of the world are undergoing a profound social revolution. Its magnitude has not been spelled out sufficiently by our social commentators, but many of us suspect that the industrial revolution, the nature of which was seen by only a few people in the mid-nineteenth century, is as nothing compared to the transformation of advanced industrialism into the first *service society*. Under these circumstances, with *the social revolution taking place first,* there are vast political maladjustments and conflicts on the part of people who are finding it increasingly difficult to find their bearings. They should not really be asking, "What is the name of the game?" Names change. They should be asking, "What *is* the game?" This is the question we face if we conceive of social planning (in the societal rather than the residual sense) as planning for changes, adaptations in various parts of a society which is already undergoing profound and unproclaimed social changes—deeply, rapidly, and confusingly.

It is argued that societal changes are meaningful only to the extent that they diminish inequality. The term "inequality" is one of the nonsense pieces of verbiage that we carry along with us. We do not mean equal in the mathematical sense. If we mean anything by "unequal," we refer to a distribution pattern which is regarded as unjust. With rapidly changing values and aspirations in society, my prognosis is that the perceptions of relative deprivation are going to change radically in this country, and that we must develop very new techniques for mapping, describing, and predicting such changes. In older societies, as in the feudal societies of the past and the present, and in many caste systems, extreme inequality existed without any perception of injustice in the distribution of man's worldly goods. Status and position was regarded as just with everybody in his proper place. Now the conceptions of what is one's due are very rapidly changing in what is becoming a sort of a muddled meritocracy, with the whole society becoming something like a civil service system, with many different and confusing career ladders intersecting at various points.

We lack, as yet, the intellectual tools with which to describe, measure, and predict the operation of this process, essentially the transformation of the familiar processes of historically identifiable industrial society into the as yet unfamiliar processes of the emerging service society. The forging of these tools for description, measurement, and prediction is the most basic challenge confronting social scientists and planners who choose to deal with societal change.

RALPH M. FIELD

Planning Consultant, New York City and San Juan, Puerto Rico. Consultant to the Puerto Rico Planning Board and the Puerto Rico Agricultural Council. Formerly staff planner, Smith, Haines, Lundberg and Wachler; Assistant Director, Community Renewal Program, New York City Department of City Planning; chief planner in study of reclamation plan of Hackensack Meadowlands, New Jersey; staff of Detroit Metropolitan Regional Planning Commission. B.A. and MCP, University of California, Berkeley.

Economic and Resource Planning in a Market-Based Economy

Economic and resource development is a topic bearing a curious affinity to that of motherhood. Both involve the act of reproduction and are embraced with like fervor as variant expressions of human nurturing. Those impatient with theory might be inclined to ascribe the motives in one to sex and in the other to profit—high in popularity with most people, difficult in either case to argue against as powerful motivating forces, and illustrative of the complexity of viewpoint inherent in the subject before us.

How economic development can better serve man, living in an environment increasingly molded by the imperatives of technology, is a challenge particularly germane to the United States. From its founding, six generations of in-migrating European whites, and transported African blacks, have peopled a continent, turned its vast interior plains into the world's most productive agricultural region, and created an economic mechanism of enormous power and vitality.

That mechanism has now freed the bulk of Americans from basic material shortages. Measured by monetary values, we are rich. But judged by other than material values, we measure up less well. We are rich—but not beautiful. Certainly we are not a contented people.

America faces many problems. The maldistribution of wealth is a major one, and continued economic growth is a precondition for its elimination. It is not, however, the sole problem, nor necessarily the most difficult one, if only because we possess many of the institutional means as well as the productive capacity to deal with it, if we have the will and the patience to do so.

Not poverty but its opposite raises questions of an even more fundamental nature. While our market economy is equipped to produce in quantity, we are less well-prepared to define—no less than to produce—the elements which insure the quality of life. Is, in fact, quality an element that can be produced with the institutional means at our disposal?

Historically, the energies that might have split a nation of such great population diversity as ours have been neutralized in quest of material gain. But today we ask—gain for what? For the multiplication of products or the enhancement of environmental quality? How successfully can the market mechanism respond to such issues?

The subject is a complicated one, with the line dividing the true from the obvious a fine one. If we succeed in establishing a perspective for fitting some of the pieces together, we shall have accomplished our purpose.

Progress toward environmental self-awareness has evolved as a series of successive approximations to a cohesive set of national policies. It proceeded on the basis of regional parochialism and the aggressive self-assertion of producer groups in agriculture, timber, power, transportation, and manufacturing, organized territorially in competing centers of power. The first stage was the longest, extending to the turn of the century. After the Civil War, development was characterized by a national free-for-all. Attention at the time was fixed on opening new territory to settlement and development. Public acquisition and private parcelization of the public domain through land grants and homesteading proved an effective means of attracting both capital and manpower to the undeveloped regions of the West. National policy aimed at speeding resource exploitation in establishing basic industry, agriculture, and continental transport. In the course of this expansion, fortunes were amassed and great economic combines created in coal, timber, oil, and other basic resources.

The period of the second approximation to a cohesive resource development policy came during the Theodore Roosevelt Administration. Roosevelt rode to power on a platform of trust busting. The conservation movement came in on the swell, with the scientific-intellectual content supplied by such men as John Wesley Powell, George Perkins Marsh, and

Gifford Pinchot. The view of then current resource practices as socially wasteful to the nation but profitable to a few was attuned to Roosevelt's political program for curbing monopoly growth. Hence, the political momentum in favor of competitive enterprise versus economic combination opened the door to the advanced resource views of Pinchot and others, on the basis of popular acceptance of the scarcity thesis.

Pinchot and those associated with him were not opposed to the exploitation of resources in the development process. Theirs was a scientific-rationalist approach to resource management in the interests of long-term development ends. The enemy was not private enterprise but narrow-minded enterprise.

A third step toward environmental self-awareness occurred as a result of World War I. For the first time, the allocation of strategically important resources was controlled by the federal government on the basis of established national priorities. The regulation of production and transportation was accomplished with government controls over prices, production, and materials allocation. The country got a strong, though short-lived, taste of how the materials and manpower of the nation could be mobilized to meet specific ends.

This third stage in the evolutionary process lapsed into dormancy after the war as the nation once more reverted to a great buying, building, and spending spree which ended abruptly in 1929. A pattern was becoming clear: resource policy and directed economic growth would arouse interest only during periods of heightened national political activity associated with national crisis. In periods of prosperity, the federal function was to make itself useful but scarce.

The fourth phase was ushered in by the Depression, when Theodore Roosevelt's Square Deal was far surpassed by the radical experimentation of Franklin Roosevelt's New Deal. Government asserted itself forcefully through the creation of the National Recovery Administration in 1933. NRA was given broad authority to fix prices and establish production quotas among participating firms in over five hundred industries.

While NRA was planning industrial recovery, the Agricultural Adjustment Administration was establishing producer controls and farm commodity prices. Both agencies were powerful instruments of economic planning. The reaction against the early New Deal policies eventually won out. But by the time these economic controls were declared unconstitutional in 1935, the organization of agriculture had profoundly changed. Present regulations governing farm production are very much a legacy of that era. From direct control, the federal government retreated to a position "of an essentially judicial character" over business practices, a policy which continued until World War II.

In the resource area, the federal impact was more enduring. TVA was established to carry out integrated development of the entire Tennessee drainage basin. National studies of soil and water resources were initiated. Soil conservation districts were established, and unemployed youth recruited into the Civilian Conservation Corps to carry out reforestation and conservation programs. While the central regulatory and policy planning agencies, including the National Resources Planning Board, may have been temporary, the ideas and concepts survived in one form or another. By 1943, other instruments were being strengthened as, for example, the Bureau of the Budget, to which some of the responsibilities of the NRPB were transferred; even in the private sector, petroleum production continues to be regulated by the Interstate Oil Compact Commission.

World War II marked the fifth stage. With the nation totally mobilized, controls were used, as in World War I, to allocate raw materials and set commodity prices. War accomplished the economic miracle. GNP soared, increasing by 73 per cent between 1940 and 1944. Full employment occurred overnight, and manpower planning, in accordance with national production priorities and armed forces needs, emerged as a new area of governmental action.

The war accelerated the long process of rural-urban movement and showed how rapidly migrants could be accommodated in new jobs and new settings. In northern California, for example, trains brought thousands of workers from the rural South to the Kaiser shipyards in Richmond. Once more, in pursuit of national objectives and under the impetus of crisis, development miracles became possible in resource planning, allocation, industrial production, and manpower training.

The war put other towns on the map—Alamagordo and Los Alamos in New Mexico, Oak Ridge in Tennessee—new towns that were to produce new products destined to revolutionize warfare, our conception of the world, and our knowledge of matter and energy. When the war ended, Oak Ridge grew but Richmond was left without an economic base. The lesson of wartime manpower training was forgotten, and instead of peacetime training programs to relocate thousands of predominantly Negro workers, massive programs of urban redevelopment got rid of the unemployed by bulldozing the temporary housing that had been constructed to accommodate them. This tale of two cities—Oak Ridge and Richmond—sets the stage for the period of the sixth approximation. However, before turning to the present, let us examine the question of resources more closely.

Webster's Dictionary defines a resource as "computable wealth . . . available means . . . immediate and possible sources of revenues." Webster must have been a drop-out economist. In actuality, resources are a function of consciousness on the one hand, and inventiveness on the other. If you are primarily aware of your poverty, resources are for conversion into material wealth. If you had been the Ford executive who shared responsibility for producing the Edsel, a resource of precious value might have been a wilderness retreat—with no roads and no automobiles.

In material terms, resource availability is also a function of science and technology. To the extent that our technology grows stronger, our concern about resource depletion lessens. Where once the emphasis was on conserving the base resources and avoiding waste as a hedge against almost certain shortages, today we see that the supply of resources is inseparable from the technology of chemical and molecular engineering through which synthetics can be made to replace natural products. We thus move from a static to a dynamic system of accounting. But even in absolute terms, we do not seem to be facing any serious shortages of our major industrial raw materials such as iron ore, petroleum or timber. Despite deterioration of its quality, our water supplies are reported to be adequate, at least in the eastern United States. The western states, with a higher rate of water depletion due to irrigation, will face definite conflicts in use as industrial and municipal water demands rise. But here, too, if we want to satisfy all interest groups by incurring higher costs, the water resources of western Canada and even Alaska could be tapped.

In terms of domestic food requirements, our needs can more than adequately be met from available agricultural soil resources. Nor do we face shortages of land. Congestion in many of our cities, particularly in the East, results from a settlement pattern influenced by complex taxation, housing market, and work-residence relationships that produce inner area land crowding and outer area sprawl, abetted in turn by a tremendous growth in automobile ownership.

Recreational and scenic resources inject a new dimension of need—that of quality. While we can live with low-grade iron ore, we are increasingly restive at the prospect of living with impure water, deteriorated air, and sordid landscapes. The middle class may have what it wants in material possessions, from outdoor swimming pools to indoor saunas, but it cannot buy clean air, pure water, quiet wilderness, reduced noise levels in our cities. And there are limits to the quality of services that are available for purchase. First-rate teaching and medical practice is limited not by consumer income but by the availability of nurtured intelligence.

Technology has been a liberating force, and we are, by its standards, the most liberated of peoples, as we enter the era of the three-car family. Technology has cheapened material goods to the point where the market has something for everybody. But it has also ensnared us into collectively accepting what individually we reject and wish to insulate ourselves against. But individual insulation becomes more difficult to achieve, for free goods—clean air and pure water—by definition cannot be purchased in the market. Neither can more ephemeral qualities like human dignity and equality.

Just as the action of a local municipality or industrial plant may have an impact on the broader geographical surroundings, so may a national industry exert an enormous impact on national environmental quality. Economists are beginning to examine these issues under the heading of "side effect costs"; those costs arising as a consequence of production, but not absorbed by the primary producer—or in the parlance of the economist —costs which represent "external diseconomies" or simply "externalities."

It is intriguing how elegant the jargon becomes when examining the problem in an industrial context. But when a slum dweller disposes of his garbage by gravity flow from the window—a least cost solution to his disposal problem—it is hardly regarded as an "externality." Nor need one be an economist to know where the responsibility lies.

Our knowledge of the environment is far from complete, yet we know more about cause and effect relationships than actions until now would indicate. The reasons for inaction can be traced to the cross purposes operating in our highly diverse society, which has stressed above all, production on a mass scale. The conflict between quantity and quality is one which must be examined in terms of the forces presently at work as we move toward a fuller awareness of our national environment.

1. Between 1950 and 1966 federal expenditures rose from $50 billion to over $142 billion. Growing federal spending, principally for weapons research and armaments, is thus a major force in the present period. It has resulted in the federal government becoming the nation's largest single purchaser of goods and services from private industry. Direct intervention, which marked the wartime period, has been succeeded by an array of indirect measures including the establishment of standards and specifications over product design and performance, negotiated profits, and a voice

in hiring practices of businesses holding government contracts. Private industry has accommodated to these new controls with relative ease.

2. A second major characteristic of this period is the consolidation of corporate strength through diversification and vertical integration resulting in corporate dominance in the production of material goods. The five hundred largest corporations now account for about half of all goods and services produced in the United States. Such corporate growth has brought extensive planning techniques to business operations, albeit along fairly narrow product lines. The techniques have extended beyond production to sales as well—to what Galbraith notes as "a massive growth in the apparatus of persuasion and exhortation that is associated with the sale of goods." In his view, corporate planning ". . . must deliberately insure that planned supply equals planned use." To do otherwise would be to jeopardize the long-term capital commitments required for new product development. The net effect is for planning to supersede the market, but according to Galbraith, "the enemy of the market is not ideology, but the engineer."

3. A third element of the present period is the emergence of a large technical and scientific estate, absolutely indispensable to the functioning of big government and large-scale business enterprise, which in turn hold a monopoly of engineering and scientific talent.

4. A fourth characteristic is the unprecedented increase in real income and consumer purchasing power. In 1967, half of American families had an annual income of more than $8000. People buy more, and their material accoutrements, of which the most formidable is the automobile, must be accommodated within more concentrated areas of national space.

5. This introduces a fifth element—a growing consciousness of people as consumers, not only of discrete goods but of the environment. The emergence of strong consumer groups to counterbalance public and private producer group action promises to be a potentially strong force. At present their efforts are particular and localized, but there is a growing community of consumer interests that transcends local boundaries. As their consciousness expands, so will their political power, and federal action will increasingly reflect their demands.

6. A sixth force in the present period is the demand for the elimination of urban and rural poverty. In 1967, 5.3 million families had incomes which placed them within the poverty category, more than 10 per cent of the nation's 49.8 million families. Thus, despite the high level of general

prosperity, serious economic problems remain, though they have become increasingly localized.

7. Related to, but also distinct from the anti-poverty crusade, is the drive for equality in social and economic opportunity. Its demands are only partially quantitative. Ask a rural housewife in a depressed farming area what her needs are, and she might pull out a Sears Roebuck catalogue. Ask the same question of a black urban housewife in a depressed urban area, and she might pull out the Report of the National Advisory Commission on Civil Disorders. It is relatively much easier to satisfy the Sears Roebuck kind of claim. We know what it entails. It is considerably more difficult to satisfy the other kind of claim—and upsets considerably more people. It even upset President Johnson.

In the first instance, the people are role-oriented and traditional. In the second instance, the people are achievement-oriented and tradition breakers. That is why the anti-poverty crusade and the fight for equality both converge and diverge. With its potentially strongest element—organized labor —largely sitting on the sidelines, to that extent the anti-poverty-equal opportunity coalition is a weak and shifting one. It is linked to a need for more jobs, a guaranteed income, and changes in the structure of welfare, as well as to the quality of education, and meaningful local self-determination. Its effect has been to catapult the race issue into the center of American political life. Despite shifting alliances, the demand for equality will be among the most persistent and critical confronting American society, giving sharper focus to the question of national development priorities.

8. A final characteristic of this period, and one with which we are thoroughly familiar, is the continuing redistribution of population from rural to urban environments, increasing the political strength of cities and metropolitan areas as contenders for a larger share of the federal budget.

Given these forces and the emerging coalitions they produce, what are the implications for national policy in economic and resource development during the next period of national life?

Two broad categories of demand confront us—the demand for greater quantity, which will draw its most consistent spokesmen from among the urban poor, and the demand for environmental quality, which will be pressed by groups whose most vocal advocates will be middle class, professional, and college educated. Neither big government nor big business can remain aloof from the issues they pose. These areas of demand place different claims on available resources. Satisfying them will call for a rigorous evaluation of national priorities among resource-related programs —as for example between urban and agricultural development.

In 1965 the federal government spent $800 million on housing, community development, and recreation. In the same year, over $6 billion was spent on agriculture and natural resources, including water programs. A plan is now under study to divert water from the Mississippi River to the High Plains region of West Texas—800 miles away and 3500 feet higher in altitude. The Bureau of Reclamation has found this project to be physically feasible. But what economic or ecological justification exists for diverting more rivers to irrigate more arid land, when we are subsidizing farmers to keep existing cultivated acreage out of production? Of course the evaluation of an individual project may show it to be feasible! But within what frame of reference is feasibility to be judged—a narrow sectional framework or one based on a consideration of national needs?

Can we afford to delay any longer the task of weighing present agricultural and water resource policies against our pressing urban and metropolitan needs? In the America of the 1960's, the most critical watersheds have proven to be the demographic ones—and these flow north, draining the alluvial agricultural areas of the Mississippi Basin and emptying into the metropolitan areas of Chicago, St. Louis, and Cincinnati. Sooner or later we will have to adjust our resource program to the facts of demographic flow.

What, for example, can be done about the continuing irrigation emphasis in water-resource development? At one symposium it was suggested, in mock seriousness, that the most direct solution might be to abolish the Bureau of Reclamation. But then we would still be faced with the dam-building zeal of the Corps of Engineers. I would propose something less traumatic than abolition—reinterpret their functions in accordance with current needs. Have every water bill under consideration by Congress evaluated by an environmental policy group in terms of its effect on pollution abatement as well as upon the more traditional purposes of waterways development. What agencies possess greater cumulative experience in water resources management? Let us harness their great expertise to the solution of today's problems by broadening their functions in accordance with their technical and professional capabilities.

With rising expenditures, the federal establishment has mushroomed into a broadening array of executive agencies, quasi-independent authorities, *ad hoc* advisory bodies, inter-agency committees, and presidential task forces—not to mention the growing role of the independent federal regulatory agencies. Congress itself has responded to greater federal responsibility by a proliferation of sub-committees within standing committees. How to achieve policy cohesion in the absence of a national planning agency—which is not a realistic prospect—is a serious dilemma, for from what policy-making locus does all of this activity flow? In certain areas we are better equipped than in others.

The greatest potential for centralized coordination is in the office of the President. At the end of World War II, Congress, fearing adverse economic effects of demobilization, passed the Employment Act of 1946, creating a Council of Economic Advisors. Its access to both the President, and to the Congress, through the Joint Economic Committee, makes it a valuable instrument in the formulation of national policy affecting economic growth and stabilization.

We are decidedly less well equipped in the area of resource and environmental policy-making or program coordination. Regrouping the great range of activities affecting environment could only prove self-defeating. Many agencies and programs should be concerned with development, conservation, and environmental quality. This new focus is to be supported, even at the risk of duplication and overlapping—decidedly lesser evils.

What is lacking, however, is the coordination of policy views at the center. Such coordination has, in the past, been associated with national crisis. How to achieve a cohesive national focus in the absence of either war or depression is a key question. The creation of the Council of Economic Advisors in the executive office of the President was a major institutional step toward comprehensive policy coordination in the economic sphere. An expansion of that concept to include a Council of Ecological Advisors has been advocated. Let me illustrate the need for such a policy-formulating group by drawing on my own experience.

The urge toward economic development has motivated the Puerto Rican government to undertake a vigorous program of promoting industrial growth. Emphasizing light industry initially, the focus has now shifted to the heavy industrial sector. One basis for this reorientation was the conclusion reached in studies done in the late 1950's showing that Puerto Rico had the potentialities for attracting oil refining and petrochemical industries. Subsequent analysis convinced the Puerto Rican Economic Development Administration (EDA) to pursue the idea. Contact was first made with Phillips Petroleum, and a development commitment was given pending approval from the Department of Interior, raising the Phillips quota on the importation of foreign crude oil. Negotiations with the Oil Import Administration began in early 1960 and led to a favorable decision, largely because the federal government recognized the pressing developmental needs of the Commonwealth. The initial exemption in oil import quotas has been broadened, and three or four oil companies are now building or planning refinery and petrochemical complexes on the island.

All went well until the biologists and ecologists began to point to the potentially harmful effects that major petrochemical installations might have on marine biology and plant ecology along the coastal rim. Also, people began to wonder about the radical change in landscape from large-scale complexes on an island thirty-five by one hundred miles. Economic values are uppermost in this developing society. The people love the land and the landscape, but they have been desperately poor for a long time.

This conflict in values is not theirs alone. Some months previously, I had been on Puerto Rico's southwest coast, and happened to spend time with a party from the US National Park Service, in the area to check into pollution dangers that might affect a coastal inlet of rare bioluminescense around La Parguera. There are few such known bodies of water in the world, the result of communities of micro-organisms dependent on a delicate and not well understood ecosystem. The Park Service people were concerned about pollutants that might flow along westerly currents from the scheduled industrial development further east. Only later did it occur to me that the survey party was from the same arm of the federal government responsible for the approval of the oil and petrochemical installations—the Department of Interior, home to both the National Park Service and the Oil Import Administration.

In one case, a bureau within a department reached a decision favoring economic development based on a pressing local need for jobs. In the other case, a sister agency was raising the red flag over the potential destruction of an irreplaceable natural phenomenon. Even on the local scene, not until after the development commitments were made did individual ecologists and biologists voice their concern. The industrial planners, who had achieved what they regarded as a major developmental coup, could be understandably miffed at the general display of ingratitude.

Such conflict is neither irreconcilable nor inevitable. Had a responsible group considered the facts before any development decisions were made, they might have suggested guidelines for the protection of the natural environment without thwarting material progress. Unfortunately, no one was responsible for taking a comprehensive view—if only because no one was aware of what the limits of comprehensiveness entailed. Ecological awareness is a relatively new phenomenon for planners, both in Puerto Rico and on the mainland as well.

I have used the example of petrochemicals in the Caribbean. Others could talk with authority of steel along the Indiana dunes, power generation along the Hudson, or highways through the wilderness areas. But, relatively speaking, these are yesterday's problems. What about tomorrow's?

By 1972, the supersonic transport will be with us. A prevalent assumption seems to be that the public's noise threshold will simply increase to levels at which it can tolerate sonic boom. We are moving along rapidly in atomic power generation for domestic use—more rapidly than solutions are forthcoming for the disposal of radioctive wastes. No group is now responsible for thinking comprehensively about these problems—the impact of past and future technology upon environmental quality, and the balancing of qualitative goals against developmental needs. Establishing a National Council of Ecological Advisors to the President is one approach. So is the creation of Regional Environmental Councils to advise state and local government. We need to move ahead on this front rapidly.

Important as it may be, the enunciation of national policies on resource management and economic growth are simply first steps. How effective are the instruments we possess for putting those policies into effect? Since 1946, for example, we have had an economic policy of maintaining full employment through monetary and fiscal controls, and government spending. These measures have proven effective in promoting general prosperity. They have not succeeded, however, in eliminating poverty concentrations and continuing high rates of unemployment and underemployment in urban slums or in Appalachia. The reason is quite simple—economic regulators are relatively blunt instruments. To tell unemployed Negro youths that GNP has risen 4 per cent last year will not "cool" them one bit, primarily because the instruments of policy have little direct impact upon them or the areas in which they live.

Over-all economic strategy without planning the specific employment consequences may simply result in aggregate economic growth without corresponding economic development. The industry focus is key, not only in planning for economic development, but in planning for environmental quality as well. Two factors—the concentration of industrial production in large corporate enterprise, and the growing dependence of corporate enterprise on government expenditures—create a new and as yet relatively unexplored potential for coordinating economic and environmental planning.

In addition to promoting the growth of key industries by centrally planned expenditure decisions, and coordinating government and corporate locational decisions, new initiatives in economic development are called for, with the means tailored to the requirements of specific groups.

The redistribution of population in accordance with area resource potential is a historic pattern in US development history. At one time, this followed from an area's agricultural or mineral reserves. Today, however, institutional resources are playing the role that natural resources did during an earlier period. Instead of promoting investment from the Four Corners to the Ozarks and Appalachia, we might be better advised to use development funds for providing people from these areas with the skills and self-assurance to migrate.

If a sixth to a third of Appalachia's population could be induced to leave, Appalachia's resources would be adequate to support its remaining population. Judging by the rate of out-migration, that is the path they are already taking. But how well equipped are they for the journey? Probably the most effective step in getting the people of Appalachia employed is through a one-way ticket to Cincinnati, St. Louis, or Chicago, with intensive occupational skill development programs at either end of the road. It is the urban centers that possess the critical combination of public and private enterprise, together with the institutional resources, either existing or potential, to absorb a redundant rural labor force. These resources, however, must be molded to the job, and in the process, new sources of employment created in the nongoods service sector of the economy. It may be a turbulent process, but if we can come through it, we will have succeeded in molding new urban institutions to eradicate the remaining vestiges of urban poverty and rural peonage.

Organized demand requires institutional means for its satisfaction. How can institutional changes affect the issues of quantity and quality? Since our major economic strength lies in the private sector, particularly in corporate business, new institutional accommodations are called for in the role of corporate enterprise, as well as in the traditional relationship between business and government. As industry becomes structurally more cohesive, it should be possible to consider industry-wide solutions to specific economic as well as environmental problems. If the automobile industry is going to produce 9 or 12 million cars per year, who is to say "stop"? If production is not to be externally controlled, can it be internally self-regulated? One way of insuring corporate responsibility may be to expand its area of functional responsibility, thereby holding it accountable for the

consequences of production decisions in terms of consumption consequences. In automobile production, for example, those responsible for the
product might also be made responsible for the path.

Why not transfer the national trunk line system of highways to a
consortium of automotive manufacturers? The object of the experiment
would be to see what innovative feedback would result from utilizing the
industry's enormous technological resources to perfect a focused and
clearly delineated functional system. By holding the consortium publicly
accountable for the efficient operation of the vehicular trunk lines, we
might force the design, the production and the replacement of automobiles
to be systematically related to the carrying capacity, design, and safety of
the entire trunk line network, including terminal facilities within central
cities. Technological improvements in the product would thus be accompanied by technological improvements in the path and in the planning and
design of terminals as well. Money now spent on styling might then become
available for research and development in enhancing private transportation. It would, in effect, present the automobile industry with a major
countertask, to balance its presently one-sided and relatively simple emphasis on production. Since state highway departments are not widely
regarded as bastions of democratic decision-making, what democratic
values would we sacrifice by squarely lodging the system in the hands of
such a private, but publicly accountable consortium of automobile manufacturers? Nor is there any inherent reason for such a group not to assume
the task of vehicular licensing and inspection—clearly a standardized,
repetitious, product-related function—superfluous to the role of government.
Democracy would not collapse even though fifty-one bureaus of motor
vehicles might.

While the foregoing may appear a bit overdrawn even as a flight of
fancy, it is not entirely beyond the bounds of rationality. As public and
private sectors increasingly interpenetrate, the public interest might be
better served through the enforcement of standards to insure uniformly
high levels of environmental quality rather than through direct public
control of operations.

We have learned to live with corporate concentration and industrial
giantism, much as the private sector has learned to accommodate to a wide
variety of direct and indirect public controls. How can we use this mutual
accommodation in the solution of economic and environmental problems?
Could we, for example, capitalize on corporate concentration by analyzing
(on an industry-by-industry basis) the potentials for integrating public

economic and environmental goals and policies, with the narrow but expert business planning for production and employment? Might it be possible to devise a list of tasks and countertasks for specific industries or industrial groupings according to their functional activities?

Industry is certainly in the best position to evaluate its short- and long-term manpower requirements. It may be in the best position to assume vocational training on an industry or inter-industry basis as a private, nonprofit function. There are obvious advantages to spinning off vocational education to the private sector, the most important of which is that it relieves the public educational system of a task for which it is unsuited, and in which it has performed poorly. If we are serious about developing our manpower resources, we must utilize those means best designed to translate potentialities into concrete accomplishments. By transferring much of vocational training to private industry, we go far toward achieving this goal. On the other hand, by rededicating public education to the nurturing of intelligence during the earlier formative years—the years when learning occurs most rapidly—we will have achieved much in assuring an integrated, adaptable population, essential to the processes of democratic development.

In conclusion, I return to the theme with which I began—reproduction in the interest of environmental enhancement. That, of course, is what economic development, as opposed to economic growth, is all about—and that is why GNP and the other usual indicies are insufficient measures in evaluating progress in economic development. Economic *development* must guarantee opportunity for advancement. Economic *growth* merely measures the increase in money values. The differences are profound, for it is entirely possible to conceive of rising development with declining growth. There are some who understand this. Stewart Udall is one. He writes:

> If we are to establish the secure foundations of an equal-opportunity society and master the sensitive arts of building a life-encouraging environment, then at this moment in history we need to realize that:
> Bigger is not better; slower may be faster; less may well mean more.

LYNTON K. CALDWELL

Professor of Government, Indiana University. Holds graduate degrees from Harvard University and the University of
Chicago. Formerly with the Council of State Governments,
the Agency for International Development, and the United
Nations. Consulting and technical assistance assignments in
Columbia, Pakistan, the Phillippines, Thailand, Turkey, In-
donesia, and with the Central Treaty Organization. Editor
of comprehensive annotated bibliography on science, technology, and public policy; currently preparing a book entitled, *Environmental Administration: An Emerging Task
of Modern Government.*

Economic Organization and Environmental Management

A COMMENT ON THE FIELD PAPER

Critiques of papers appear in many forms. They may range from comprehensive and detailed analysis of a paper under review to essays that are
critiques in name only, using the review merely as a point of departure.
This critique will avoid these extremes. It will offer a critical analysis, but
one that is limited to what I take to be the principal thesis of Ralph Field's
paper.

It will not review the extended middle section of the paper, which
describes a series of historical stages in the evolution of American attitudes
toward the functions of government in relation to resources and the environment. The historical section provides a good description of the
lagging transformation of American values and political expectations in
relation to environmental quality. It affords a background in pragmatic
political theory for the thesis toward which Field's paper is directed. This
thesis, as I read it, is not stated explicitly in any single sentence or para-
graph. And so, in stating it here, I may be expressing merely my interpretation and not the author's intent, but this is what I understand Field, in
effect, to say:

71

The historical evolution of the American political economy has resulted in the institutional malplacement of certain major responsibilities for the protection and management of the nation's physical
environment. The unique role of government as "guardian of the
public interest" has been confused by making it responsible for a
large number of operational and developmental activities which could
be performed more economically and with greater social efficiency by
nongovernmental (private) economic organizations. The production
sector of American society—agriculture, manufacturing, and the ex-
tractive industries—has been generally relieved of responsibility for
the social costs incurred by its operations (the so-called externalities
of the economists). The consequence has been that neither government nor the private economic sector performs responsibly in relation
to the quality of the American environment. Institutional reform is
needed, and in Field's words, ". . . social control in private decision-
making and democratic control in public decision-making are the institutional objectives that we should seek to promote."

I am in general agreement with this thesis, although I am not persuaded
of the feasibility of some of its applications that Field suggests. For example, although it would be very instructive to observe the outcomes of
a policy by which the automotive industry was made responsible for the
construction and maintenance of public highways used by automobiles, I
question its feasibility under present circumstances. More importantly, I
believe that Field dismisses too readily the possible efficacy of federal
administrative reorganization. He writes: "Regrouping of the great range
of activities affecting the environment would probably be no more than an
exercise in futility." This surmise seems inconsistent with Field's belief in
the efficacy of institutional reform, and inconsistent with his earlier statement that ". . . a constant process of rethinking appropriate functional
groupings within government is necessary." The question of whether the
federal government can be reorganized on behalf of a national policy for
the environment more truly in keeping with the public interest is crucial to
Field's thesis. Consequently, my commentary will be directed primarily to
this question.

Whether reorganization can provide a remedy for organizational ills
depends upon many variable factors. It is not a question to be answered in
the abstract. The failure of particular reorganizations to yield desired results does not necessarily indicate that reorganization per se is futile. There
are many forms of organized relationships in society, and no student of
organization has been known to argue seriously that each of them is
equally suitable for any type of collective enterprise. If the effects of re-

organization were always superficial, it is doubtful that the very threat of reorganization would bring the anxiety that it inevitably does to organizational personnel.

There is a tendency among critics of reorganization to take as a remedy for organizational malfunctions an unduly limiting and superficial view of the meaning of organization. Reorganization may be merely a reshuffling of bureaus (which may or may not bring improved performance), or it may be much more. Reorganization can bring about a fundamental change in the structure of power and influence in organizations; it can alter expectations and can open or foreclose opportunities. Reorganization can be a profound and subtle tool of policy, and this is why it is so often feared and resisted.

Organization involves both technical and political aspects, and they are frequently so intermeshed that unless all major aspects of an organizational problem can be dealt with effectively, no part of the problem can satisfactorily be resolved. Much of the pessimism regarding the efficacy of governmental reorganization reflects disappointment in the results of reorganization plans based largely on technical considerations, and which failed to cope adequately with political realities. To be effective, reorganization must restructure not only the form but also the substance of power. Particularly in democratic societies, the pluralism of interests, and the penchant of politicians for compromise, leaves the reorganizing reformers with the aesthetic satisfaction of a rationalized organization chart, and the tough-minded intransigent political realists in full possession of their traditional ways of doing business.

The lesson which this exercise in futility teaches is not that reorganization does not solve problems, but that complex political problems are not solved by naive reorganization. Only the politically inexperienced would believe that merely to move the Bureau of Reclamation, the Bureau of Public Roads, or the Corps of Engineers, from one department to another would seriously impair the enormous independent power of decision enjoyed by these agencies. If, in the interest of national environmental policy, it would be desirable to bring these technocratic baronies under full public control, the primary objective of a reorganization effort must be to displace the bases of their political power. Reorganization in any meaningful sense is not an innocuous substitute for politics; it *is* politics in the most definitive sense, with outcomes that entail political and economic life or death for many of the contending parties.

Reorganization measures that successfully "liquidate" long-standing

political and economic arrangements are almost inevitably crisis phenomena. The traumatic shock of military or economic debacle disorganizes
"normal" political responses and relationships. The farsighted reformer is
prepared to take advantage of a temporary breakdown of countervailing
inhibitions. Disaster strikes, and the public is alarmed and confused. Calls
for action resound. The "public interest," normally an abstraction, takes
on a special and urgent meaning, overriding long-standing and seemingly
impregnable obstructions. A new order, that few would have believed
possible, comes into existence—seemingly overnight. In fact, most fundamental reorganization measures have a long period of gestation. The labor
pains of their birth and the accompanying cries of political anguish are
merely the culmination of events long in the making.

Large numbers of Americans, including some of the most intelligent and
sophisticated, seem strangely oblivious of these simple behavioral realities—the common historical experience of the rest of mankind. There
appears to be a tacit assumption among Americans that Providence has
granted them a perpetual dispensation from what may informally be called
"the laws of history." The indignant and bewildered reaction of many
Americans to riots and racial conflicts on city streets and college campuses
is only the most recent manifestation of a pervasive political naïveté among
the American people. And the "liberals" are no less naive than the "con-
servatives"—only differently so.

A reading of the *Report of the National Advisory Commission on Civil
Disorders,* of official and unofficial explanations of the origins and conduct
of the Vietnamese war, or of conjectures as to how the nation will accommodate more than 300 million inhabitants by the year 2000, leave one with
the feeling that the nation is becoming one vast Disneyland of make-be-
lieve. When national explanation fails, the human mind seeks recourse to
proverbs that presumably contain basic truths beyond the test of science.
But proverbial wisdom tends to contradict itself. We are told that whom
the gods would destroy, they first inflict with madness, but we are also
assured that God takes care of little children and Americans. Thus, folk-
lore does not offer a promising avenue to the solution of America's fantasyland fixations. And if large sectors of American society *are* out of touch
with important sectors of reality, the circumstance has serious implications
for the nation's future.

Such evidence as we have indicates to me that American society, as a
collectivity, is not realistic in relation to man-environment relationships.
The network of causality interconnecting the effects of science, technology,

economic growth, population dynamics, and human behavior, is poorly understood at best. But even poor understanding might induce a concern and a caution in the informed mind that appears to be utterly absent among the great mass of the people and their political, economic, and spiritual representatives. People who are "insane," that is to say those out of touch with reality, are potentially dangerous to themselves and to others. But the danger may be magnified exponentially when the insane have at their command the powers of science-based technology. Flying through fantasyland at supersonic speed is a model for a journey to disaster.

The technoscientific society of late twentieth-century America has no historical precedent, but neither is there evidence of its immunity to the cause-effect sequences of the natural world. Under the so-called laws that appear to govern nature, ours is a most improbable society on a most improbable planet. The very limited scope of human experience permits us to be largely unaware of our great and increasing vulnerability. Our society seems to have moved into a paradoxical situation in which the practical man's "reality" is based on fantasy, and the reality perceived by science seems unreal and hence irrelevant to practical men. Our so-called conquest of nature—and especially of the atom—has increased our vulnerability to the operation of physical laws.

These considerations lead me to three questions concerning economic and political organization for environmental management. The first of these concerns the "reality" problem: How can the belief-patterns of American society be restructured so as to permit a reordering of national priorities consistent with environmental realities?

Philosophical objections may be interposed against the assumption that there are knowable, demonstrable environmental realities, understood with a certainty sufficient to provide a basis for rational public decision. The answer, of course, is that to *perceive* the human environment holistically does not imply an attempt to do the impossible by *managing* it holistically. The feasible philosophical approach to the environment is through general systems theory which, like *ad hoc* methods, deals with specific objects and events, but unlike the *ad hoc* approach deals with them, in so far as feasible, in relation to the total systems of which they are interrelating components. Fortunately, in the intellectual world of the physical sciences, engineering, and biology, the whole-parts concepts of field theory, systems theory, and ecology are demonstrably valid means of understanding and manipulating complex realities.

Operational models in submarines and spaceships, and theoretical models for moon ports, and terrestrial megastructures, have conditioned an influential minority of the more highly educated members of society to think ecologically, or in terms of parts-to-whole relationships. But this kind of thinking is alien to the prevailing assumptions and practices of law and government. The generation gap between the middle-aged and youth in contemporary society is paralleled by an equally wide gap between the scientifically sophisticated minority and the conventional-minded mass of common men. Whether this mass can be persuaded by rational evidence to support a change of economic and political priorities, or whether it must be stampeded under crisis to accept the better judgment of an informed minority, is presently a moot question. But a greatly upgraded public understanding of the need for wise social control over the uses of science and technology is essential to the survival of democracy as Americans like to think of it.

The second question asks: How can responsibilities for custody, care, and future development of the American environment be reallocated to maximize beneficial results? Implicit in this question is Field's assumption that the present allocation of "public" and "private" responsibility for the state of the environment tends, in fact, to produce irresponsibility and a resulting decline of environmental quality. This question, however, generates a series of sub-questions that must be answered before it can be intelligently considered. Some of these collateral questions are, for example: What specific responsibilities is it proposed to reallocate? From whom, to whom? Under what safeguards or conditions?

The "under-what-conditions" question may be the most important of them all. This is because that which can be reallocated, or in any case administered in the public interest, depends upon the capacity of the agency—whether "public" or "private"—to receive and to carry the burden of responsibility. The considerable reservations that I have regarding Field's suggestion that certain operational environmental management tasks be allocated to private enterprise are related to this question.

In my view, the distance one may safely go in transferring (or imposing) responsibilities for environmental management on the economic enterprise system of American society, depends greatly upon the degree to which that system can be transformed from what it now is to what it would need to become were we to rely upon it for the performance of what are essentially public functions. I do not disagree with the desirability of the reallocation of environmental responsibilities between the economic and governmental sectors of society. The difficulty I find with Field's suggestion is not in principle—for I think his objective ultimately must be realized if we are ever to obtain a rational and effective management of spaceship earth. It is rather his formulation of the issue that troubles me. My objection has more to do with his semantics than with his reasoning.

The semantic difficulty that gives me trouble is the public-private dichotomy. Field's difficulty, and mine, is that our language is obsolete. We are attempting to deal with concepts and relationships for which conventional language offers no convenient terminology. Our language carries the richness and the burdens of the historic past. The terms "public" and "private" in the complex technoscientific society that is now emerging do not and could not have the same connotations that they traditionally have carried. To speak of large-scale publicly chartered corporate enterprise as "private," is to extend the application of the concept to a point beyond any useful meaning. Privacy is a concept that our society might do well to treat with greater care. Its properties and values will need to be specified more closely in the future, for the reality of privacy is threatened by almost every trend in the technoscientific society, and those who declaim most loudly in its behalf are often the most effective engineers of its demise.

Field recognizes that " . . . public and private sectors increasingly interpenetrate." But his formulation of their relationships is old-fashioned. The new-fashioned relationship, which appears to me to be the systems-structured integrated relationship of the future, has been presaged in the organization of the agricultural, aerospace, and defense sectors of the economy. Biomedical services are well on the way to joining these forerunners of an emergent form of political economy for which no name has become common. It might be called free-enterprise-socialism over the objections of ideological free-enterprisers and socialists. But each word in the epithet carries a burden of common usage that is at variance with the emerging pattern of economic-political relationships.

John Kenneth Galbraith has perhaps come closer than others to describing its characteristics in *The New Industrial State*. Little as the term "technostructure" may mean to most people, such meaning as it conveys is consistent with an important aspect of reality in the American political economy, whereas the conventional expressions "private business" or "corporate enterprise" refer either to organizational characteristics that are relatively unimportant (the legal status of incorporation) or are not true (i.e., that nongovernmental business is a private affair). The political economists have failed to provide us with an everyman's language to describe the realities of the technoscientific industrial society to which our destinies are committed. But the shaping of popular language has been more often the work of poets than of economists. It should not be surprising that those political economists who have taken liberties with conventional language to make it more descriptive of reality have, like Galbraith and Boulding, been possessed of more than a touch of the poet.

We may be grateful that "the dismal science" has occasionally been illuminated by a touch of poetry. And this illumination is especially needed if, as political psychiatrists might say, our society is suffering from a reality crisis. Of all men, the poet—who among other things may also be a scientist, a politician, or even an engineer—is most sensitive to realities. He may misunderstand and misinterpret the reality that he senses, but he is not—like most of us—intellectually and emotionally insulated against it. We need the help of poets to induce in us an awareness of reality that science cannot provide. That awareness is a sense of the relative importance of things.

Technoscience, through incredibly accurate and sensitive instrumentation, can provide us with evidence concerning the state of reality that our own senses cannot detect or measure. Where science alone cannot help is in evaluating the importance of its findings in the lives of men. Neither poetic ignorance nor science irrelevant to the real needs of man will help society transcend its present critical juncture. We cannot accomplish the institutional reforms and the reallocations of social responsibility that Field and I both advocate unless, to use poetic language, a national "change of heart" occurs. How much change, with respect to what beliefs and values, and by whom, are questions worth exploring, but not manageable within the confines of this critique. What can be said, however, is that a fusing of the scientific and poetic aspects of life could do much to bring people closer to a realistic appraisal of their environmental situation.

Although I have not contracted to answer the questions that Field's paper brings to mind, it may be useful to offer a summary answer to the question which has been given random exploration in the foregoing paragraphs. The question is, in essence: How can we improve the management of the American environment by a more appropriate allocation of social responsibilities? The answer, implicit in the foregoing discussion, is that we can wisely reallocate these responsibilities only as fast and insofar as we can define more clearly than we do now what the environmental needs, values, goals, and responsibilities of America really are.

To do these things we need a far clearer perception of the realities of this world than most people, and their leaders and managers, possess.

Instant enlightenment is what is needed, but it is not likely to be forthcoming. We shall have to rely instead on the slow and uncertain processes of education and experience. But somehow people must learn that the wonderful new world of technoscience exacts a price in human behavior that previous generations were not required to pay. To manage an environment in which nuclear energy, chemical biocides, supersonic transport, and possibly the genesis and perpetuation of life itself are among the manageable variables, requires more than optimism, good intentions, and hard work. If the nation, in some fashion, can decide what kind of environments it wishes to protect, remake, or create, it will then be possible to determine, more accurately than at present, the allocations of responsibilities that can best be relied upon to attain the objectives. Pending this possibly Utopian state, another political strategy, based upon the assumption of disagreement, may be more practicable.

This conclusion brings us to a third question suggested by Field's paper: What kind of organizational structure is indicated where concurrence on objectives is weak relative to the strength of antagonistic forces, but where the costs of error are too great to permit differences to be settled solely through trial by political combat? This is a simplified description of the political circumstances of environmental management in the United States today. An overly-simplified answer might be: The system indicated is the one that we have—its evolution being the natural consequence of the interaction of political and economic forces.

This interpretation is most plausible to those observers who see politics as a market phenomenon, with bargains, trade-offs, pay-offs, risks, profits, and losses. But the circumstances of technoscientific society complicate the market process to an extent that threatens its utility as a model for political decision-making. The primary complicating factor is knowledge, which in its rate and volume of increase, and its impact upon society, may accurately be described as "explosive." But possession of this explosive knowledge is distributed very unevenly in all societies and among societies. Its most disturbing manifestation is galloping obsolescence that makes the technoscientific world, for all its creature comforts, a place of instability, insecurity, and anxiety. Man has always lived with these discomforts, but their presence in the technoscientific world is in new and unpredictable ways. The fears that men have learned to live with are being replaced by new dangers which most men can no more than vaguely sense, and against which history offers no counsel for avoidance or protection.

Opinions will surely differ over whether this nation suffers from a "reality crisis." But there is ample evidence of widespread, although not unanimous, agreement that it is confronted by an environmental crisis. The word crisis is overworked in our communications media. I use the word to describe a juncture at which, if the critical situation does not stabilize or "improve," it will inevitably, perhaps irretrievably, become worse to a point of ultimate disaster.

The difficulty with popular understanding of most crisis situations is that they become critical before they become apparent. For example, a population time bomb is ticking off the minutes between now and seemingly inevitable demographic catastrophe for large areas of the earth. The crisis is not the final phase of the explosion, but it is the critical period during which the so-called bomb might be defused. Unfortunately, relatively few people hear the ticking, and, among them, fewer are agreed on how the bomb *should* be defused. Public opinion, therefore, tends to react to the noisy crises, not to the quiet ones—which are often the more deadly. Symptoms, such as war in Vietnam or crime in the streets, are made into public issues, obscuring the real issues—the more fundamental circumstances that gave rise to these events and which will continue to produce similar manifestations in one form or another until the basic causal factors are removed.

Historians of the future may cite as a major indication of the severity of contemporary America's reality crisis the obsession of her people with the wrong fears. They may find that seldom in history were a people more mistaken regarding the dangers that threatened them. The dual threats of irreversible environmental deterioration and pathogenetic over-population may, a century hence, be perceived to have been the most serious dangers to the America of 1968, but they are not the issues that most contemporary Americans believe to be of critical importance.

Yet even now there is widespread dissatisfaction with the management of the nation's environment and growing skepticism concerning the desirability of indefinite and unchecked population growth. Legislation to establish national policies for the environment has been introduced into the Congress, hearings have been held, conferences convened, and action on behalf of environmental quality has been recommended by a series of high-level scientific and civic committees of inquiry. Enough concern with the state of the environment has been generated to make probable some change in the near future in the organization and management of public policies for natural resources and environmental quality.

When the *need* for remedial action is more widely accepted than the *choice* of remedy, some method of resolving differences or delegating the power of decision is often sought. For many reasons the political and economic market mechanisms for allocating priorities in the use of natural resources operate very inperfectly. Large numbers of Americans, as individuals and interest groups, have no real access to the marketplace. They have no seats, so to speak, on the Board of Trade. The structure of government in the executive branch and in the Congress is designed to favor certain interests and policies as against others. Environmental quality, as a general political objective, has no official home in the federal structure comparable to agriculture, forestry, mining, transportation, or urban affairs. The organizational cards have been stacked against environmental quality considerations and in favor of economic and developmental interests. If the operations of the market-based American economy have produced some environmentally damaging side effects, it would seem desirable to restructure the government so as to countervail or to correct deleterious operations of the economy.

It is easier to say how the government *could* be reorganized for a more responsible and ecologically intelligent management of the environment than to foresee what may be politically feasible. What needs to be done is relatively clear considering the complexities of environmental problems. What may be politically feasible is less certain, and may be subject to abrupt and unpredictable changes in the wake of events. For example, some observers believe that a major environmental catastrophe will be required to jolt the nation into political action commensurate with the environmental need. Under the circumstances now prevailing in American society, public responsibility would seem to be promoted most readily by a greatly strengthened and centralized executive authority accompanied, perhaps, by a strengthened regional basis for intergovernmental initiative and cooperation.

A mere regrouping of federal agencies in a new department of natural resources would not provide what the need requires. What is needed is first of all a focus consistent with the constitutional purpose of the federal government—to promote and protect the national welfare. In the technoscientific society, this focus must be primarily on maintaining the fitness and quality of the environment, and only secondarily on the conservation or development of natural resources. To create a federal department of natural resources during the latter decades of the twentieth century would be to offer nineteenth-century concepts as answers to twenty-first-century needs. Man's environment, or at least that part of it that sustains and enriches his life, must now become a major object of public responsibility. The technoscientific revolution that has in some measure rendered natural resources issues less urgent, has also made concern for the state of the environment of critical importance. A few random terms not found in the dictionary of conservationist President Theodore Roosevelt suggest the nature of the evidence supporting the thesis. They are atomic energy, pesticides, smog, sonic boom, epoxy, automation, beneficiation.

A restructuring of federal agencies would certainly be indicated if protection of the environment became a major national responsibility. But with this restructuring, a revision of some basic laws would also be necessary. The power base of an agency should be consistent with its function. If its function directly concerns the entire American people, and not merely particular occupational, regional, or economic interest groups, its mandates, authorities, responsibilities, and procedures must be rewritten to insure so far as possible that it will be responsive to the interests of the Americans as a people. And because there is a logical relationship, although imperfectly expressed, between the committee structure of the Congress and the administrative structure of the executive branch, some measure of Congressional reorganization is implicit in an effective restructuring of the administrative agencies.

In summary, I share Field's preference for a rational and harmonious society in which each sector—economic, technical, and governmental— would do the thing best suited to its capabilities and to the needs of society. But I do not now see the market-based economy of twentieth-century America as prepared to assume the kind of responsibility implicit in Field's proposal. Consequently, I look to more broadly responsive government for protection against the adverse side effects of the enterprise system and the errors of government itself. To effectively protect the environment, the focus and structure of the federal administrative establishment must be changed. In the aggregate, the policies of the federal agencies must be consistent with a generalized set of national policies for the environment. Greater responsiveness to the needs of all Americans as consumers of the environment must be built into governmental operations, and bonds of interest binding particular agencies to particular client groups may have to be replaced by new and more numerous connections. Of course, none of these developments necessarily *must* happen. But unless they *do* happen in some significant degree, it is difficult to see how the nation will surmount the crisis of environmental deterioration that existing institutions have been unable to forefend.

MALCOLM D. RIVKIN

Director of the Department of Urban and Regional Development, Robert R. Nathan Associates, Inc., Washington, D.C. Consultant on economic impact of Delaware River Basin National Recreation Area, economic development assistance in Appalachia, and a review of major city plans for Israel. Formerly resident planner for Cleveland's University Circle development project, and regional planning advisor to the Government of Turkey. Ph.D. and M.C.P. from M.I.T. and a Fulbright Scholar at the University of Amsterdam. Author: *Area Development for National Growth, the Turkish Precedent*.

Structural Change Needs National Commitment

A COMMENT ON THE FIELD PAPER

Ralph Field makes an excellent review of resources development history in America. He points out the complexities and the conflicts of managing our national heritage. He sets forth environmental preservation as a positive goal, even while the growing country requires far more of the environment to be transformed by the works of man.

Field closes his analysis by posing a set of questions: "In short, can we satisfy a spectrum of objectives, efficiency in developing our economy, quality in the results of development, equity in the distribution of the products of development, cohesion among our people in the course of development, improvement in the mechanism of development, and the application of new areas of knowledge to the processes of development?"

Affirmative answers to these questions imply, I believe, the existence of a stable, unified society. Such a society would be kept firmly on course by the gyroscope of national leadership. Such a society would possess a strong sense of values and the ability to make hard decisions, even to undergo sacrifices in pursuit of these values. We would all, I believe, wish to live within such a system. As I regard contemporary America, however, the evidence warrants a regretful "no" to Field's hopes for harmony and balance in resource development.

This is a society which can still afford to waste, and waste on a lavish scale. What other nation is so rich as to allow a body of water such as Lake Erie to die before its eyes? What other nation is so able to allow sections of its inner cities to be laid waste, and then let the wreckage sit and smolder for all to see? I have often wondered when work would begin on all the ambitious schemes for rebuilding the riot-torn areas of American cities. Evidently the urgency is not great, for out of some national sense of masochism, Washington's Fourteenth Street, Newark's Springfield Avenue, and Cleveland's Hough are fast becoming tourist attractions in their bombed-out states.

How can we seriously consider conservation and quality in a society which, unlike any other in human history, has unleashed expectations of material and social advancement so far beyond the society's capability to match that frustration is commonplace?

This is a society that favors instant gratification. When aspirations can not be instantly gratified, disappointment leads to destruction of the very material and human resources we talk of preserving. For both the haves and the have-nots, short-run immediate returns are paramount. Our local communities are the chief custodians of our resources, and they, too, are prey to pressures for the quick return. Thus when a community gives up parks for an expressway, or encourages land development that brings sprawl, this is a part of the same pervasive tendency to sacrifice the future and its value.

America is still a land of riches. It is still a land of vigor and hope, but these dark clouds on our horizon cast doubt upon our survival as a society, not to mention our ability to manage what is left of nature's gifts or construct new cities at acceptable aesthetic standards.

Field has proposed that a Council of Ecological Advisors be created on the national level to provide advice to the President on resource development. He further advocates that such councils be established on a regional basis as well, providing advice to state and local governments. These are good structural proposals. The councils would certainly provide better information to policy-makers. They would provide a channel for sound ecological thinking at all levels of government. But they make little sense in view of what is really happening in America today. This is an America which lacks commitment. Indeed, lacking commitment, no structural changes will help.

In reviewing the prospects, my pessimism is not total. I believe that it is possible to move more closely toward a harmonious management of resources. But fundamental changes in the way this nation operates must occur first, along with some alterations in the way planners approach their tasks.

America must first resolve to confront its domestic crises. Those of us who prize the environment must begin to mobilize political power behind its preservation. Furthermore, we must put efforts into building up the positive role of local communities in environmental affairs and pull back on what has become an over-dependence on federal action.

Preliminary estimates of the costs to implement the Kerner Commission recommendations have been made by the National Planning Association. These amount to more than $40 billion annually beyond current levels of expenditure on housing, employment, welfare, and education. About $23 billion must come from the public sector.

Pragmatically, it would be impossible to divert the entire Vietnam budget to domestic affairs. Yet even 50 per cent, if devoted to critical social problems at home, would go a long way toward restoring America's credibility to herself and to the world. I believe little of value can be accomplished in meeting these problems, or in restoring the battered physical environment, until that commitment is made.

When the time for domestic confrontation comes, however, planners and ecologists will need political power on their side. No longer will we be able to "poor mouth" about quality and salve our consciences with the plaint that no one listens. It is easy to criticize the manner in which resources are abused. The hard and necessary job is to start using the other fellow's weapons and bring positive environmental change into the political arena. Social justice is now a political issue. Why not better cities? Why not pollution-free streams? Why not protected countryside?

The beautification provisions of the highway act were decimated in the 1968 session of Congress. It was concerted political pressure by the billboard and highway lobbies on the congressmen that left a once-heralded piece of legislation a monument to tokenism. Yet contrast this use of political power in Washington with the passage by the Vermont legislature of a billboard banning act far more sweeping than the original federal law. This, too, was a demonstration of political power. For the politicians in Vermont recognized that their interests were in jeopardy if the vacation state were to become a clutter. Public opinion and party machinery were mobilized to drive home to the legislators the importance of the tie between natural resources and economic self-interest.

The new law in Vermont, and the circumstances of its passage could be a bellwether for America. We know increasing numbers of citizens are concerned about the environment and the more obvious signs of its malaise. We know that the majority of Americans will be living in cities and suburbs where this malaise is most apparent. The concern can be converted into political issues, into the meat of political campaigns.

It can be so converted, however, if the pseudo-scientific mystery and the wordiness are stripped away from environmental problems; if the citizen and voter understands the problems and what must be done about them. Professionals bear much blame for the confusion. We have too often poured jargon over straightforward issues to keep them our own special preserve. We professionals can take the lead by de-escalating the verbiage and by realizing that the goals we claim to champion can be achieved as issues in the political arena, intelligible and compelling to those with political power.

The search for quality and the mobilization of political power to that end must focus more on the smallest units of government—the communities. Only when local communities across this land want and demand high standards of environment will effective national policies be possible. Cities and metropolitan areas must themselves organize to conserve resources, must themselves sacrifice funds and efforts to maintain decent human and physical environments. This is still a federal nation, one in which local and regional attitudes govern what is actually accomplished.

Local and regional attitudes have a far greater impact on national policy than many planners even now wish to believe. In our frustrations with narrow, parochial communities we have expected too much from the leadership of the federal government. We have vested the men in Washington with too many responsibilities they cannot assume.

This over-dependence reminds me of King Henry's soliloquy before the battle of Agincourt:

> Upon the King, Let us our lives, our souls
> Our debts, our careful wives,
> Our children, and our sins lay on the King.
> We must bear all, oh hard condition!

And Washington cannot bear all. Even if the federal government were prepared to set standards and to encourage lofty goals, recent years have vividly illustrated what happens when communities are unprepared to accept these standards, when communities meet these goals with hostility. I do not mean to minimize the vast resources which Washington can manage and allocate. Unless pressures come from below, however, unless a receptivity for new approaches exists where those approaches are to be applied, the federal effort is wasted. It is within local communities that the greatest challenges exist to the ecologist's skill and persuasive abilities. The degree to which these challenges are met will determine both the communities' and the nation's performance.

My final proposal is one often cited by the Cassandras of urban affairs. It is nonetheless important for repetition. The machinery of government is past due for an overhaul. Relationships between federal, state, and local government in environmental affairs must be altered. Suitable instruments must be devised to attack the problems of today. The mind boggles at more than two hundred federal programs that stumble over each other in dealing with the environment. The games of grantsmanship which communities must play with the federal Establishment are a national disgrace. So are the fragmented patterns of metropolitan government. So are what Donald Canty calls the "sleeping" states who, with a few notable exceptions, stand by while the "Feds" and the locals slug it out. A day of reckoning must come, when the logjam will be broken, when local and federal activities will be streamlined, when the states will use their significant powers over community affairs and act. It can come when the environment and its preservation are in the political arena, and when the demand for change emanates from the local jurisdictions themselves; then the needed commitment will be found.

HANS BLUMENFELD

Consultant to the Metropolitan Toronto Planning Board, the City Planning Department of Montreal, and the Vancouver City Planning Department. Special lecturer at the University of Toronto. Previously architect and planner in Moscow, Gorki, New York, and Jersey City. Formerly research director of the Philadelphia Housing Association, and Senior Land Planner and Chief of Planning Analysis for the Philadelphia City Planning Commission. Degree in architecture from the Polytechnical Institute at Darmstadt. Author: *The Modern Metropolis.*

The Rational Use of Urban Space as National Policy

The implication that without a national policy urban space is not being and cannot be rationally used is far from being self-evident. Nobody has yet, to the best of my knowledge, asked for a national policy for the rational use of shoe leather. We leave that quite confidently to dealings between the sellers and buyers of shoes, to the rationale of the market.

In a market economy all resources, whether they be natural, or man-made, or labor-power, must be transformed into capital before they can be used. They become "factors of production," which are bought, sold, and substituted for each other in terms of value, as commodities; to be combined in such a way as to add at least as much value as any other possible combination. To say that land should be regarded as a resource rather than as a commodity makes no sense in this context, because nothing can become a resource without first becoming a commodity. The combination of commodities adding the highest value is called, in real estate terminology, the "highest and best use." Within the conceptual framework of a pure market economy, the highest and best use *is,* by definition, the rational use. If the goal of national policy is defined as the creation or maintenance of a pure market economy, the real estate market provides for rational use of urban space. However, it has been a long time since we have left decisions on the use of urban space entirely to the market.

Why don't we deal with it as we do with shoes? What is so different about urban space?

What is different is, first, that it is space, and second, that it is urban. Let us look at these two aspects.

Space, in the sense we are discussing here, consists of defined parts of the surface of our planet, extended for undefined distances downward towards its center and upward in the opposite direction. It is not made by man, but, in traditional parlance, by God. Traditionally, it was therefore regarded as the property of God, to be managed by its earthly representative, the king, for the benefit of God's people. The king could not and did not give it away to any individual, but only loaned it, retaining the right of eminent domain. This right is still retained by the king's successor, the state.

Because the earth has not been made by man, it cannot be reproduced by man. This may be of little practical significance as far as the total of the 197 million square miles of the planet's surface is concerned, dire predictions about impending "standing room only" to the contrary notwithstanding. What is important is that each part of it is unique and irreproducible. It is unique in its relation to all other parts. What happens on any one piece of land, potentially affects all other pieces of land. Normally, any market transaction concerns only two persons, seller and buyer who, under the not entirely realistic assumptions of perfect competition, both maximize their benefits. But, in the case of a piece of land, benefits and "malefits," or "costs," accrue to third persons. If a man sells two right shoes, he is likely to hurt his customer's left foot, but he is not likely to hurt anybody else. If a man engages—to use the most hackneyed example—in the manufacture of glue, he is not likely to hurt the buyers of glue, but he may inflict a serious "malefit" on his neighbors. This is the basic reason why the most rational use of land cannot be produced by the market, but is a legitimate concern of public policy. This applies to all land, but with particular force to urban land, or urban space, a term which is preferable because it emphasizes the three-dimensional character of "land."

There are many definitions of the term "urban," none entirely satisfactory. However, they all contain as a necessary, though not sufficient condition, a relatively high concentration of persons and activities in a limited space. They are drawn together by the need for cooperation which requires mutual accessibility. Any piece of land, or water, can be made urban by making it accessible to other urban activities, existing or newly established. Urban space is thus man-made space; and, as it at present covers only an insignificant part of the globe's surface, its potential expansion is practically unlimited. A given piece of space is made accessible, and thereby urban, by two types of action. First, the locational decisions of all other "urban" persons and establishments. In our society the majority of these are private, a growing minority public. Second, by the provision of means of access for persons, messages, and goods (including water, power, etc.). At present the majority of these are provided by the public, a decreasing minority by private enterprise.

It is thus the actions of these "third" persons which determines the urban character, and the value of a given piece of land, not the action of the owner. However, a very large and financially powerful owner, public or private, may be able to locate *all* urban activities and means of access on his land and thereby create urban space *de novo;* or may be able to do the same by locating activities of decisive importance and thereby induce decisions of other locators and providers of access.

Consequently, public policy can exercise a decisive influence on the use of urban space, both on its distribution within urban regions and on the distribution of urban regions within the national territory. While the former is the main concern of professional planners, the latter is dependent directly on national policy and will be discussed first.

All over the world governments are concerned with the distribution of the rapidly growing urban units. While this concern ranges from the purely verbal, as in the United States, Canada, and most "developing" countries through varying degrees of directing financial support to certain regions, as in most countries of Western Europe, to actual government construction of new towns, as in Great Britain, Israel, and Eastern Europe, the proclaimed intentions are remarkably similar. They tend to be rich in emotional appeal, but poor in clear definition and quantification of objectives.

"Balanced distribution" of the population seems to be considered desirable. The balance is variously interpreted as to be achieved between regions, between the urban and rural population, and/or between large and small cities. However, no criteria are available by which it could be determined why one distribution is more "balanced" than another. Subconsciously, the present or past distribution may be seen as "balanced"; but maintenance of the *status quo* is hardly a valid and certainly not a realistic objective.

A somewhat more rational formulation is the claimed objective to equalize the levels of income and opportunity of all regions. This objective has particular validity where regions have strongly distinctive ethnic and cultural characteristics, a rather exceptional case in the United States. Here two questions arise. First, why are governments so much more concerned with differences of income and opportunity *between* regions than with the much greater differences existing *within* regions? I am afraid that I will have to leave the answer to someone more experienced in electoral and parliamentary tactics than I am. Second, in the excellent formulation of Edgar M. Hoover, is it people prosperity or area prosperity that we want? Certainly the latter has value only as a means to achieve the former. If jobs, or well-paying jobs are lacking in a region, it is because certain conditions make productivity lower than in other regions. The choice is between bringing people to jobs or jobs to people. Bringing people to jobs means emigration of the most productive people and a shrinking of the market for local services, a very painful downward spiral which, however, may end with a higher level of income and of services for a smaller population. This may be preferable to prolonging the agony by keeping a nonviable economy half-alive by continued subsidies.

The case is different if the conditions responsible for low productivity of a region can be permanently changed. These conditions all amount to accessibility, both to other regions and to other activities within each region. The latter is entirely, and the former is to a considerable extent dependent on attainment of a certain minimum size. Only in an urban area of considerable size can the great variety of specialized establishments and skills find the market and the supply which each represents for all the others. Also, only such an area can support the long-distance terminals and lines required for good access to other regions, such as large jet airports with frequent flights, harbors for large ocean-going ships with frequent sailings, and any future means of high-speed ground transportation. The minimal size for an adequate complement of establishments and skills is growing with increasing specialization, and the minimal size of long-distance terminals is growing with increasing size and speed of vehicles. I am fairly certain that the minimum is a population of at least half a million, and probably is rising to a million or more.

It is clear that no individual decision-maker can build up such a unit; he has to locate where the complementary establishments are. Decentralized decision-making, such as prevails in the United States, inevitably leads to ever greater spatial centralization. Spatial decentralization can be brought about only by a central decision-maker, who can locate all required establishments simultaneously, or at least in a scheduled sequence. This is confirmed by the experience not only of Communist-ruled countries, but also of those Western nations who have achieved some success in spatial decentralization, Great Britain, the Netherlands, and Israel. This dialectic appears to be overlooked by most decentralists who want decentralization both of decision-making and of location.

Governments and public opinion have been less concerned with minimum than with maximum size. Indeed, ever since big cities have appeared, all, from Queen Elizabeth the First of England, the Czarina Catherine the Second of Russia, and the Prussian Junkers on the right, to Thomas Jefferson, Karl Marx, and Peter Kropotkin on the left, as well as all shades of opinion in between, have condemned them. Nobody has ever defined when big becomes too big; it seems always to be about the size attained by the biggest city at a given time and place. Attempts to stop their further growth have always failed. Even the countries which have succeeded in decentralization can at most claim to have slowed it down. The only exception is the German Democratic Republic, East Germany, where the population of the three largest cities is well below the prewar level, while the population of the smaller ones, especially in the 20,000 to 50,000 range, has grown considerably.

France is now trying to slow down the growth of the Paris region by building up a few cities in the half-million to one million plus class quantitatively and qualitatively so as to make them countermagnets. If the United States wants to limit the giantism of its largest metropolitan regions, this would be the most promising way.

Current discussions about "New Towns" appear to be concerned primarily with the creation of "satellite" cities within the orbit of a large metropolis. There are indeed strong indications that smaller towns, existing or new, thrive best if they have easy access to the services, supplies, and markets of a metropolitan center. Two hours traveling time seems to be about the limit for easy access. With modern means of transportation, the metropolitan region may cover an area considerably larger than Belgium.

It has been noted earlier that the market cannot be relied on to produce rational use of urban space because the close interdependence of all urban activities produces effects on third parties not included in the market transaction. This does not preclude, however, a strong element of rationality which must be understood before the irrationalities can be identified.

The market organizes the city through the differential rent, which reflects the price which a user is prepared to pay for differences in accessibility. Under the American system of "fee simple" land ownership, the differential rent is capitalized as land value.

Normally the point to which access is sought is the original core of the city. If this core is located in an open plain, subsequent development spreads evenly in all directions, and the original core remains the point of maximum accessibility. If topographical conditions prevent development in one or more directions, the point of maximum accessibility tends to shift away from the original core. However, here we will ignore this modification and assume that there is a definite center which is both core and point of maximum accessibility.

The greater the distance from the center, the less the accessibility; therefore, the land value would be lower, even if the volume of land supply would be the same at all distances. In fact, the supply increases with the square of the distance; in a ring ten to eleven miles from the center there is twenty one times as much land than within one mile from the center. Therefore, even if accessibility would be the same, land value would be much lower.

As a result of these two factors—less accessibility and more supply—land values decrease regularly from the center to the periphery. As, for a great variety of reasons, users desire more space, density drops with land value. This density gradient is entirely rational.

Accessibility is determined not only by distance in space but by means of communications which overcome the friction of space, in terms of time, money, and inconvenience. As they do this more and more effectively, more and more land becomes accessible. The gradient of land values and of densities flattens, and urban development spreads out further and further at lower and lower densities. It does not make much sense to call this natural and rational process a "flight." There is nothing irrational about "spread city" per se.

What happens is that each locator trades space against accessibility. In the competition for the scarce space at the center, those for whom accessibility is most important, pay the price and remain. This is facilitated, usually, by their demand for space—both on the site and on the access roads to it—being relatively small; all others move out. Generally speaking, those dealing with bulk goods—manufacturing and warehousing—move out; those dealing with persons, business and consumer services, remain. Specifically, those consumer services of the "highest order" which can only exist by serving the entire metropolitan area, remain; those which find a sufficient market in one outlying sector, move out. Those business services, primarily the offices of private and public managers and their advisors, to whom mutual accessibility is even more important than access to the entire metropolitan area, remain; routine office functions move out.

A similar process of natural selection goes on in the surrounding area. Labor-intensive plants to whom access to the centrally located business services are important—notably small, new, more or less experimental industries—locate in the old loft buildings near the center; other industries establish themselves in new one-story plants on the periphery. In the residential sector, access to the jobs, educational, and recreational services of the center is important to adults, in particular young white-collar workers. On the other hand, pre-adolescent children have little need for access to the center but great need for access to open space which is more plentiful at the low density periphery. The predominance of one- and two-person households near the center and of households with growing children at the periphery is entirely rational. There is no sound reason why the same mixture of age and family groups should be found in all parts of the urban area.

We have so far only dealt with accessibility to the center. However, as all functions—manufacturing and services as well as residence—establish themselves on the periphery, mutual accessibility between them becomes more and more important, while accessibility to the center becomes relatively less so. Little is left of the huge difference in accessibility which once gave areas near the center a near-monopoly on urban land use. It is therefore, anything but rational to expect or demand that the monetary expression of this difference, the land value, should be maintained or restored. This notion reflects a fetishistic attitude which regards the value of a piece of land as a kind of immortal god of the soil.

So far, so good. The market produces a rational distribution of urban space. All is for the best in the best of all possible worlds.

We noted that the difference in type of household between center and periphery is as rational as it is voluntary. There is, however, another difference between the households living in these two areas: the poor are concentrated in the central sections, while the periphery is almost entirely inhabited by middle- and upper-income groups. This division is not voluntary. It is forced on the poor because they do not have the money to pay for the new housing at the periphery nor for the transportation required to provide mobility in those areas. Here we meet a problem which is deeper and more general than the previously discussed impact of use of urban space on third persons. Our society operates on two different and potentially contradictory principles of equality. In the legal-political sphere, all men are equal. Here the rule is one man, one vote. But in the economic sphere, in the market, the rule is one dollar, one vote. There is no pre-stabilized harmony between these two types of equality; it is not one man, one dollar. The distribution of resources by the market is rational in terms of effective demand, but it is not so if the democratic goal of equal opportunity is accepted as rational. Political democracy has attempted to come closer to this goal by an ex post facto redistribution of the incomes after their primary distribution by the market. The current proposals for a "negative income tax" are such attempts. But it will certainly be a long time before the gap is closed between the cost of new housing and the amount of money which a large proportion of American families are able and willing to pay for housing.

In the United States class division has been immeasurably deepened by race division, with the resultant confinement of the Negro population in the black ghetto. The most urgent task of national policy for the rational use of urban space is to open up all parts of the urban area for people of all classes and races, by a massive use of its financial power to subsidize poor families to rent or buy a decent dwelling of their choice; and an equally massive use of its legal and police power to overcome the resistance of white prejudice.

It is sometimes proposed to overcome the class and race division between center and periphery by the opposite process, by "bringing middle-class families back to the city." I consider this fashionable slogan to be entirely wrong, for two reasons. First, because the familiar statement that "only the very rich and the very poor" live in the central city simply is not true. Even in the most extreme case, Manhattan, in 1959, over one-third (34.4 per cent) of all families were middle class, narrowly defined as the $5000–$10,000 income bracket. The percentage of middle-class nonfamily households was certainly even higher. The poor in the central city can see plenty of the rich and middle class. It is the upper and middle class in the suburbs who never see how the other half lives.

Second, and far more important, "bringing the middle-class families back to the city" means displacing low-income families. But there are better reasons for the poor than for anybody else to live close to the center. In their households there are frequently several persons looking for employment, much of which is casual, part-time, or at unusual hours. The jobs open to them may be either in the center or at varying points at the periphery which can be reached by public transportation only from the center. To destroy the homes and neighborhoods of thousands of poor families in order to replace them with so-called middle-income housing, is a crime little short of genocide.

There is no secret about the motives for this crime. They are spelled out in many urban renewal reports. The purpose is to improve the finances of the city. Poor people can pay only little in taxes and need many services. Wealthy people pay higher taxes and need fewer services. From the point of view of the municipal treasurer, the most desirable land uses are industry—clean, of course,—commerce, and wealthy bachelors.

The suburbs have for a long time based their policies on these considerations. In the words of the late Hugh R. Pomeroy: "They have been zoning the poor out into the Atlantic Ocean." Now the cities are trying to beat them at their own game by means of "urban renewal." It is futile to blame municipal councilors for this competitive chase after "good assessments" which makes a farce out of any attempt at rational land-use planning. They are probably neither better nor worse than you and I, and certainly act with the backing of most of their constituents. They are forced to act this way because their main resource to meet their rising expenses is the so-called real estate tax. This tax lumps together two entirely different economic categories, land and buildings, the latter quaintly listed in tax records as "improvements." The value of the land, the capitalized differential rent, is created entirely by others than the owner, and the tax on it cannot be passed on. It could well be increased. The tax on buildings is passed on. As at least half of the building value is residential, it acts as a sales tax on housing that narrows the market and lowers the standards with much greater effect than is achieved by all the government aids adopted to widen the market and raise the standards of housing. As the percentage of income spent for housing increases with decreasing income, it is a strongly regressive tax. A family with an annual income of $3000 is likely to pay 6 percent of it for real estate taxes; one with a $30,000 income, about 2 per cent of its income.

No other single measure of national policy could do more for the rational use of urban space than the replacement of this tax by allocation of a share of centrally collected revenue, such as a per capita share of the federal income tax. It may here be noted that the cities of the Netherlands, who receive 89 per cent of their income from the national government, exercise in fact greater autonomy than American cities who have to go hat in hand to the higher levels of government for practically everything they do.

The zoning policies of the suburbs, supported by lending institutions, including the FHA, have also worked to make peripheral densities even lower than they would be as a result of market forces. Perhaps the greatest disadvantage of low densities is the fact that they have to rely entirely on the private automobile. Public transportation requires concentration at least at the destination end. As noted, all kinds of potential destinations, both places of work and services, are establishing themselves at the periphery, but generally all in different locations. As a consequence, both travel to and from them, from and to the dwelling, and travel between them, are almost entirely by private automobile. If they were concentrated in one location, access to them could be largely by public transportation, and between them on foot. Such centers could be surrounded by high-density housing and also by some labor-intensive, non-nuisance manufacturing establishments. They should be genuine secondary downtowns, serving populations of a quarter million or more. As such, they would create identification with a district within a large metropolitan area and could become seats of elected district governments.

Such centers cannot be created by the dispersed decisions of many individual locators, but only by a metropolitan government or publicly-owned land. As this land, by the very fact that it is to be developed as a center, would have a much higher value than the surrounding land, this may be possible only on the basis of extended public land ownership of the entire area ripe for urban development. The planners of Stockholm always emphasize that it is not their superior ability but public land ownership that enabled them to make Stockholm a model for other cities.

In Stockholm the policy of public land ownership was established more than half a century ago by a conservative city council. Public land ownership, metropolitan-wide government, and adequate financial resources are the three main tools to bring about a rational use of urban space.

Without a radical housing policy, as outlined above, New Towns in America can only be bigger and better upper- and middle-class suburbs, however high-minded their sponsors may be. If and when such a radical policy should become a reality, New Towns on the English pattern would have their place in the United States. It should, however, not be overlooked that mutual choice of employment and of employee, as well as many other choices, are more limited in New Towns than in a large city. As work becomes more and more specialized, and as changes of product and of process become more frequent, a decreasing percentage of persons and of establishments will be willing to forego that wider choice.

It is human for planners to want to escape from the many and troublesome constraints of existing cities and to design an urban environment closer to the heart's desire, starting from a clean slate, be it a New Town on open fields or a big urban redevelopment on a man-made desert. The time has come for the planning profession to shun this dual escapism and to concentrate on tackling the problems where the crucial changes are taking place and the most critical decisions being made—on the expanding fringes of our big urban areas.

ROBERT N. YOUNG

Executive Director, Regional Planning Council, Baltimore.
Vice President, AIP, 1966–69. Chairman of the Governor's
Steering Committee for Mass Transit, Baltimore, and Chair-
man of the Metropolitan Water Supply Steering Committee
also in Baltimore. Former Executive Director, Tri-County
Regional Planning Commission, Lansing, Michigan; Direc-
tor of Planning Research Associates, Los Altos, California.
B.A., M.A., from the University of Washington. Ph.D.,
University of Wisconsin.

Planning Can Harness the Profit Motive

A COMMENT ON THE BLUMENFELD PAPER

A major conclusion of Hans Blumenfeld's paper, as seen from the vantage
point of a practicing metropolitan planner, is the suggestion that the only
practical method of implementing a "better-for-the-public" use of urban
space in the United States is through some form of metropolitan government. The implication is that a "Metro" like this would have powers to
purchase land for satellite development, though primarily to house and
serve its middle- and upper-income people. This government would be
financed in part by a per capita rebate of federal income taxes.

I find the "metropolitan government" implications unrealistic. Serious
considerations of metropolitan government have been la·gely discarded;
and, at least for most areas in the United States, they will very probably
not be revived in the foreseeable future.

Instead, there is in prospect a strengthening of existing institutions and
processes, with private and public efforts more precisely focused than
before and with social and economic objectives more clearly defined.

First, Blumenfeld recognizes the significance of the free market, while
pointing out that we long ago abandoned the idea of leaving "decisions on
the use of urban space to the market." The trouble is that in our efforts to
influence decisions, we have used fairly weak techniques. Blumenfeld sug-

gests stronger methods, including higher taxes on land as well as income tax subventions to some centralized urban government. Britton Harris, William Wheaton and, no doubt, others have pointed out in various ways that the market is a very powerful force, and that unless the controls are stronger than the market, they probably will not work.

This has been amply illustrated by much of our experience with zoning and other control devices used in America. Our postwar efforts to subsidize or otherwise bring about *desired* kinds of decentralization have not worked out too well either. Yet some programs have managed to bring about *undesired* decentralization, such as suburban sprawl—decentralization gone berserk. Some multi-state regional development programs show considerable potential for exerting tighter control. But, still, it is obvious that most attempts at curtailing metropolitan development, however well intended, have been too weak to counter the market fully or effectively.

It is likely that cooperation between the private and public sectors in the near future will take advantage of the powerful forces of the market. In the Baltimore region, James Rouse, the builder of the new city of Columbia, is demonstrating that the profit motive can be harnessed to create new and better places for people to live and work. However, his technique of land assemblage—of, essentially, buying "incognito"—would not be successful a second time in the Baltimore area.

Given a revised set of market-oriented "rules" established by government to establish both incentives and development controls, private enterprise would likely be more than willing to take the initiative in establishing environments which would use urban land space more rationally than at present. For instance, perhaps some of the speculative private profit derived from urban development which capitalizes on publicly financed improvements—such as roads, utilities, open spaces, schools and so on— should be added to the existing federal income tax structure. Then an income tax rebate representing that "recaptured" gain could go to existing state and/or local governments, who would set up the mechanisms by which private enterprise and public agencies might most effectively tackle a given problem.

For instance, fairly tight governmental control might be needed in the center of a new town, while the market could function more freely on the outskirts. Some sort of government action would, of course, be required to assemble the critical land at the center.

In another situation, as in the provision of region-serving green space, the action would have to be entirely governmental. On the other hand, a large industrial development might require minor governmental participation, with the private sector constrained only by standards protecting the public interest.

To summarize, radical departures from our present balance of private and public interests are not visible at the horizon, in this country. We should, I think, prepare ourselves to work in today's world, doing what we can to improve existing institutions, helping to create new ones where desirable and possible—and certainly keeping open various options as we go along.

It is recognized that in a market economy, land cannot become "a resource without becoming a commodity." Immediately, money casts its shadow over the picture. Long-range plans are not all that real planners should be concerned with. This real world includes private sector measures of value other than money. Power, prestige, continuity, and tradition, to name a few, all take their places beside money. Still, money is almost always of more than passing interest.

It is not certain that the participants in the market have really learned to maximize their benefits. Both buyer and seller could learn to be much more sophisticated for their own long-term interests, and additional benefits would automatically accrue to "third persons"—the public.

Perhaps a "marriage" of more effective market-countervailing forces and such indicative measures of how things might be "better" can help structure these forces for useful results. To plan toward "better" metropolitan results soon enough to be useful may itself be "better" than planning for some ephemeral—and unattainable—"best" of all impossible worlds.

Along these same lines, why should not we be concerned about both people prosperity and area prosperity, about differences between regions as well as within regions?

The point that decentralization of decision-making and of location do not go hand in hand is a good one, and one that has not been made clear before. Blumenfeld has a way of translating difficult concepts into understandable language.

RITA D. KAUNITZ

Coordinator, Urban Affairs Study, Fairfield University, Connecticut. Currently member Advisory Council on Community Affairs and Clean Air Task Force. Formerly member of the Legislative Commission to Study the Feasibility and Necessity of Metropolitan Government. Served as consultant to the Centre for Housing, Building and Planning, the United Nations Secretariat, on problems of rapid urbanization in developing countries. Ph.D. in Regional Planning, Radcliffe College, Harvard University.

The Emergence of the States in Urban Affairs

Each time the nation has faced a domestic ordeal, in redefining the role of government, it has of necessity redefined the federal-state relationship. Over our nation's 193 years, the power of the national government has grown while that of the states has dwindled. The two great nationalizing forces have been the income tax amendment and the Great Depression.

The national desperation of the Thirties called forth unprecedented measures to prevent violence and possibly even revolution. Former Governor Terry Sanford of North Carolina recalls how the Depression ". . . forced the nation to reach back for all its historic powers in political, wartime, constitutional and fiscal experiences, and convert them to massive action across the nation." Reacting to the urgent pleas to get the country moving, the federal government entered many fields of activity formerly the prerogative of state and local government. The states as a viable entity were virtually written off and have since tended to be on the defensive.

Today's domestic crisis, that of our cities, is also occasioning a rethinking of the role of each governmental level and their interrelationships. This time it is not only the federal government which is reaching out for yet more power, but it has been joined by the states which are rediscovering their authority.

Perspective on the changing role of the states and the cities is needed if we are to understand why the states have re-emerged at this critical juncture, and how they are likely to contribute to the future direction of what is evolving into a national urban policy.

The intensity of the present urban plight makes it hard to recall that there was a golden age of cities following the Civil War which lasted until the 1930's. The cities at their prime were where the action was in a far different sense than today.

The decline of the central city was set in motion by decentralization, caused by radical technological and economic changes in transportation, communication, and production methods. High-income citizens—the middle and upper classes—were replaced by high-cost citizens—the poor and the educationally deprived, many of whom are young and old, unable to compete for gainful employment. The urban condition has steadily worsened, and the once proud municipalities can no longer cope with their grave and incredibly complex difficulties, which for a number of reasons lie beyond the impact of any one city to control.

The opening out of the suburbs has made the geographic confinement of the cities more evident, and the line between city and suburb has become harshly drawn. There is separation not only by income, housing type, and economic activity but also by race; there is quality public education and services on the periphery and squalor and overcrowding at the center.

The average central city spends more taxes per capita than do the suburbs or the remainder of the country. Paying for the poverty-related functions of education, health, welfare, and police has created a municipal overburden, causing a decline in the property-related services, with resultant deterioration of the city's physical plant.

Cities as creatures of the state lack the legal authority to solve their new intricate development problems. The city is still shaped far more by its zoning map, a negative and limited tool, than by its community plan. The land-use controls "beyond zoning," badly needed if the city is to maximize its social and economic potential, are barely in use.

The perennial hope that new metropolitan agencies, most recently the councils of government, will become the instruments for urban change and metropolitan governance, falls short of the political reality.

As the cities became more impoverished, the states tended to turn a deaf ear to the mounting urgency of their pleas for help, and the initiative passed to the federal level. Direct federalism, originally forced in the aftermath of the Depression, has steadily grown, except during the Eisenhower years. The new order of metropolitan difficulties which faced Presidents Kennedy and Johnson again brought widespread federal expansion. During their administrations, urban affairs became the nation's paramount domestic issue. In response to recognition that the problems created by unprecedented change and urbanization are nationwide and not local, a national urban policy has begun to emerge from the mosaic of federal programs for housing, urban renewal, and mass transit, to combat pollution, to war against poverty, and to provide civil rights.

Direct federalism is entrenched, and domestic problems have become so dominant that national administration, controls, and financing reach out to almost every segment of the society. The federal government and the cities in combination have been unable to resolve the metropolitan dilemma. The exclusive relationship between the federal and the local levels has become more cumbersome and questionable. The choice is continued bypassing of the states and further national intervention in local affairs, or a genuine not ersatz federalism, which means state involvement, backed by the "full faith and credit" of the federal government.

I will examine how our number one domestic issue, the revitalization of the cities and metropolitan areas can be resolved: whether by the federal government working directly through city hall and/or the new metropolitan bodies, leaving the states as supernumeraries; or whether the states can provide answer to little government (fragmentation and inadequacy), and to big government (over-centralization and undue bureaucratization); and whether the states are the logical political instrumentality to move into the vacuum of municipal breakdown and metropolitan impotence. The emergence of the states as a full-scale partner in urban affairs can be viewed as a study of dynamic forces and the resulting tensions. I will attempt to assess the trends and prospects to determine whether they favor further centralization or a return to federalism, and the resurgence of the states as viable and dynamic governmental institutions.

What is striking about the upsurge of state energy is how much of it has occurred just within the past few years. As recently as January 1967, the Advisory Commission on Intergovernmental Relations questioned whether the revitalization of the states was too little or too late, but just a year later, it called state government a new frontier.

The forces for a strong state role have been growing, and by 1968, what had seemed scattered instances of state resurgence added up to a trend, and the bulletins continue to pour in. The National Governors' Conference regards the years 1967–1968 as the turning point in improved federal-state relations, with both the state and federal levels acknowledging the new state competency to deal with compelling metropolitan difficulties.

Many structures at the federal level have contributed to the state awakening, including the Advisory Commission on Intergovernmental Relations, the Office of Emergency Planning, and the Intergovernmental Relations Sub-committees of the House and Senate Committees on Government Operations.

The states, too, have parallel new structures. The National Governors' Conference, recently stationed in Washington, has been the cornerstone. The conference has particularly contributed to far better communications among the governors themselves, and among the governors, the Congress and the federal agencies, substantially modifying legislation and executive guidelines.

Other innovations which are altering the passive state image include the States Urban Action Center, the Institute on State Programming for the Seventies, which is the first of the Institutes for Excellence in State Government, and the Education Commission of the States, the latter founded on an unusual working relationship among the governors, legislators, and educators. The governors' coordinators for federal-state relations, a crucial addition, could provide a strategic bridge between the federal and state layers, if adequately staffed and funded.

Since the 1930's, many have regarded the states as obsolete, a fossil form of government. As the forces build up for a renascence of the states, it is essential to understand the unique qualifications of state government to deal with our metropolitan problems.

The states have extensive legal powers including the police powers, the constitutional authority to conduct basic governmental functions, and the direct power to tax. Unlike the federal government, states are closest to the needs of the cities, and they can avoid a concentration of power, while allowing for regional diversity and adaptation. They also can respond more quickly and with flexibility.

The states are better situated than local government to establish priorities and to provide a perspective often lacking at the municipal or regional level; they can balance off conflicting claims over a wider area, and they are more able to resist the pressures which stem from local crises. The states already bear major responsibility for many functions closely bound up with metropolitan requirements (transportation, health, education, welfare, recreation, water supply, and resources development), and as the middle government they can exercise both supervision and leadership and serve as brokers for cooperative intergovernmental action. And not only do they have special legal, administrative, financial, and coordinative powers and resources, but they are the focal points for the country's politics.

They also offer what Lyle Fitch has called "the only organizational building blocks below the federal level," essential for the state-to-state action which will be needed since many of our problems are no longer metropolitan but megalopolitan. New regional operating instruments of government such as the Appalachian Regional Commission and the Delaware River Basin, which brings the states into partnership not only with each other but with the federal government, are likely to become more numerous.

The states have seized the initiative, and many are rapidly and dramatically cementing their status as an indispensable partner in federalism. But why now?

The states themselves, through their vehicles, among others, of the Council of State Governments and the National Governors' Conference, have been working toward revitalization for some years. By now a number of states have made significant reforms. The stage was set.

With reapportionment completed, the realignments in the state legislatures furnished the script. The "one man, one vote" redistricting stimulated many state governments to take a hard look at their metropolitan areas, providing a climate for an aggressive state stance. The spotlight on the legislatures brought awareness that executive and administrative capacity must likewise be strengthened and reoriented.

The urgency and acceleration of urban unrest made it evident that action could no longer be delayed. The governors of many of our urbanized states found themselves the leading actors. As the new demands flooded in on the states, a number moved decisively and unequivocally to stage center with the formation of pioneering departments of community or local affairs, or of new corporate mechanisms. The legislative declaration of Connecticut's unprecedented Community Development Act epitomizes the states' new posture: no longer could the state, prosperous as a whole, turn its back on its deprived citizens and their decaying environment.

A governmental vacuum exists at the metropolitan level, characterized by municipal impotence and metropolitan fragmentation. Despite tremendous effort by successive waves of reformers to create metropolitan-wide governmental institutions, only a handful of such bodies have been created, and resistance seems even greater than before. A staff study for the National Governors' Conference has pointed to the difficulty: barriers to metropolitan area action arise from tax-payer concentration in the suburbs while the beneficiary concentration is in the core cities.

With metropolitan political solutions virtually ruled out, the federal government provided inducements to metropolitan planning agencies, and more recently to councils of governments, to serve as the executors of federal programs and the recipients of federal funds. Federal policy for metropolitan program development, review and action, and the accompanying leverage possibilities, have not yet crystallized, however.

Most of the councils of governments are still hardly more than voluntary forums and only a few, the Association of Bay Areas Governments and the Washington Council of Governments, have advanced to significance. Undoubtedly, many more councils are having a positive effect on their regions. But by and large, they all suffer from a lack of institutional ties to state government, although the states play a major, and in some cases, predominant role in a broad range of programs upon which the implementation of metropolitan decisions depend.

The American Law Institute's draft Model Development Code runs counter to the current preference for independent metropolitan planning agencies or councils of governments, providing instead for the creation of an executive department with broad powers to act in the interests of the states and regions, on the premise that ultra-municipal planning must reside at the state level.

Hybrid agencies, which are formally linked to their states as well as to their metropolitan areas, offer a promising departure from the usual council of governments pattern. The Metropolitan Council of the Twin Cities, which has more extensive responsibilities than most COG's, was established by the Minnesota legislature in 1967 as a unique legal entity halfway between state and local government. A study commission of the Connecticut General Assembly which debated metropolitan government, urged the state to consider the possibility of creating councils of government composed of the chief elected officials of a region's cities and towns and the state's legislative delegation from that area. Ernest Erber[1] has proposed that the reapportioned state legislatures enact metropolitan plans as a binding instrument, with one of the benefits the rise of a metropolitan caucus, along or across party lines.

Nor should we overlook the possibility of greater utilization of the urban county. The county fills a need at the sub-state level for governmental

1 "Urban Land as a National Resource; The Public Interest Vis-à-vis the Market"; mimeographed, privately published, p. 54, 1967.

coordination and the provision of essential functions which cannot be met by suburban communities, even acting through area-wide planning agencies. Counties, however, have tended to be the most backward of the governmental units and surprisingly, many of the larger counties still lack land-use controls. Urban counties require substantial upgrading to fill the important intermediary role between the states and the localities.

In the quest for a regional body to fill the metropolitan void, we may have been going up the wrong path. Regional and metropolitan bodies cannot be politically responsible as long as they lack a legislature and a regional constituency, nor are they likely to be given the sovereign powers to tax, to regulate, and to condemn.

There is reason for concern about the organizational pattern of state, or as in the New York metropolitan area, interstate agencies which have few links to local government. Yet by turning to what can only be ineffectual and irresponsible metropolitan agencies such as councils of elected officials, we are foregoing the use of constitutionally empowered state agencies which, with their far greater powers and resources, can solve metropolitan problems. A wiser course would be to build into the state and interstate agencies the means to make them locally responsive.

The Connecticut study commission was probably prescient when in its deliberations it considered the state itself as the metropolitan area. It is likely that as the growing metropolitan population urbanizes more and more of a state's land area, and as urban problems continue to multiply, a number of states will come to serve as metropolitan governments for all practical purposes. Since two hundred of the nation's 230 metropolitan areas lie within the borders of one state, a strong state position on metropolitan problems could have far-reaching effects.

The rapid growth of state agencies for community and local affairs provides the strongest evidence of the new state initiative. The number has risen from eleven in 1966 to nineteen, and seven of these new offices are lodged in the Cabinet, a recognition that urban affairs must be managed at the highest level of state government. (Connecticut, New Jersey, Pennsylvania, Ohio, Missouri, Vermont, Wisconsin.)

The full-scale agencies for community affairs are charged with broad responsibilities:

1. Provision of advice, information, and technical assistance in the widest sense.
2. Enlargement of the research function, developing it in depth as well

as in breadth, and serving other agencies and branches of state government, including the legislature, and the localities.

3. Coordination of the range of aids and services available to a locality from the state, where federal programs have a state component, the departments serve as intermediary.

4. Provision of financial assistance to the communities for an increasingly wide variety of programs including housing and urban renewal, such human resource development activities as job training, basic education, ghetto recreation, summer employment, day care centers and social services in public housing projects—and the list keeps growing. There are also grants for demonstration projects such as rat control and modular housing.

5. Direct programs, largely in the housing field, include the construction and rehabilitation of moderate-income housing.

The new community affairs departments have come into the limelight because they provide a much needed framework for organizing the resources of state government to confront the problems of the cities. By dealing with their responsibilities in a forthright, continuing and integrated manner, these agencies furnish the missing link between Washington and city hall, and give the localities a unified voice in the statehouse. The Departments of Community Affairs (DCA's) substantive line responsibilities, and their provision of significant financial as well as technical assistance, distinguish them from the other state agencies for local government. Such DCA's include Connecticut, New Jersey, Pennsylvania, and Washington, and the latest addition, Massachusetts.

Missouri's department of community affairs represents a similar but scaled-down approach to the state role in urban affairs since it lacks broad financial powers, as do the agencies of Nebraska, Ohio, and Vermont. The more conventional and limited pattern is found in the local affairs agencies of Minnesota, Montana, Virginia, and Wisconsin.

Neither California nor New York State utilizes the community affairs approach. New York, long accustomed to providing urban assistance, has moved on to an even more positive state role, which is discussed below. California prefers its advisory Intergovernmental Council on Urban Growth and has "found it neither possible, even if it were desirable, to compress all those agencies concerned with local government and local affairs into one department . . ." The monumental 1968 State Development Plan Program has set forth the dimensions of what could be a far-reaching urban program for the state.

Innovations with great possibilities have been fostered by the new state-level departments, notably Connecticut's Community Development Action Plan (CDAP), New Jersey's unique community service programs (including "one stop" direct help to municipalities, a personnel interchange, and interns in community service), Pennsylvania's Partner Cities, Wisconsin's ghetto program for Milwaukee, and the state Model Cities programs. These unprecedented direct action programs indicate that a number of states are prepared to meet urgent community needs without waiting for Washington. In the case of the state Model Cities programs, the state-level counterparts may have as great an effect, if not greater, than the federal prototype. The excitement, creativity, and diversity of these programs fulfill the great tradition of earlier state experimentation and pace-setting.

The growth of state planning agencies has been rapid, and forty-eight states now have such offices, as against only nineteen in 1960. State planning was born during the Depression, stimulated by the National Resources Planning Board, and eclipsed by World War II. It is sobering to recall that in state planning's earlier heydey, the number of agencies reached forty-six.

State planning's formal rebirth was brought about in 1959 by an amendment to the Housing Act of 1954 which authorized grants-in-aid for state planning programs. Many of state planning's limitations can be traced to the inability, since then and until recently, to distinguish between the vastly different needs of state and local government, and to link them to common policies and objectives.

State planning has suffered from two defects: its failure to take advantage of new management technology (PPBS, information systems and analysis, modeling and simulating), and its insensitivity (along with most local and regional planning, one might add) to the social implications of its physical schemes. Social planning is beginning to be understood and used, although not to the extent of the systems and related approaches, which have recently caught on. Where the DCA's have strong commitments to human as well as to physical renewal, as in Connecticut and New Jersey, social planning is being joined to economic and physical planning, though its local impact is still confined largely to central cities.

As the new community and local affairs departments increasingly rationalize and coordinate the state grant-in-aid programs, state planning will become an integral part of the total state operation. Should the federal government change to a system of block grants, the state planning function will become crucial to the setting up of priorities and the allocating of governmental resources.

The Committee on State Planning of the National Governors' Conference has been seeking to make state planning meaningful to the states, and that means to the governors, the states' chief planners. Their criteria are relevance, reliance, and realism. The governors' group doubts that most state planning agencies have focused on the real issues which face state leadership. They fear that planners will find themselves working outside the context of government unless they cease acting largely as information scientists and deal in issues, problems, and controversy.

The Urban Development Corporation (UDC) created by the New York legislature has received the most sweeping powers yet conferred by a state. Governor Nelson Rockefeller declared that the time had come for the state to take "extreme measures" since the cities, with all their local powers, had done little to resuscitate the slums and curb urban blight. Pre-emption by the state of the powers of condemnation and the setting of zoning and construction standards signals the reclaiming of what is "inherently" the right of the state.

Enactment of the UDC should not have occasioned surprise, since New York State has been sensitive to urban problems for many years and has provided substantial urban assistance. UDC is a state agency authorized to carry out projects to alleviate unemployment, revitalize industry, expand community facilities, and replace slums with low- and moderate-income housing. Inducements for private industry include tax exemption, the capacity to speed renewal and to assemble large tracts of land, and a revolving fund totaling $1 billion.

The Urban Development Corporation is controversial because it has been given the power to acquire land by condemnation and to waive local zoning and building code requirements. Its first executive officer, Edward J. Logue, is equally controversial. His extensive experience, including the rebuilding of Boston and New Haven, makes him one of the most seasoned development administrators anywhere.

Enactment of the UDC legislation brought sharp objections from Mayor John V. Lindsay of New York. He asked that the localities be given a veto power over all slum rebuilding projects and countered with an "urban bill of rights" to accomplish similar ends.

UDC can only override local zoning and building construction laws when "compliance is not feasible or practicable," and it would then have to meet the standards of the state building code, followed by most cities in New York. The Corporation points out that it seeks to be asked into the community since, if it expects to accomplish its objectives, it would be foolhardy not to win local approval first. As a creature of the state, it is responsible to the legislature, which could remove or modify its powers were it to act irresponsibly. Furthermore, it will take a two-thirds vote of its Board of Directors to overturn local objections.

Most mayors around the state reacted to the Corporation's formation with approval, and some expressed gratitude that the state was going to step in and "save the communities." A number of mayors have already discussed with UDC the possibility of building urban renewal projects in their cities.

The Urban Development Corporation's powers are large, commensurate with state's urban problems. With its great authority and the huge sums it can probably generate, it could operate on a vast scale, rebuilding large areas quickly. If it can avoid the arrogance, so often coupled with power, of the older authorities and demonstrate a sensitivity to each community's requirements, the options it offers to cities of all sizes are new and extraordinary.

The dynamics of the emergence of the states in urban affairs is reflected in the tensions that have resulted as Washington and city hall resist the states' new urban role. The prospects of the states' sustaining and enlarging their role in urban affairs are linked to complex political, legal, administrative, and fiscal considerations. These are inflamed by issues of class and race which reach down into the nation's very vitals, its neighborhoods.

Direct federalism, developed in the 1930's, has intensified in this decade. Twenty-four of the forty grant programs which by-pass the states have been enacted since 1961.

A different posture toward the states has characterized each of the three federal agencies—HEW, HUD, and OEO—with vast and ambitious urban empires. HEW has long been sensitive to the state role in urban affairs since so many of its grant-in-aid programs flow through the state governments. HUD, and its predecessor, the Housing and Home Finance Agency, has preferred to deal directly with the cities. OEO, until the amending of the Economic Opportunity Act in 1967, completely by-passed the states.

The Secretary for Health, Education and Welfare, Wilbur J. Cohen, has given the Model Cities program "the highest priority." HEW, unlike HUD, prefers to work through the states, and its lead has recently encouraged HUD to consider utilizing the states more directly in its own Model Cities effort. It was the intent of the Congress, as evidenced in the hearings on the legislation which created the Cabinet-level housing office, that the states play a significant role in administering HUD's programs. HUD, in practice, has tended to side-step the states, failing to use them effectively.

The Model Cities act provided no scope for state participation. Its implementation has occurred while the new state-level community affairs departments were gaining momentum. New Jersey, which had a Model Cities Task Force even before it had a community affairs department, provided strong impetus for a number of states to supplement federal Model Cities efforts with state funds, manpower, and technical assistance. Many states, in fact, have considered the Model Cities program an opportunity to sharpen the focus of state government on urban problems. But so far, it is largely a one-way effort. HUD as yet does not recognize the state component and has made arrangements, *ad hoc* at that, only with certain states. The initiative shown by some states, gubernatorial prodding, and the HEW example may persuade HUD to give the states a piece of the Model Cities action. This would mark a turning point in the department's whole attitude toward intergovernmental cooperation.

Several other HUD programs now further a positive relationship with the states, including the Community Development Training Program, the State Technical Assistance, and Urban Information Services (the Title 8 and 9 programs). Improving the management capability of state and local government and strengthening public urban manpower resources are areas the states consider their own and where they are convinced they can perform well, given sufficient federal backing. The unexpected reaction of the states to Titles 8 and 9 is a measure of their alertness to urban aid programs. Even before the ink was dry on the program guides, forty-four governors had organized state agencies to administer one or both of the new grant programs.

HUD has considered the cities, and more especially the large cities, its natural constituency. With a little effort on the part of the department, Lester S. Hyman, reporting to HUD on its posture toward the states, feels that the states would be every bit as "natural" a constituency.

OEO's programs not only by-pass the states, but some of its activities also by-pass the cities to deal directly with nongovernmental agencies. This use of "direct" and "private" federalism ignores the considerable resources many states recently have put at the service of the disadvantaged. States with strong DCA's particularly have a broad and increasing arsenal to combat poverty, and their outlays represent a considerable increment which is beyond OEO's ability to finance. Yet OEO has not recognized the impact of the financial and technical assistance provided by the states through these new agencies. Although the 1967 amendments to the OEO Act called for active state participation in the administration of the community action programs, most of the states which have formally applied for a major role in coordinating OEO programs have been denied the opportunity to participate meaningfully.

HEW has emphasized its concern about the involvement of the governors and the state agency heads in the human resource component of the Model Cities program, noting that since state agencies administer more than three-fourths of the regular HEW appropriations, their participation is critical to program success, and that the cities simply cannot afford not to have them involved. Many states are obviously ready, willing, and able to play as responsible and substantial roles in the HUD and OEO programs as they now do for HEW.

The federal approach to manpower problems has also discouraged state initiative. In fiscal 1968, the federal level gave out over $2 billion in manpower grants, administered by eighteen different agencies. A number of states, disturbed by the coordination difficulties these scattered grant-in-aid programs pose, have instituted a state-wide approach. Utah has placed the CAMPS program (Coordination Manpower Planning System) right in the governor's office, and California has created a state-level Department of Human Resources.

Where states have community and local affairs departments and have demonstrated that they are geared to tackle the mounting difficulties of the cities, they should attain a special relationship with the federal establishment. The possibility of having these new state departments function as *"ad hoc* regional offices" for such agencies as HEW, HUD, and OEO should be carefully considered. Decentralization of federal agency functions to regional offices has not facilitated federal-state relations. Education Commissioner Harold Howe, recognizing this limitation, reorganized the Office of Education in 1968 so that it can work through the states.

By the same token, where the largest cities have the authority and have demonstrated the capacity to handle their problems, the direct relationship between Washington and the city should be retained, provided the appropriate metropolitan and state agencies are kept advised.

The present system of administering grants-in-aid through special separate programs has reached the point of diminishing return. It is profuse, overlapping, and conflicting. The number of aids—over five hundred—has multiplied unduly, and remedial action is necessary. A report to the Committee on State and Local Revenues of the governors' conference has pointed out that although the matching provisions of the existing grant programs vary markedly, the differences do not reflect national priorities. Nor do they stimulate the states and localities to determine their priorities since they have to spend more effort in chasing after what money is available than in determining what needs to be done. Perhaps unwittingly, the narrowly-defined categorical grants encourage piecemeal solutions to public service needs.

The federal establishment, aware that it has reached a management impasse, has instituted some machinery for improvement. The Partnership in Health Act, passed in 1966, may have started a healthy countertrend. The first significant federal legislation to provide block grants, it gives the states discretion to allocate previously earmarked funds; in this case, to design their own public health plans. The Act was the impetus for utilizing a consolidated and flexible (but not state) approach in the Model Cities and Metropolitan Development Act. The Joint Funding Simplification Act of 1967, which would combine related grants into a single package, may point the way to replacement of categorical grants with block funding. The Bureau of the Budget has provided procedural devices to facilitate cooperation and communication between federal and state officialdom, notable Circulars A-80 and A-85, but these need firmer implementation if they are to have an impact. But these measures are just a beginning.

Federal agency heads and state leaders disagree over the channeling of federal grants through the states. Federal officials indicate that they will give the states a more substantive role in federal programs when they "buy in." In the states where this has already happened, there seems to be little meaningful change in the federal-state relationship.

The federal government has not yet acknowledged that the nineteen departments of local and community affairs provide an important new link in the federal-local grant-in-aid chain. Governor Richard J. Hughes sees his New Jersey department of community affairs as "the vehicle through which the State can re-emerge in our federal system" to provide the needed coordination, rationalizing, and blending of federal programs.

There is a trend toward combined funding of local projects by federal agencies whose programs impinge on a target problem or target group. The most far-reaching extension of this concept is The Urban Development Fund, now under consideration, an enlarged and broader version of Model Cities. One of the basic questions which must be settled is whether these funds should flow directly to the cities or should be transmitted through the offices of community affairs, where these exist. As we move away from categorical grant programs, to the degree that state organization and capability make it possible, qualifying states should administer federal block grants, as in Partnership in Health, as opposed to direct federal-city channels, as in Model Cities.

With the steady erosion of the cities, the fiscal disparities within metropolitan areas are becoming extreme. The nation's wealth lies increasingly beyond the central cities' boundaries, while its gravest problems of poverty and segration are found within.

In many other countries, costs for health, education, and welfare are assumed by the national government. This needless municipal overburden may explain why our urban plant is deteriorating and even our greatest cities are shabby, compared to a London or a Paris.

The traditional approach to the financing of what are now recognized as national problems has been challenged. The questions at issue are *who* is to play Robin Hood and redistribute the money from the rich to the poor, from the suburbs back to the cities; *how* shall this redistribution occur; and *what* will be the new roles of the three governmental levels.

The Regional Plan Association of New York has proposed a fiscal strategy, developed by Dick Netzer, whereby the federal establishment would assume fiscal responsibility for poverty-related health, welfare, and special educational services, and double the investment now being made in assisting the poor. The states would finance about 60 per cent of school costs, and the older cities would use the released funds to finance essential community improvement and housekeeping programs.

The achievement of these goals may not be as far off as we think. Thirty-one states have assumed some responsibility for welfare. The proportion of school financing from state revenues already exceeds 50 per cent in twenty-one states, compared with only nine states in 1939–1940.

Dr. James B. Conant has called for a thorough investigation of the proposal that the localities' share of school financing be transferred to the states, eliminating local authority to levy taxes for schools. Dr. James B. Allen, Education Commissioner of New York State, believes that this shift would contribute to school desegregation and reduce the extreme variations in per-pupil expenditures among school districts, even in prosperous states.

States and localities make a far greater fiscal effort than is generally known. While state and local expenditures doubled in the past decade, federal expenditures rose by only 25 per cent. Moreover, since the end of

World War II, the states have multiplied their own aid to municipalities more than seven times. State aid to localities is actually greater than federal aid to state and local government.

We tend to forget that the urban states provide the federal government with far more dollars than is returned to them. Connecticut taxpayers, for example, paid a "premium" of 56 cents in 1967 for each dollar they received in grants, as compared with 44 cents in 1966.

A financial strengthening of federalism requires not only that those states which can, raise more taxes, but that national revenue transferral, the essential mechanism in the adjustment of metropolitical fiscal disparities, be redesigned to relieve cities of the burden of poverty-linked services.

Block grants are unlikely to be legislated until there is an extra fiscal dividend. When this comes to pass, such grants will be a long overdue vote of confidence in the states. Walter W. Heller, revenue sharing's leading proponent, believes that it is precisely to enable the states to overcome their weaknesses that broad-gauged grants must be utilized.

States have performed urban functions or provided urban facilities in the past, largely for mass transit, air and water pollution control, and to assure an adequate water supply.

New York State's recent wide-ranging urban legislation indicates that the state no longer considers it sufficient to provide money and technical assistance to its localities. Where the municipalities have shown themselves unequal to meeting a problem, whatever the reason, New York State now feels that it has the obligation to perform the function itself, to achieve the broadest and fastest impact. State agencies have been established to perform functions already undertaken by New York City, namely transportation, housing, and urban renewal, and urban parks.

S. J. Schulman, General Manager of the unusual new State Park Commission for New York City, considers it a first cousin to the State's Urban Development Corporation and the State's Metropolitan Transportation Authority. He believes that direct performance has become New York State's "basic thrust," expressing a new assumption of responsibility by the state to assert its urban concern.

The states have a vast reserve of power which they continue to exercise sparingly. Carl Feiss, consulting to the study commission on metropolitan government, urged Connecticut in 1966 to attempt to recall to the state level in the course of four to six years "certain zoning powers which it has granted to the towns and municipalities over the past forty years." He stated that he was aware that it would entail "a long and agonizing effort."

Hawaii has state-wide zoning, and the state now exercises controls over the open and rural lands while the urban areas retain their own zoning. William Whyte points out that Hawaii is a special case and that it is too early to say how well the zoning will stand up, or how applicable it might be to other states. Like Feiss, he believes that the states should protect the larger public interest if the local governments do not.

The American Society of Planning Officials (ASPO) prepared the first state-wide study of the operation of zoning for the 1967 Connecticut General Assembly. ASPO's consultants suggested that local zoning ordinances be subject to review at the state level by an administrative body which could compare the objectives of such local regulations with regional and state plans. The states are a long way from taking on state-wide zoning, but the institution of a state-level appeals mechanism seems likely.

In all the furor engendered by the Urban Development Corporation over the possible loss of New York City's home rule, too little was said about the onerous effects of the local code and how much it discouraged technological advance, which could mean less expensive and better housing. It is also curious how little attention was given to the possibility that the Corporation could equally use its sweeping powers to open up the suburbs to the poor, who may well be black.

Local building and zoning regulations are suburbia's traditional instruments of exclusion. It is quite clear that the needs for housing and access to suburban employment will cause state governments to assert their sovereign police powers to override home rule in the rich, restricted suburbs. This is likely to become one of the major issues of the Seventies.

Since the crisis in urban education is part of the greater metropolitan crisis, the solutions reflect the power struggles of society at large. These include a bewildering number of approaches to the vexing problem of educational inequality of the urban poor, particularly in the North. The two main strands which can be sorted out from the tangled skein—a pressure for regionalism and consolidation on the one hand, and pressure for local control on the other—seem contradictory. Since the state has the legal responsibility for education, it finds itself in the middle of powerful cross currents. These are further complicated by the states' rights stand in the South, in opposition to the federal desegregation guidelines.

It was all so simple years ago when the neighborhood school in the old-fashioned neighborly sense provided planners with the parameters for one of their pet concepts, the neighborhood unit. Now we are seeking ways by which the favored can help improve the achievement of the neglected, by their presence and also by their money. This comes down to bussing, educational parks, financial equalization of the rich and poor areas within a state, the merger of city and suburban school systems, or some combination of these volatile elements. We are, at the same time, searching to find ways to capitalize on the ghetto community's determination to administer the education of its children without wrecking the educational system.

It is paradoxical that at the same time there is active consideration of proposals to expand the boundaries of school administrative areas, New York City's racial minorities have been fighting for community control. Yet both types of solutions are necessary. Stripped of its excessive demands, local control can be viewed as the painful start toward a necessary and inevitable decentralization of a remote and gargantuan school system.

During the New York City confrontation between the black parents and the teachers' union, Mayor Lindsay called upon the state Commissioner of Education to resolve the deadlock, since only the state has this authority. The New York legislature has entrusted this office with extensive judicial powers, including the right to order racial mixing. The use of equally strong power to prevent desegregation has been advocated by former Governor George C. Wallace, who claims that there will be such a public outcry against the federal government's school desegregation efforts, that states like Alabama will resort to their police power to "physically" take over the schools.

Our public educational institutions have become a proving ground for intergovernmental relations, and battles over their management threaten the viability of the country's largest city; and in the future will test to their limits, the authority of the states and of the federal government itself.

Local control and home rule have become shibboleths proclaimed under the different banners of the radical right, the black separatists, and the middle-of-the-road white suburbanites. We cannot measure home rule by the emotion it evokes but by how well it actually operates when viewed in terms of the larger public interest. Confrontations over zoning and the schools are altering the meaning of home rule, and this is to the good in our rapidly urbanizing and highly mobile nation. At the hearings on the Urban Development Corporation, the governor's representative had to remind the legislators that "Citizens of the cities are also citizens of the state."

Now that reapportionment is completed, there is doubt that it will be as clear a force for bringing urban needs to the forefront as was hoped right after the Supreme Court's landmark decision in Baker *v.* Carr. The newly districted legislatures in many states may prove to be more responsive to suburban than urban concerns, their legislation static rather than dynamic, with the primary goal being maintenance of the *status quo.*

Urban aid has been a hot issue in New Jersey since Governor Hughes' Select Commission on Civil Disorders indicted the state in 1968 for failing to respond to the needs of its deeply torn inner cities. Hemmed in by a politically hostile Republican legislature, the Democratic governor had reluctantly cut the budget request for his new community affairs department almost in half (from $24 million to $13.1 million). Responding to an outcry from the states' enlightened interests, the governor reversed himself and in a special urban message, proposed a $126 million urban aid program and a "moral recommitment" to meet "a New Jersey crisis of massive proportions."

The governor's courageous action was buttressed by an unprecedented "rich people's march" on the state capital in May 1968, composed of those who took to heart their select committee's conclusions that city problems and remedies are the responsibility of the white majority. (When the crowd was asked "Do you want to pay an income tax?" it roared back "Yes.")

New Jersey's intense conflict may mirror similar cleavages in other heavily urbanized states. This new backlash line-up of wealthy suburbanites with President Richard M. Nixon's "the forgotten people," many of whom probably respond more to former Governor Wallace than to Nixon, may prove a formidable force. This new alliance could slow down or even block the urgently needed social legislation for the urban poor, "the left-out people" of former Vice President Hubert Humphrey, in many of the state legislatures as well as in Congress.

Before a working equilibrium can be achieved between the two principal centers of constitutional power, the states and the federal establishment, many substantive changes must occur. Relationships have become lop-sided, and consolidation, packaging, and simplifying of the grant-in-aid programs are essential to restore balance. Social and economic disparities within the metropolitan areas can be reconciled only by recourse to a new fiscal strategy which is able to relate needs and resources. Unless the anti-state tendencies of the federal agencies are modified, their urban programs will prove too vast and complex to be administered from the center alone.

Within the states themselves, direct performance by state government of urban functions, or in a new relationship with the cities, will complement their increasing provision of technical and financial aid, particularly in the critical areas of transportation, low- and moderate-cost housing, ghetto rehabilitation, and the acquisition of open space. Many of the contests over open housing and racially balanced schools will take place in the no man's land on the metropolitan frontier, with the states asserting their powers, to build "new towns" or to expand old towns for new people. The schools in particular will personify the perplexing philosophical rift in the nation, between the need for increasing regionalization and inner city demands for intensifying local control.

The heavily urbanized states will have to face up to the tough issues of urban aid and racial balance. Confrontations between the formerly dis-enfranchised and the growing voting bloc of new and old suburbanites and the lower-middle-class whites, will bring to the surface deep cleavages between governors and legislatures, or within the legislatures themselves. Reapportionment, instead of rescuing the cities, could solidify the suburbs. The latter, however, will find it increasingly difficult to exclude urbaniza-tion and become susceptible to urban problems.

Yet, on balance, this is hopeful. The resurgence of the states, as spenders and as policy-makers, frankly as forces to be reckoned with, has reminded us of what our country is all about. We chose a federal form of govern-ment because we were a dynamic, restless, enterprising people, welcom-ing diversity, encouraging innovation. Federalism has permitted us to operate fifty political laboratories. Much of the experimentation has been good, and the most venturesome legislatures are setting higher standards than the Congress, to fight pollution, to open up employment opportunity and housing, and to save dwindling open space. (We should remember that much of the New Deal's social legislation was pioneered in states such as New York and Wisconsin.)

The enabling acts of the new state agencies for local and community affairs are redefining the public interest to incorporate, even single out, the long-neglected claims of the poor. In these states, the entire machinery of state government is being retooled to be socially responsive, while state planning is now encompassing human as well as environmental issues.

As state government becomes more potent, flexing its unaccustomed muscles, it is also reaching out to its constituency. The localities, by means of the regional planning agencies can move upward, while state administra-tion, through field offices and district coordinators, can move down. Pos-sibly most encouraging is the growing insistence that where state money is given to a community, those whose needs are greatest but whose voice has been least, must also have a say.

Today's political climate favors decentralization, a yearning, probably fanciful and romantic, to return government to the people, and the people to a simpler life. In this reaction to bigness and concentration, we must be aware that those most ardently anti-federal government may well be anti-*all* government, when government threatens their way of life.

A continental democracy, as sprawling, as geographically and ethnically diverse as the fifty United States of America, can rarely speak with a unified voice. The voice from the states will be getting louder, from those that refuse to feed their hungry and school their children in equality, as well as from those that do. The states will become stronger, because they are the logical political instrumentalities to mediate between big and little government, and they have discovered this at a critical moment in our nation's history. As they emerge, some will opt merely for states' rights but most, we trust, will also move toward states' responsibilities.

Measures taken by the federal government since the New Deal have moved the country toward national government and away from historical federalism. Unless the states emerge, the national government's power will continue to grow. However, despite its increasing reach, the federal level will be unable to solve metropolitan problems because it cannot create a mechanism that can deal politically, legally, and financially with the entire metropolitan areas, and more and more, with megalopolitan areas. The inability to solve metropolitan problems means also an inability to resolve the problems of race and poverty, the essence of the urban crisis. The awareness that only the state has the authority to cut across municipal boundaries has stimulated the rethinking of the role of each governmental level and has caused the emergence of the states in urban affairs.

PART 2

THE STATE OF THE ART

HENRY FAGIN

Professor of Administration, Graduate School of Administration; Research Administrator, Public Policy Research Organization, University of California at Irvine; Registered Architect, New York. Previously Professor of Planning, University of Wisconsin; Executive Director, Penn-Jersey Transportation Study; Executive Director, Regional Plan Association; Research Professor, University of California, Berkeley, 1958; Director of Planning, Churchill-Fulmer Associates; Architect, Mayer & Whittlesey, 1939–42; Architectural Editor, Federal Writers Project, 1938–39. Member, AIA (1941–46). Co-editor: *Urban Research and Policy Planning.* Co-author: *Planning and Community Appearance.*

Advancing the "State of the Art"

Competent city and regional planners, even in the years when they focused mainly on guiding the physical aspects of development, have always been concerned with the social and economic factors that act on a physical environment, no less than with the physical factors. This wide spectrum of factors composed the input side of the planning process. It has always been an aim of planners to understand and communicate to other people the potential impacts of their land development and public facilities proposals on the social and economic qualities of the environment, no less than on the physical. But traditionally, the measures proposed by planners have been expected to express policies fundamentally about "land use and land occupancy and the regulation thereof," to use the phraseology recently erased from the constitution of the American Institute of Planners (AIP).

Put positively and simply, the change placed on an equal footing planning for the social, the economic, and the physical aspects of unified community development. Thus, the change removed a previous self-imposed constriction in planners' search for solutions and therefore a harmful bias in the nature of their actual recommendations. The change was pointed at the output side of professional work. Rather than limit recom-

125

mendations to measures designed primarily to guide or bring about physical changes in the environment, planners now would give equal status to
the design of all sorts of measures to be taken to handle peoples' problems
in the whole hierarchy of jurisdictions, whatever realm of human action the
measures might entail. We would insist only that the quality of work performed meet a professional standard, systematically focusing what is
known about time, space, resources, and human beings on the creation of
an endless stream of policy to solve problems of community change.

It is from this newly legitimized and broadened orientation that I
propose to consider "Advancing the State of the Art." But first, I wish to
propose a more precise subtitle for my paper: "The Profession and the
Discipline of Planning." There are those among us, on the one hand, who
practice the planning *profession.* They mainly apply what is already
known generally to determine what should be done in specific situations.
On the other hand, there are planners motivated mainly by an urge to
increase the general store of knowledge as to how to plan better. They are
the primary builders of the *discipline* of planning. The first group works
mostly in on-going public planning agencies and in the consulting firms that
serve them. The second group is concentrated largely in the universities but
also includes important scholars working independently or often in the
action agencies themselves. Hans Blumenfeld, J. Douglas Carroll, Jr.,
Britton Harris, and Alan Voorhees, for example, come readily to mind as
men who have contributed important conceptual elements to the discipline
of planning at times when they were working within basically action-
oriented frameworks. Conversely, such academics as Professors Robert B.
Mitchell, T. J. Kent, Jr., Kevin Lynch, Harvey Perloff, William L. C.
Wheaton, and Louis Wetmore have served from time to time as planning
professionals seeking solutions to current community problems largely on
the basis of what they already knew.

In the end it is perhaps a difference in time scale that most distinguishes
the two modes of planning service. The academic pursuing the discipline in
the university is more inclined to work today on concepts that may have
direct utility only some time off; to fill in pieces of knowledge for particular
purposes still to be discovered; to prepare students for a world with issues
different from our own. The practicing professional is more driven by
the urge to do something now about the problems already insistently
demanding action. As an Institute of Planners, of course, we are fully
concerned with both time scales and with both modes of service.

With the foregoing distinctions in mind, I come to my first point about the state of the art. Looking now at the profession of planning and at the discipline of planning, our greatly expanded definition of the "what" that is the concern of planning ought to have an immediate and sobering impact. It should remove once and for all a pretense that never was valid but did appear at least plausible in times past. This was the notion that the individual planner practiced a field sufficiently narrow for him to be an independent master in all of it. His special sector of competence, as it was frequently phrased, was bounded by the general, the comprehensive, and the long-range aspects of physical development. Within this sector, it was held, the planner could and should develop a personal mastery of the survey, analytic, design, and advocacy skills essential to a role as the community's expert in the design of the general plan and its implementing instruments. Following the image of the architect as master builder, expert in his knowledge of every phase of the building process, the planner was viewed as the master city builder, expert in every phase of the city building process.

Whether or not this particular image of the sectoral but comprehensive expertise expected of the city planner ever had relevance, it clearly has no application to many essential kinds of planners at work today—planners who take part in the planning processes now defined in AIP's constitution, described in its journal, educated in its planning schools, and active in its planning offices. In the past, even when we sought to restrict our scope to recommendations in the physical realm, most of us were aware of collaborating with other members of the "design" professions—and planners were not necesarily the masters of such collaborative efforts, as we might remind ourselves. Leadership in a cooperative undertaking is largely an ineluctable quality of personality, not a prerogative bestowed by definition or by legal victory won by some profession's lawyers.

The fact is that collaboration among limited individuals really was of the essence, even when the thing to be designed was the physical environment. How much more so must collaboration become a hallmark of planning when we address all the program areas of our communities—and at every scale from the neighborhood to the nation and beyond. What is signified most by our changed perception of planning is the character of our specialization. We propose now as an Institute to specialize not so much in *every* aspect of land planning as in the peculiarly "planning" aspects of all the functional activities of government—including physical development activities, but not limited to them. Whatever the particular function, we propose to offer expertise in something we name a "planning" dimension.

(I shall describe this dimension presently when I discuss the discipline.) But, and I wish to underline this, in the case of every function to whose planning we contribute, we depend heavily on collaboration with persons who are specialists in various specific aspects of the precise function, as well as on collaboration frequently with other specialists in planning.

A difficulty with survey papers of this kind is their tendency to sprawl over large areas and to leave somewhat vague and disconnected impressions, hard to grasp and to remember. We feel the need for some simple organizing and unifying concepts on which to hang the separate strands of investigation. Accordingly, what I attempt in the remainder of this paper is to provide a structured way of relating to each other and to the whole of planning the many diverse elements of the art that are about to be discussed separately and intensively. For this purpose I offer a pair of frameworks—one for the profession of planning, the other for the discipline.

I distinguish seven major functions of the practicing planner: he is analyst, synthesizer, collaborator, educator, mediator, advocate, and administrator. These seven words serve as my check list for organizing an evaluation of the profession's competence. In the following pages, I shall present a second framework for evaluating what I call the disciplinary aspects of planning. (As will be seen, these latter relate mainly to the first two functions—the analyst and synthesizer roles of the profession.)

I suggest that the state of the art of the *profession* of planning is best judged by looking at people's capabilities as practitioners rather than at their development of ideas. Here, the state of the art is embodied in the levels of competence planners have reached in the performance of the seven essential professional roles. When we seek to evaluate the discipline, the situation is reversed—the focus is on the evolution of concepts.

First, the role of analyst. I refer here to the basic role of the planner that is highlighted by terms like policy analyst, systems analyst, planning analyst. I have already noted that the roles of analyst and synthesizer, more than the others, related directly to the disciplinary aspects of planning. Accordingly, my meaning of these roles will be further elaborated in the concluding pages devoted to the state of the discipline. In the present context, I suggest that analysis is the systematic clarification of a whole and its component parts so as to gain a knowledge of what something is and how it functions. Analysis is the aspect of professional planning most capable of being advanced in a social sense as well as within the arc of a single career. That is, there is transmittable progress in improving the role of the planning professional as analyst—not merely personal progress tied to years of practice directly experienced and solely possessed by the single planner involved. Advances in what might properly be called the science of analysis are transmittable; advances in the capacity to synthesize are somewhat less so; but advances in the capacity to perform the other roles—to collaborate, educate, mediate, advocate, and administrate—tied more closely as they are to the evolving capabilities of particular individuals, are buried largely, alas, with the planner in his grave; largely, but not fully.

Second, then, the role of synthesizer. If the function of analysis implies clarification of wholes by taking things apart so as to examine component elements in detail and in interaction, the function of synthesis is to assemble parts in new ways so as to create wholes or systems—that is, to invent new constellations of ideas, arrangements, programs. Applied to the physical environment, the planner as collaborating designer is a synthesizer. But increasingly we speak, too, of designing organizations, designing social programs, designing financial plans, designing models of virtually anything on earth or elsewhere. The art of synthesis has had long attention in planners' drafting rooms, the methods used growing largely out of the practice of architects, engineers, and landscape architects. Synthesis has had some systematic and new attention among us in recent years. Decision-modeling is one expression of this interest. Christopher Alexander's lively paper on design at the 1966 Portland Conference demonstrated that the state of the art of synthesis can be materially advanced by the contributions of thoughtful and imaginative people among us. But in a professional sense, Clarence Stein and Henry Wright were masterful synthesizers fifty years ago. So was Ictinus in fifth-century Greece. It is the combination of the greater complexity of our problems and the greater range of design subjects that marks the planner's more difficult task today and challenges his synthesizing capabilities.

Third, the role of collaborator. I already have referred to the dramatic shift in viewpoint concerning the planner's potential subject matter that led to our changed definition of the general role of the planner; and I have stressed the impossibility of operating within this widened scope except through a sharing of responsibility for planning through extensive collaboration. Let me now indicate something about the necessary scale of this collaboration. It implies a process and structure of collaboration, a capability to cooperate, for which we are as yet quite unprepared. The planner ought to operate as part of a collaborating structure with a great many other specialists speaking in many other tongues. These include (1) at least twenty other important disciplinary and professional contributors—economists, ecologists, lawyers, statisticians, engineers, political scientists, agronomists, etc.; (2) administrators and functional specialists in each of the organizational divisions used to make the total governance task tractable—highway transportation and labor relations, waste management and equal opportunity, housing and medicare, public safety and higher education, and all the rest; (3) other planners in the whole intricate web of planning, working in every kind of planning agency, and at all the levels of government, and in all the private or voluntary enterprises that interact with public activities; and (4) representatives of the scores of interest groups that constitute the planner's clientele (including the political parties) with whom and for whom the planning process is conducted and plans are made. Real collaboration with all of these is of the essence. More effective performance of this collaborative role hinges on the development of better institutions, instruments, and personal skills for collaboration—and especially on a fuller sense of the importance of collaborative capacity. One crucial measure of the progress of the profession will be the extent to which it is transformed into a meeting place for all the collaborating planners.

Fourth, the role of educator. The planner is paid to dream with very open eyes. He is a professional visionary. To paraphrase Lewis Mumford on the city, the planner functions to overcome separation in time and in space. But until the planner's insights come to suffuse the outlook of the larger community, the planner's plans remain inert, possessing no power to inspire action. It is in this sense that every effective planner plays a role as an educator. To assess the state of this component of the art, I ask: How far do planners project their best visions beyond the immediate and traditional circle of planning commissioners, ladies of the League of Women Voters, and other planners? At a different level the professional planner must serve as an educator for planning throughout whatever organization he works in. We are painfully discovering that planning must be going on throughout organizations and not just in specialized units labeled "planning." If there is any single lesson in the current experience with PPBS—planning, programming, budgeting systems—it is that improved methods require the development of improved skills from top to bottom. Re-education is the key.

Fifth, the role of mediator. The idea of mediation applies to situations involving competing interests. The concept is that some "highest" level of compromise can be attained in actions collectively taken that affect diverse interest groups. The major responsibility for mediation, as part of an essentially political process, is placed on politicians. But the planner has a special role in the mediation process, concentrated on raising the quality of what is debated and therefore decided and done. This notion of mediation among differing interest groups, rather than service to an abstraction called the public interest, squarely recognizes and addresses the fact of cultural, social, and economic diversity among people, and the perpetual presence of validly particular interests. The planner's special contribution to the mediation process is the systematic discovery of previously unseen options. He offers these thoroughly described, examined, and compared as to their respective potential impact. This service significantly increases the available range of possible actions, hence enlarging the scope and content of the mediation process. The concept of the planner as a mediator is very different from the idea of the planner as the master designer who alone can perceive the one best plan to fit a situation that he alone grasps (a caricature to be sure). But it is also very different from the concept of the economic market, guided by Smith's "unseen hand," or the political market, guided by Lindblom's disembodied "intelligence," or both operating together, producing a sequence of activities automatically leading to optimal solutions.

Sixth, among the roles of the professional planner is the role of advocate. This is by no means a new role. Some city planners, along with other concerned reformers, were passionately and prominently advocating measures to relieve poverty, reduce disease, eliminate illiteracy, end overcrowding, and introduce amenity for disadvantaged people when the twentieth century opened. Whatever their motivations, wisdom, or success, they were advocates of a better life for the people described so ringingly in the rhetoric of the day on the Statue of Liberty:

> Give me your tired, your poor,
> Your huddled masses yearning to breathe free,
> The wretched refuse of your teeming shore,
> Send these, the homeless, tempest-tossed, to me:
> I lift my lamp beside the golden door.

What is new in the current discussions of "advocacy planning" is the notion that more planners today ought to devote all or parts of their lives to the service of particular interest groups not now adequately served with professional advice: the poor, the young, the victims of racial or other prejudice, the aged, the physically handicapped, the foreign—at home and abroad—not to mention that overwhelming unvoiced majority, the not-yet-born, who most desperately need advocates.

Paul Davidoff and his colleagues in Planners for Equal Opportunity have labored effectively in recent years to rekindle the spark of social concern that inspired the earlier generation. Yet who among us can deny that the special problems of the millions of persons in the neglected groups named, far too seldom hold a central place in the attention of professional planners? Even when we do look at their problems, is it not generally over the shoulders of mayors or governors or civic leaders—who too often are troubled only by some special manifestation of a problem rather than its fundamental substance? If the hippies cluttering streets and ruining central districts would only move away, they feel, the problem of alienated youth would evaporate. If the angry black youths could only be sent back to the cotton fields, there would be no problem of urban unemployment and unrest.

The truth is that for half a century our profession has specialized predominantly in advocacy planning for the business community. In the cities, we have helped maximize functional efficiency for America's industrial and commercial enterprises; and, again serving its owners and managers we have protected the affluent in their suburban home communities from unduly high taxes, residential and school overcrowding, "undesirable" neighbors, and the collapse of commuter rail service. The investment of the time and talents of planners to keep the two-dollar-a-day commuter trains running at rush hour, or to substitute a ubiquitous network of freeways that slice through the slums as they go downtown far exceeds planners' occupation with the travel needs of the autoless, ordinary, twenty-cent mass rider.

If we assess the state of the planning profession's capacity to play fully the role of advocate—advocate for every legitimate group—then surely we have made but a most modest modern beginning. This, despite the honorable tradition I have already cited—a tradition that goes back through a long if thin line of planners to the days of the early housing, health, and welfare reformers. We today do not yet know very much about how to arrange effective advocacy for the groups that now lack the services of planners, how to find the essential resources for such planning, how to practice from this unaccustomed perspective, and how to relate to the groups involved.

Finally, seventh in the role of administrator. With the trend toward a more central placement of planners in the structure of government has come the vesting of greater responsibility and the provision of much larger resources for planning. Consequently, many planners now find themselves administering substantial and complex organizations. Their effectiveness has come to depend on their competence as administrators no less than as plan makers. They learn this role mainly on the job. I suggest it warrants much greater attention in formal education for planning practice.

Having proposed a basis for considering the state of the art of the *profession* of planning, I turn now to the state of the art of the *discipline* of planning. Some might venture to refer to this second subject as the state of the science rather than art, a useful distinction though perhaps not thoroughly scientific. My immediate challenge is to offer a second evaluative framework, a counterpart to the foregoing check list covering the roles of the planner. This second framework is intended to help assess where we are in the evolving methodology of planning. The framework I offer grows out of two problems that occupied me during much of the past year; and I propose to present it in terms of a model derived mainly from thinking about these problems. (Its outlines were sketched very briefly in my review essay entitled "Perspectives on the City," May/June 1968 *PAR*.)

But first, the two problems. Both involve wholes and parts and the implications of fragmentation. The first problem arises from societal pressures to separate our capacities for feeling, knowing, and acting. The conceptual distinction among these is valuable enough for many purposes, including, I hope, the use I am about to make of it. But the distinction also tends to deny our experience as whole human beings. To the extent that we organize responsibilities, learning, or action separately around any of these conceptual categories isolated from the others, we risk producing warped results—including, of course, warped people. Yet all sorts of circumstances press us toward suppressing one or another of the three modes of experience. Sometimes when we have to act, we feel forced to anaesthesize our feelings about what we do. Sometimes action is paralyzed by what we know and feel about its consequences. Sometimes we wish not to know what is happening. Integrity is a painful condition to win and hold.

The other problem is the widespread difficulty of resolving the tension between the perspectives of persons responsible for parts and those of persons responsible for wholes within various organizations. Even the tension between short-run and long-run considerations may be viewed as a special case of the problem of parts and wholes.

In my consideration of these organizational issues, I have been viewing and defining planning as an action-producing activity which combines investigation, thought, design, communication, and other components. But in another sense, planning is a special kind of pre-action action. The immediate output of the act of planning is a decision about action—still an internalized action rather one turned outward with direct impact on the environment. Thus, planning is two steps removed from an actual environment-shaping activity. It informs the decisions that direct the ultimate actions. In this sense only can one properly make a distinction between planners and decision-makers, since planners are in fact decision-makers in everything they do.

Planning at its best is an efficient substitute for trial and error regarding the relations of wholes and parts. It is at the level of planning, rather than of action that produces outer changes, that potential combinations of actions can first be investigated for their combined effects and for their mutual interactions, without incurring the heavy penalties that may come from real-life tests. Examples of fresh approaches to the study of parts and wholes are the system of policy development that has come to be known as policy planning and the related work in planning-programming-budgeting systems.

A number of considerations of this nature suggest that a framework for evaluating the state of the discipline must embrace all three primary realms involved when people carry out the planning process—feeling, knowing, and acting—as well as the relation of these realms to the changing contextual constraints of time, space, and other resources. This framework might also be thought of as a model of the societal processes that concern public planning. It may be useful also as a general model for public administration.

In the form I present it, the model describes public action as a system comprising three sub-systems, each with further sub-system components—altogether a hierarchy of several interacting systems and sub-systems. The primary sub-systems focus respectively on realms for which I use the shorthand titles feeling, knowing, and acting. (Parenthetically, it should be emphasized here that a linear, analytic description of the model is forced on me by the nature of discourse. But in concept, the sub-systems of the model all exist, interact, and change simultaneously. Each is a perspective for looking at the others. The order of treatment is arbitrary. Interaction may be initiated from changes in any part of the total system. Some directions of influence can even reverse.)

To begin somewhere, the discipline of planning has an extensive concern with the realm of *feeling*. We have created the notion of this realm as a way of naming our perception of the wellspring of human energy, choice, will, action. Feeling is necessarily idiosyncratic, since it is an individual experience. The realm of feeling is a complex system, however. It is not simply emotions as felt by individuals. It comprises also the feelings people have about particular things and the feelings shared within groups. Values, a concept closely related to feelings, may be regarded as a language for distinguishing and measuring feelings. For a man to state his values is to assert the strength or persistence of his feelings about one class of things or another. To say that someone places a high value on privacy, for example, is to predict that in situations involving choice, this person is very likely to feel strongly enough about privacy to sacrifice feelings about other elements of existence to it.

At a given time in his life, a person possesses a structure of values with some degree of stability. This has been referred to as a preference profile or preference curve. The larger society is composed of groups within each of which there is some characteristic value structure that provides cohesion. The value systems of such interest groups are the driving force of politics. The differing value systems are the sources of the criteria used by the groups respectively to weigh choice and determine action. Thus, this major system comprises feelings, values, interest groups, preferences, sources of choice, motivations, and similar matters. An understanding of the system and its component sub-systems involves matters of basic human psychology—how values are generated, transmitted, modified, suppressed; how people group and regroup in response to feelings of common or divergent values; how people draw on their values to direct attention, to evaluate alternatives, to motivate decisions, to energize actions, to criticize results.

In anticipation of moving on from feeling to another major realm, knowledge, we may note important interface elements connecting the two systems. The system of concepts encompassed under the generic term goals is such an interface component. As basic, generalized feelings increasingly become infused with specific content derived from the realm of knowledge, values crystallize progressively into goals. Along a continuum from vague, generalized feelings to precise, attainable benefits informed by the realm of knowledge, lies a range of objectifications of values that we call aims, objectives, programs, projects. The capacity to articulate the existing goals in a way that makes them operational at each step is an important concern of the discipline of planning. Even more fundamental, however, is the capacity to invent new options, since the best solutions grow out of the particulars of unique situations and never really pre-exist. But this latter function of creative design, or synthesis as it was called earlier, is deeply embedded as part of the realm of knowledge and will be more extensively considered there.

Before leaving the sub-system of feeling, a word more about interest groups—basic elements in the politics of planning. Interest groups tend to organize not so much around shared general feelings or values as around the embodiment of particular clusters of values in objectives held in common by the members of such groups. Thus it is that individual persons find themselves in kaleidoscopically shifting constellations of different interest groups, sometimes seeing the same faces, sometimes quite different ones, as the agenda of issues and objectives change with the passing of time. I suppose personal membership in the Automobile Club is the most embarrassing reminder of this coalition concept that I can think of for professional planners. Just think with whom and on what issues annual AAA dues associates planners.

A word in passing about a special class of groups very much concerned today with issues of urban life. Religious groups seem to be a reverse of interest groups. Where the latter are usually united on programs, however diverse the moral expectations of the members, many religious groups, oriented largely around nurturing a unique cluster of values, often find it very difficult to agree on common action toward other particular objectives. Given their central focus on the articulation and transmission of values, religious groups and their secular equivalents, including the conservationists and philosophers, have a special importance to planners. This is related to the advocacy question raised earlier in the discussion of professional roles. Somewhere in this component is the source of that sense of responsibility for the stranger and the unborn to which I alluded before. In any event, given our stake in the outcome of political decisions—these in turn the result of the continual interplay of interest groups—a fundamental part of planning discipline must be addressed toward understanding more about the nature and dynamics of interest group formation, operation, and interaction.

I come now to the next major realm, for which I have chosen as shorthand the term knowing. This realm draws on information to modify preexisting feelings, values, goals, and interests; thus it sometimes produces changes in the components of the realm of feeling and in the interface elements as well. In particular, however, as I already have suggested, the knowledge realm contains the sub-system I've termed options, within which are invented the alternative objectives, programs, or projects that become subject matter for political decision and subsequent action. It should be emphasized here again that public actions cannot be any better than the options devised—hence the extreme importance of this creative, synthesizing component of the discipline. Its state of the art is measured by our capacity to generate manageable but thoroughly explored ranges of action alternatives, with their crucial respective consequences spelled out in terms both adequate and understandable to each interest group with stake in what might result. Granting that the creation of options for action is and must be a cooperative effort of planners with many other collaborators, it remains true that the planners' capacity to innovate options is exercised at present primarily in relation to designs for community layout, with ancillary attention to economic improvement, but with little involvement in social program development, and that of recent date. There is an urgent need to devote to the processes of designing options for social and economic aspects of community change, the same kinds of imaginative spirit that Alexander, Lynch, and Safdie have demonstrated in the creation of three-dimensional options. To use a figure of speech, thus far planners have stressed gaining some analytic understanding of the world of social space. Planners now must move into the redesign of social space.

The major knowledge system also comprises several other subsystems. The next one is the whole context within which proposed options would operate. A disciplined approach to the contextual system involves knowledge of alternatives of a sort different from the action alternatives, the options already alluded to. These other alternatives are due to uncertainties or indeterminacies in the environment itself. But, more broadly, planners must gain understanding of the larger societal processes that provide them their opportunities and constraints. We need historic perspective on the present, greatly increased clarity about what is, and what affects what, what can be changed, and what is beyond our influence.

A grasp of today's dynamics and of the nature of the uncontrollable variables in the environmental context has an important bearing on the third subsystem of knowledge—prediction. I speak of prediction here not in any pretentious sense but as an integral and inescapable part of the discipline of planning. Always, in even the simplest possible exercise of planning, there is an essential element of prediction. We say, "Here's a plan and a course of action you might wish to follow; if you do so, this is how it's likely to come out." Prediction is implied in every architect's plan, in every budget, in every program policy proposed. Of course, given the magnitude and complexity of life today, we seldom encounter simple situations in which cause and effect can be demonstrated conclusively in advance by simple logic.

Most often, the options planners test are complicated, and the contexts in which they are forced to project their impacts are variegated and dynamic. Even with what we can observe about the past projected into the future, utilizing fully the findings of the statistical and probability and simulation fields, prediction is just about as difficult as invention, which is to say very hard indeed. An invaluable model-building group within the planning discipline has been working on the improvement of planners' capacity to predict. This thrust goes back at least to the enormously significant grouping of social scientists and planners in Columbia's Institute of Urban Land Use and Housing Studies in the 1940's under Ernest T. Fisher, with David Blank, Henry Cohen, Leo Grebler, Robert B. Mitchell, John Rannells, Chester Rapkin, Louis Winnick and others contributing. Another great advance toward prediction capabilities came from the Chicago planning school under Harvey S. Perloff, which inspired the model-building work of John W. Dyckman, Britton Harris, Richard L. Meier, Ira S. Robinson, and Lowdon Wingo, Jr. in the 1950's and subsequently. Other transportation and land-use modelers and predictors—J. Douglas Carroll, Jr., Stuart F. Chapin, Jr., Roger Creighton, John Friedmann, Edgar M. Hoorwood, Ira S. Lowry, John R. Meyer, and Alan M. Voorhees —have steadily sought to increase the time-range and the reliability of our capacity to predict. One is tempted to declare that more time, energy, and brainpower in recent years have gone into the component of the discipline of planning that deals with prediction than into any other comparably important element. Yet the other disciplinary components appear to be equally important. Do we need to manage a better balance?

Moreover, there is still a fundamental difficulty with the state of our ability to predict. The physical bias of the profession has thoroughly dominated the subject matter we have been concerned to predict. For example, our models are intended to predict the future movements of Chicago's automobiles twenty years hence, but not tomorrow's movements of black people in response to the outrage of Chicago's planned housing slums. Planners have not yet tested Bayard Rustin's Freedom Budget to predict whether its realization would be the end of free enterprise in America, as some claim, or its savior, or neither. In brief, to plan for auto traffic and related aspects of land development, we possess elaborate models back by mountainous quantities of data. To plan for economic aspects of development we have a growing body of macro-economic theory, backed by some input-output data and the maintenance of extensive records of various economic accounts. But to plan for the crucial social aspects of development, the social well-being of people, rich and poor, we have virtually no workable models, little significant data, and a large lack of predictive theory. We are just beginning to talk about social accounting. Our data about social phenomena are a collection gathered largely for other purposes, frequently as not misleading.

To sum up the state of our second major realm relevant to the discipline of planning—the capability for knowing—we are of necessity aware of huge gaps. The fact that we have this awareness is itself an important gain. The American Institute of Planners' three-year national consultation, focused though it was on the substantive issues of the day, revealed how rapidly the felt need for knowledge still tends to outstrip the expanding level of knowledge. And here, of course, lies the symbiotic relationship between practice and theory, the profession and the discipline, that ties together the two halves of my paper and, within the profession, the practicing and academic wings.

Before turning finally to the third primary system, which for convenience I term the realm of acting, let us observe an interface already remarked that represents the link between knowing and acting. This is the decision sub-system; and it encompasses the organization and functioning of a special set of activities that I earlier called pre-action actions to stress their internal nature. To understand this sub-system, planning discipline draws on emerging bodies of theory about decision processes, gaming, consumer behavior, group bargaining, voting behavior, and other aspects of how people organize, delegate, conduct, and modify their decision institutions and behaviors. It might be noted that items arrive on the decision agenda also from changes arising within the realm of feeling itself, as when aspiration levels rise and new goals appear.

Major gaps in the functioning of our decision processes result from manifestations of America's widespread social disorganization. Substantial population groups remain outside either or both of our two primary decision-registering webs—the market and the democratic political processes. Their members are the victims of poverty, illiteracy, ignorance, apathy, or outright denial of political rights. How to render these groups effective in the community decision structure, a desperate societal need nowadays, is a conceptual challenge to the planning discipline.

I wish to make two further observations on the subject of decisions. First, decisions are distributed in hierarchic fashion throughout organizations; hence, there is a certain misleading implication in the fashionable notion of "The Decision-makers," with capital T and D, to which I alluded earlier. Everyone in an organization is a decision-maker. The quality of organizational output is a direct result of quality all along the line. Hence the need for a high quality of planning suffused throughout organizations. Second, however, some people in any hierarchy are 'more equal than others, as George Orwell once put it. Accordingly, we identify certain important classes of decisions, reserving these for elected officials and the judiciary—executives, legislators, and judges. The latter and their various advisors most frequently call upon planners to sort out knowledge needed in decision-making. Indeed, their future decisions largely set the planners present agenda. The planning discipline as a whole, however, ought to have a broader agenda than just the concerns of the governmental bureaucracy, as I intended to suggest earlier in my mention of advocacy in the profession.

The realm of our third primary sub-system, acting, is generally denoted in planners' jargon as implementation or execution. To insist that the action is a concern of the planner is healthy. Indeed, until plans are spelled out and evaluated in terms of the actions they imply and the consequences of those actions, the plans remain lifeless. But what precisely should be the planning discipline's concern with action? I earlier described a pre-action planning function. This was to help prepare the informational conditions for decisions that generate actions or by which actions are constrained. Similarly, there is a post-action planning function: observing the actual performances of activities and evaluating these against the expectations embodied in plans—the post-auditing of predictions, so to speak. Both the actions and their impacts need to be monitored, judged, and reported. Such observations and evaluations, when fed back to the other sub-systems, become evidences of change and in turn produce further changes. And a new round of interactions proceeds on the basis of modified feelings, values, interest groupings, goals, alternative probabilities, option possibilities, decision agendas, etc.

Given the importance of the foregoing realtionships between the realm of acting and the interactions of the model as a whole, the planning discipline obviously has vital involvements in the realm of action. I wish to caution a limit to such involvement, however. Thus I raise a question about where most usefully to place a boundary around the discipline of planning, if indeed such a boundary is needed. A brief excerpt from a recent planners' local newsletter epitomizes the problem I am here raising. In context, the statement is perhaps defensible since it intends elected officials rather than planners to exercise the described functions. Nevertheless, it illustrates the issue. The statement reads in part: "The authority to plan must be broad enough to include power to exercise controls sufficient to implement regional plans and policies, and . . . should include: regional planning, resource allocation, intercounty freeways and bridges." The underlying notion, as this phrase might be interpreted, would appear to incorporate in the authority to plan the whole remainder of the administrative process, including particularly the enforcement of controls over public and private developmental activities and the actual allocation of public resources through budgeting and budgetary controls. Whether or not this was intended in the case cited, the idea appears with some regularity in discussions about how to strengthen planning. For myself, I do wish to include the primary sub-system of acting in the model that illuminates the discipline of planning, while at the same time noting precisely the limited nature of the planner's responsibilities in regard to the action realm. He prepares and he reviews, but he does not manage action except for the activities of his own planning office.

A concluding word—I began this final section by asserting the importance of viewing the foregoing model of the administrative process as a single unified system, even though its description requires its unfolding as though it were a series of separate subsystems. I remind you again that the model is intended here today as a heuristic, that is, as an aid to evaluating the state of the discipline of planning. I have suggested in passing some opinions of where we have arrived in the state of the art. I have done so in terms of our evolving capacity to understand and operate the various subsystems and their interfaces and interactions. In my view, this capability measures our progress in the discipline of planning. Moreover, it concerns that which is essentially planning and cuts across all the special varieties and applications of planning.

My emphasis has been on the presentation of evaluation frameworks, not detailed views as to planning's attainments. Let me observe that our progress seems extremely uneven—we have devoted large resources to grasping the workings of some sub-systems and components, while we have all but neglected others that are equally vital.

PETER A. LEWIS

Assistant Director, Bureau of the Budget. Previously Deputy Assistant Secretary for Metropolitan Development, Department of Housing and Urban Development; financial analyst, International Cooperation Administration in Taiwan, 1956–57; investment banking, 1958–66. B.A. and M.A. from Harvard University; M.B.A. from Harvard School of Business Administration.

The Uncertain Future of the Planning Profession

A COMMENT ON THE FAGIN PAPER

That the concern of planning should be broadened to include all aspects of government presents no problem. Even the Congress had accepted this principle in the 1968 amendments to the legislation providing for federal grants to state, regional, and local planning (Section 701). Further, as Henry Fagin points out, good planners have always taken into account the nonphysical ramifications of physical planning. Yet, merely to say that planning ought to concern itself with all functions of government does not solve any problem. It may increase the problem. For if planning for social concerns is only as effective as planning for physical concerns has been, then the road looks very long and bumpy indeed. In addition, disregarding past effectiveness, as planning's concern broadens it seems to me the planner's role might well be re-examined.

I have a simplified theory of the evolution of the role of the planner which goes something like this: City governments have suffered from lack of professionally-trained people. The planner was probably one of the few people in city government who had any claim to a systematic way of thinking, or had any claim to general experience outside the city in which he worked. Of course, there might be a capable engineer in the city, but this did not help the mayor or city council very much when it came to multifunctional questions or questions relating to a problem that had not previously confronted them. So the planner moved into those areas in which there was an intellectual or professional vacuum. The reason he did not get deeply involved in social matters is that the city did not. The reason the planner is now more deeply involved in social matters is that the city is involved.

What I see on the horizon, however, is that we will get more and more professional help in specific areas of concern. Eventually, we should have reasonably able finance administrators, safety directors, welfare directors, and traffic engineers, etc. One cannnot expect these people, if they are able, to be pure technocrats, nor can we pretend that they have no view as to the interrelationship between their areas of interest and the rest of the city nor that they will have no direct access to other departments. I would assume that if sufficient staff were available, each of these functional areas would have their own planning group, although dominated by their specific areas of interest. What I am pointing out is that the planner should look ahead to the time when public administration in a city is much improved. This will occur at the same time as the planner wants to broaden his concern. Thus, the planner must define his role in light of more effective competition from traditional areas of administration—at a time when the planner wants to concern himself with everything. The inclusiveness of the planners' concern is unmistakable, if we are to accept Fagin's version of it:

> Rather than limit recommendations to measures designed primarily to guide or bring about physical changes in the environment, planners now would give equal status to the design of all sorts of measures to be taken to handle peoples' problems in the whole hierarchy of jurisdictions, whatever realm of human action the measures might entail. We would insist only that the quality of work performed meet a professional standard, systemically focusing what is known about time, space, resources, and human beings on the creation of an endless stream of policy to solve problems of community change.

This is a sweeping mandate. Though I am sympathetic with the aspirations, I find it difficult to understand exactly how such inclusive planning will operate within city administrations. Probably more importantly, I cannot conceive how you train someone for this function. However, the question that troubles me most basically is whether or not, considering the proclaimed scope of the function—almost as broad as the world around us—there is a profession involved. Fagin says little that is explicit on how the planner might fit into the community in his new role, and how one might train him.

Fagin's description of what the planner does, the six essential roles of analyst, synthesizer, collaborator, designer, educator, and mediator, are applicable to almost anyone and certainly to the role of any boss. It does not describe the roles of planning to me in words which can distinguish the profession of planning from the profession of businessman, governmental administrator, or lawyer.

Are we talking about the transportation planner, the recreation planner, the housing planner, or the health planner? Or are we talking only about the elusive comprehensive planner? Fagin does not address himself to how functional planning is to be handled in the future. Assuming that there is something which can be called comprehensive planning, what is it? How do you organize for it? How do you train people for these functions?

However, let me try to develop—hopefully within the framework of Fagin's conceptions—a description of planning which might fit the future.

I would start by elevating functional planning to a greater degree of respectability than it now appears to have and separating it from what I might term comprehensive planning. I would do my best to improve functional planning as part of the traditional government machinery. I would do my best, for example, to see that the recreation department, the welfare department, and the transportation department all had a planning section. I would not be unhappy if each department considered coordination to be a secondary function. I think we spend altogether too much time on coordination. For every example of lack of coordination, we have fifty examples of inertia. I would have the planners at the departmental level be experts first in their functional field and second in planning. I do not know if I would be happy with a planning staff in the welfare department which knew much about planning and little about welfare. I might, in fact, prefer the reverse.

Now what about the comprehensive planner? I believe we all would agree that before important decisions are taken that there be some overview—a *control* point. In my model, the comprehensive planner should act as a policy and strategy advisor to the chief executive. By this I am not asserting that he would be looked upon to set independently the priorities among problems. He should be prepared, however, to enliven the discussions about them. I know this may be anathema to some, but I am not unhappy about relying upon the market place of interest groups. I have heard frequently how nice it would be to compare the benefits of one dollar spent on health with one dollar spent on housing, but the Secretary of Health, Education and Welfare and the Secretary of Housing will make their own and separate cases—and if these gentlemen are any good, their cases will be pretty good.

And how does one measure these cases objectively? By searching for community goals? By laying out seventeen alternatives? Lacking the ability to compare expenditures for health with expenditures for housing, comprehensive planning now turns to both: alternatives chasing goals, goals chasing alternatives.

Thus, comprehensive planning, when it survives, becomes diffused and frequently irrelevant to decision-making.

I would not expect the comprehensive planner to advance solutions for our problems, although I would expect him to impress upon others the necessity to propose solutions. I would not be too concerned if he did not analyze the ramifications of every proposal for twenty-five years in the future. I think we all tend to exaggerate our ability to project consequences very far in the future.

What I would expect this policy advisor to do for the chief executive would be to identify and quantify problems and measure progress. I would expect him to recommend quantitative targets for solving problems. I would expect him to keep the functional agencies intellectually honest. Again, I would not be overly concerned if he did not devote all of his time to analyzing the interrelationships of problems, although he should not be totally unaware of them. If there is to be an educative role, I would have him educate the functional agencies and the chief executive on the importance of quantitative analysis.

Thus, I would pull back comprehensive planning to a simpler state than at present. This might in many cases mean the total withdrawal of what we know as comprehensive planning and a substitution for a much more immediate attack on problems.

Maybe some day in the future, in a far-off age, the state of the art will be sufficiently developed to allow us to compare benefits objectively and to weigh community values. A paper on the state of the art here and now, however, must recognize reality.

It may be useful to speak briefly about one form of governmental planning, using the model of the federal government's Bureau of the Budget: the bureau does not have a grand master plan. It works primarily through the functional agencies, acting as a gadfly, moving in where there is a vacuum, mediating between conflicting points of view and preparing for the President a package of proposals, sometimes, but not frequently, with alternatives. The package is basically a compromise among competing forces. Every once in a while, to everybody's surprise, the bureau devises its own solution to a problem.

The bureau has a total staff of some five hundred people, compared with a bureaucracy of 3 million. This would be the equivalent of a planning staff of five, including clerical, for a city of 1 million.

The bureau's entire responsibility could, of course, be handled in a different manner. It could take the form of a planning agency, with a very detailed, large planning program, such as devising a five-year plan for the entire governmental apparatus, weighing alternatives, measuring needs, devising solutions, and finally directing the agencies on the steps necessary to reach these goals. It could do this in every area of the federal government's activity. It is an article of faith within the bureau that it should not.

My model for planning is not so very different from the present practice within the Bureau of the Budget—corrected and improved to quantify problems and targets. If this does not sound very much like planning as it is taught and practiced today, I should add that I can see the day when the schools of planning as we know them will be replaced by schools of administration, such as the Harvard Business School. They, too, can prepare graduate students to analyze, synthesize, collaborate, educate, mediate, and advocate. The functional planning we know today, largely projection-oriented, would be added to the curriculum of schools of engineering, transportation, social studies, health, economics, etc.

A logical extension of the same planning model would, of course, lead to the planning profession absorbing other professionals or being absorbed itself into something quite unlike what it is today.

THEODORE E. HOLLANDER

Dean for Planning for the City University of New York and Professor of Accountancy at the Bernard M. Baruch College. Served as the Research Director of the Educational Task Force of the Mayor's Temporary Commission on Finances. Coordinated the preparation of the 1968 Master Plan of the City University. Co-author: *Six Big City School Systems—A Study in Institutional Response.*

How Encompassing Can the Profession Be?

A COMMENT ON THE FAGIN PAPER

Henry Fagin has presented a comprehensive, systematic, and perceptive analysis of the state of the art, both of the profession of planning and the discipline of planning. My comments will be limited to three points raised in his paper: the boundaries of the discipline and the profession and how they interrelate; the role of the planner as a decision-maker (because that is what makes it all worthwhile); and the advocacy role of the professional planner.

What planners do must be differentiated from the discipline of planning. The discipline encompasses the common body of knowledge which every planner must assimilate; it is the field of inquiry that is uniquely the province of the planner.

If the discipline of planning is to define its own "turf," if it is to accept the concepts of a "territorial imperative," then I suggest that the boundaries of the discipline circumscribe an area within which it can best advance the frontiers of knowledge.

Fagin points out that the professional planner functions in many roles—as an analyst, synthesizer, educator, mediator, collaborator—and that the professional planner must be sophisticated in using tools drawn from many disciplines. But this does not mean that the *discipline* of planning should be delineated to encompass all the disciplines that the professional planner needs for proficiency. Fagin himself recognizes the importance of defining boundaries. So much more so is this true in a field that has just been redefined to encompass several professions, several of the applied sciences, and almost all of the social sciences.

Defining boundaries is of critical significance if the discipline of planning is to continue to mature as a legitimate field for inquiry and study. It is the need to define boundaries that is suggested after reading Fagin's paper. Though the profession of planning must have an extensive concern with the areas of "feeling" and "acting," I would urge the discipline to leave "feeling" and "acting" as fields for inquiry to other disciplines and confine itself to the area of "knowing."

Despite large gaps, I am nevertheless impressed with the great advances made by experimental, behavioral, and social psychologists in the realm of "feeling."

For example, psychologists have mapped the culture of poverty; the ways in which social class and physical deprivation relate to the incidence of mental illness and the motivation for its cure. They have found ways to identify pre-delinquents and how to treat the pathology. I doubt that planners have the competence, background, or even the inclination to improve upon such accomplishments except in collaborative efforts.

Fagin does recognize the limited nature of the planners' concern with the sub-system of "acting." Planners should be informed about the research of behavioral scientists in this area, but I believe this sub-system also falls outside the purview of the planning discipline.

As an applied discipline, planning is a field of inquiry with its roots in economics, applied mathematics, design, and engineering. It should be concerned with the highly sophisticated art of model building of economic and social systems which encompass within them physical, financial, and social sub-systems.

The discipline of planning should focus on analysis and synthesis. The planners' unique contribution is the development of tools that will carry model building to a highly sophisticated art.

Planners must utilize pertinent knowledge in related disciplines, and, clearly, planning as a field of study must be interdisciplinary. But the discipline of planning itself should be concerned with advancing the frontiers of knowledge in the sub-system of "knowing," where major gaps have yet to be filled.

Fagin points out that the sub-system of "knowing" requires that the planner be able to offer a manageable but thorough range of action options, with their crucial respective consequences spelled out; that the planner be able to appreciate the uncertainties and the indeterminacies in the environment itself; and that the planner be able to utilize and improve predictive mechanisms. These areas for inquiry are common to all planners—environmental, social, political, and financial. The agenda for future development of the discipline of planning must concentrate on improvement in these areas—and especially for their application to ecological and social problems as well as to physical problems.

If there is such a thing as a profession of planning, it exists because there is a body of knowledge common to all planners; the credentials of a planner are identified in terms of the common body of knowledge. I wonder whether the present state of the discipline is sufficiently well developed to support planning as a unique and distinct profession. Even as a layman, I know what a physician knows, I have some idea of a lawyer's frame of reference; the standards of professional competence are well defined for the public accountant. But the planner—how do I identify him? What distinguishes him from the practicing economist, behavioral scientist, statistician, demographer, architect, consultant?—at the moment only his membership in the American Institute of Planners.

What planners should have in common, regardless of origins and special orientations, are the minimum levels of competence in using the planners' tools. The discipline of planning should focus on these tools. I fear that a broader role for the discipline will dissipate efforts to the point that essential gaps in methodology will not be filled.

This is not to suggest that the planner is simply a technician; on the contrary, his perspective must be broad, his talents many, and his education interdisciplinary; but competence in the methodology of his profession is the source of his power and his influence.

Without disagreeing with Fagin, I should like to comment on the role of the planner in the decision-making process. Fagin states that planning informs the decisions that direct the ultimate actions. In identifying the issues to be raised, the questions to be posed, and the interests to be served, the planner does not merely inform the decisions, he influences the decisions. If he goes about his work appropriately, he also directs the ultimate action with an "unseen hand."

In broadening his role from physical planner to planner for the general betterment of the human condition, the professional planner is more likely to advocate the public interest in the broadest social sense. He now—even when engaged in a specific role by a particular client—is likely to raise issues that are tangential to the initial objective of his client but which have long-range impact on the social and political well-being of his client, though I question how well he functions in his advocacy role.

Let me cite as an example my own limited involvement in planning—the development of a Master Plan for the City University of New York. The legal requirement for planning was established at the beginning of a period of massive expansion of public higher education in New York so that physical planning could proceed in relation to over-all enrollment needs. As the planning proceeded, it soon became apparent that physical planning could not proceed until certain basic issues could be re-examined. What were the objectives of the institution? How many and what kinds of students would be served? What was the relationship of graduate to undergraduate education, of academic programs to career training? What was the optimum size of an institution and where should new institutions be located? Few, if any, of these questions had any direct relationship to physical planning, but the physical plan clearly would be influenced by the answers.

The process was traditional. Faculty and student committees developed recommendations while administrative personnel projected enrollments by race, ethnic, and social characteristics, identified job vacancies in the New York City labor market, and examined new professional and occupational opportunities. Without going into details, the result was a major change in institutional objectives, a massive expansion of educational opportunities for the black and Puerto Rican minorities in the city, a change from admission policies that had a one hundred-year-old tradition, a new plan for university financing, a re-examination of the relationship of the institutions to the community, and a re-examination of a clearly obsolete method of program planning and budgeting.

These changes resulted from the fact that both the governing board and the faculties, for the first time, examined the university's objectives from the broader perspectives of urban need, and, for the first time, utilized data about the communities we serve. If planning had proceeded from the perspective of the physical planner alone, many of these questions would never have been raised.

The decisions have been made and the "unseen hand" of the planner is helping in their implementation. Early in the planning process, both faculty and students helped design the plan; they now are committed to its implementation.

Through his involvement in social planning, the planner's influence and power will increase in areas where it really matters—that is, if planners get close to the decision-making process. This responsibility is an awesome one; it suggests further the need for clearly defined professional and ethical standards.

Fagin correctly notes that we do not really know how to arrange effective advocacy for groups that now lack the services of planners.

There clearly are limitations to the individual professional planner who has been professionally engaged by one interest group to advocate the interests of another group which are not compatible with his client's interests. True, the planner can and does educate his client to sacrifice short-run interests for long-term benefits. But we would be deluding ourselves if we really believed that such an approach had much meaning. The statement, "that in the long run we are all dead," is especially pertinent to public officials, especially at the local governmental level.

I know of no professional practitioner, even those with highly developed codes of professional conduct—law, accounting, medicine—where the "credo" of public service takes precedence over a client's interests. I doubt that we can expect a "greater good" from the individual planner. It is the profession which must exercise leadership in this area.

If the planner's role as advocate is to be more than token, the profession must continue to press for expanded arrangements to assure that those presently under-represented have a meaningful voice in the planning process. This can come about only if planners are retained to represent communities now under-represented, and if the communities have resources available to give meaning to plans. Power in the political and economic market place is far more meaningful to those without voice than the pleadings and concerns of a thousand advocates.

I would argue that the most important contribution that the American Institute of Planners can make to planning is to assume responsibility for defining and pressing for national, regional, and local arrangements that will increase the power of the under-represented in the planning process. And this means something more than adopting a "credo."

WILLIAM L. C. WHEATON
AND MARGARET F. WHEATON

William L. C. Wheaton—Dean of the College of Environmental Design, University of California, Berkeley. Former director of the Institute of Urban and Regional Development, University of California. US representative to the U.N. Committee on Housing, Building and Planning. Current chairman of the Intergovernmental Council on Urban Growth for California. B.A., Princeton University; Ph.D., University of Chicago. Consultant to the US State Department, HUD, the agency for International Development and Urban America. Co-editor: *Urban Housing, 1966*.

Margaret Fry Wheaton—Ph.D. candidate, City and Regional Planning, University of California at Berkeley; degrees in architecture from Radcliffe College and Ecole des Beaux Arts; served on staffs of National Capital Planning Commission and Alan M. Voorhees and Associates, Inc.; currently analyzing statistical data and reports systems of California Division of Highways for Legislative Analyst Office.

Identifying the Public Interest: Values and Goals

Planners have always believed that there is some unified public interest or general welfare which was the special responsibility of the planning profession, at least in the field of environment. The American Institute of Planners constitution states that "its particular sphere of concern shall be the planning of the unified development of urban communities and their environs and of states, regions, and the nation." Dunham notes that planners believe they are best qualified to evaluate land-use proposals because they are experts in the interdependencies of land use; they have a general or comprehensive viewpoint; and they can coordinate specialist plans for the benefit of all.[1] Altshuler adds that "their [the comprehensive

---

[1] Dunham, Alison. "A Legal and Economic Basis for City Planning," Columbia Law Review, LVIII, May 1958.

planners'] claims to comprehensiveness, therefore, if they are to be persuasive, must refer primarily to a special knowledge of the public interest."[2]

But Altshuler goes further when he states that public planners must have "some conception of the public interest. Since plans are proposals of concerted action to achieve goals, [the planner] must express his conception [of the public interest] as a goal or a series of goals for his community . . . [and] the goals must win approval from a democratic political process." Altshuler goes on to say that "the comprehensive [public] planner must assume that his community's various collective goals can somehow be measured at least roughly as to importance and welded into a single hierarchy of community objectives." Often the public assumes that the planner does indeed have a special responsibility for the public interest in urban affairs. "Many [people] do believe, however, that professional planners can come closer to achieving [comprehensiveness] on numerous vital issues than other participants in the urban decision process."[3] Where planners are called upon to arbitrate public conflicts, the public defers to the professionals' judgment as if it were authoritative and based upon some final principles. Such convictions are part of the ethical and ideological base of all the professions. Perhaps they are necessary to maintain morale. Certainly they are helpful in maintaining ethical standards because the very pursuit of the public interest is one of the base criteria by which society defines professions.

Altshuler's analysis of the planning process deals with the substantive element of the planner's special skills and responsibility for the public interest, and ratification or legitimation of his judgments by the procedural element of guiding and terminating public discussion. Thus we have the two-headed problem in identifying the public interest: the method by which the public interest is defined, and the content of that public interest.

Recent planning thought tends to recognize that all individuals have competing goals. We all want rest; we all want excitement; we all wish to be rich, and in some degree we all wish to be lazy. Society, being made up of individuals, naturally includes groups who have special interests in one field or another. The conservationists place an unlimited value on every redwood tree, while the industrialist sees no reason why society's needs for lumber cannot be served with profitably exploitable trees. All of us as automobile users want better highways, and on direct and level routes,

[2] Altshuler, Alan. "The Goals of Comprehensive Planning," JAIP, 31:3, August 1965.
[3] Ibid.

while some of us who will be affected by this goal resist relocation, the destruction of the city, the separation of neighborhoods, or the ruination of the natural landscape. In the end, there is bound to be competition between these interests, there is bound to be conflict between ends and means, and there is bound to be bargaining as a means of reconciling competitive or conflicting goals.

Our society has happily relied upon the market as the main means for bargaining and resource allocation. Indeed, some recent actions by local governments suggest the reintroduction of the market as a distribution mechanism for those public goods which satisfy the market criterion of substitutability. For example, refuse collection can be divided into two services: two cans once a week is one good, or one can twice a week is another and competitive good. Price differences in the cost of the service provide a market mechanism whereby consumers can express their utility differences in demand for convenience. It is clear beyond question that the market has proven to be a superior means of adjudication, if only in the sense that it produces a substantially larger pie to be divided. There is some evidence, further, that the "smaller" shares of the larger pie derived from the market system are substantially larger than the proportionally larger shares in smaller pies derived from "more equitable" systems. But these facts, if they are facts, do not relieve us of controversy. Indeed, they exacerbate it, and they certainly do not relieve us of the problem of the allocation of nonmarket goods, a steadily increasing proportion of the total pie in all societies.

The market cannot allocate merit goods: fresh air, safety, education to some level, have no readily ascertainable market price. Some of these goods must be allocated by political means in any society. With growing urbanization and increased interdependency among groups of the population, the proportion of such goods rises steadily.

Planners have shared at secondhand in the philosophical debates about the general welfare. Too often, as we now recognize, planners have merely reflected the narrow class bias and values characteristic of their social origins. They have placed great emphasis on long-range values which they felt to be neglected by others. They have tended to emphasize the preservation of nature over the needs of man. The main body of their work has been concerned with property values rather than human values. Within property values their chief concern has always been with the property of those who were better off in society rather than the property—or, rather, lack of it—of those who were less well-off.

Despite these persistent class biases, every history of the planning movement also stresses the extreme concern of its leaders with problems of greater equity and justice for all; their important role in establishing movements in the fields of housing, health, welfare, recreation, and education, which were concerned with the lot of the underprivileged; and their persistent concern with the development of institutions and professional procedures which would give the needy the support of the profession in public and private decision-making. Indeed, the few systematic histories of the planning movement which we have, including Scott's exhaustive work now about to be published, stress the broader welfare interests of most of the founders and leaders of the movement, and their persistent frustration over the fact that the clients of planning have often been disinterested in the welfare goals of planning and chiefly concerned only with their own goals.

In recent years, we have benefited from an increasing concern with welfare goals within the profession, largely reflecting society's more intense concerns with the problem of equity. In addition, however, the profession has begun to draw more heavily upon the larger body of thought in economics, political science, and sociology which expounds the biases built into our institutions and which explores in theory and in practice the processes of decision-making, the gaps between the rhetoric of the public interest, and the performance of some narrower interest. This literature has contributed considerable depth to our thinking and accelerated the search for better means of defining the public interest in any particular situation. Only in planning reports do we find a continuation of the naive assumption that there is a general public interest and, as we will indicate later, there will be very good reasons why this is so.

Politics as the means for the identification and allocation of the non-measurable, nonmarket goods has always been an acute concern of planners. However, the economists have pursued the method of politically defining the public welfare with considerably greater rigor than the planners. Arrow's analysis of the procedure in a democratic society was a classic statement in the field. His contribution was to outline the conditions for voting in a democracy, and to analyze the results of majority rule for terminating the voting.

His conclusion, the "general impossibility theorem," says that there is a paradox in voting with the majority rule, and thus there was no decision rule which was democratic. The solution to the paradox has been suggested by several authors, and essentially involves relaxing one or more of

Arrow's five conditions for a democratic decision process:[4] a free triple, or at least three alternatives; the positive association of individual and social values, or the transivity of (adding) individual votes to get a social choice; the irrelevance of independent alternatives, or that other alternatives do not influence the preference among those under consideration; nonimposition, or not unanimity; and nondictatorship.

Rothenburg observed that one solution to the impossibility theorem lay in the social decision process of the family.[5] Family choices are group choices, and continued harmony suggests a minimum consensus on operating decisions. Family choices reflect interpersonal comparisons of utility, delegation of decision-making, authority within functional limits to a working stability, and temporal development of a common value system. Rothenburg's "family" analysis actually attacks several of Arrow's conditions, but two are most important. First, interpersonal comparisons of utility imply differences in the intensity of preferences, a murky area that political economists have tried to avoid, and this relaxes the condition of the irrelevance of independent alternatives. Second, a common value system implies an underlying unanimity of values, which violates the condition of nonimposition.

Tullock exorcises the ghost of the Arrow problem by demonstrating its irrelevance in realistic voting procedures, such as Roberts' Rules or its variants.[6] This involves a theoretical analysis of voting strength on different proposals, given some rule by which all the proposals are available for analysis and discussion before the voting begins—that there is some information about each other's position on each alternative and the relative intensities of preference, and that each alternative is taken up in a certain voting order, i.e., pairwise comparisons of alternatives. This very realistic procedural model relaxes Arrow's condition of a free triple and permits bargaining between alternatives rather than a yes-no vote on each. Further, Tullock's model assumes an underlying single-peaked preference curve, or some common value system in which unanimity occurs.

The most interesting solutions to Arrow's voting paradox seem to relax the condition of the irrelevance of independent alternatives. Both Rothenburg and Tullock use it, in combination with others, to provide their solu-

---

[4] Arrow, Kenneth J. *Social Choice and Individual Values,* New York: Wiley, 1951.
[5] Rothenberg, Jerome. *The Measurement of Social Welfare,* Englewood Cliffs, New Jersey: Prentice-Hall, 1961.
[6] Tullock, Gordon. "The General Irrelevance of the General Impossibility Theorem," Quart. Jour. Econ., 81:2, May 1967.

tions; Rothenburg in the interpersonal comparisons of utility, and Tullock in relative intensities of preference. The irrelevance of independent alternatives assumes an equal intensity of each vote, and the independence of the preference between the available alternatives and some other alternatives. However, other alternatives do influence voting on the available choices, as is seen in Tullock's model where all the choices are proposed before the voting begins. The fact that other alternatives, than the two under consideration at the immediate moment, affect one's voting behavior on these alternatives, implies differences in the intensities of preferences for the different alternatives. This has led Coleman to construct a very interesting vote exchange model, where low-valued votes are traded for high-valued ones.[7] Though Meuller correctly analyzes the logical imperfections of Coleman's model in the abstract, such as the influence of dissembling and Indian-giving in the vote trading, still Coleman's model more closely approximates the real world political process than Mueller's highly idealized vote market model.[8]

The general conclusion from these models is the importance of bargaining in the political process. Different people and groups which have different concepts of the public interest must somehow find a common ground by bargaining. The ends of some groups require the adoptions of means which conflict with the ends of other groups. Only in the haggling of the market, the adjudication by the courts, the enactments of legislative bodies, and the administrative acts of legitimate authority, can we discover what that balance between conflicting ends and the means to achieve those ends may be.

In the past, the standard procedure for defining the goals of a plan involved only staff responsibility. While we can find efforts to involve wider groups in goal formulation in the "Action for Cities" plans of the 1930's, in the use of simple polling techniques in the 1940's and 1950's, these efforts have not altered basic reliance upon professional judgment. Poverty programs, "maximum participation" theories, and the critics of past procedures have changed all of that. Today the profession is groping, somewhat ineptly, for new methods.

Three recent efforts at identifying the public interest are interesting because of their very different approaches to public involvement in the goal definition process. The City of Chicago 1964 report, "Basic Policies for the

[7] Coleman, James S. "The Possibility of a Social Welfare Function," Amer. Econ. Rev., 56:5, December 1966.
[8] Meuller, Dennis C. "The Possibility of a Social Welfare Function: Comment," Amer. Econ. Rev., 57:5, December 1967.

Comprehensive Plan of Chicago," takes one approach.[9] A "series of regional meetings was held" to explain the policy proposals. Oral and written comments and criticisms were received, and subsequently modifications were made in the basic policies. Unfortunately this summary treatment of the process by which the basic policies were made does not provide much illumination into the very intricate decision-making processes which are the meat of the theoretical models. There is no indication of how widely copies of the proposals were circulated, or whether they aroused any general public interest. There is no way of knowing the extent to which comments and criticisms were incorporated in the final report. There is no indication whether the modified policies were accepted by vote or by some less defined form of consensus. Thus only an elementary level of community participation can be presumed. At least the informed and concerned citizens of the city had some opportunity to be "involved" in establishing these goals. The planners or politicians were not alone in this endeavor.

In 1966 and 1967, the city of Los Angeles sought citizen participation in the definition of its planning goals.[10] It convened a number of meetings of representatives from professional societies whose professional responsibilities were concerned with the "environment." Less than twenty such societies are listed, including architecture, landscape architecture, city and regional planning, transportation, interior design, and environment (the local AIP chapter was among them). There is nowhere in the report a tabulation of the number of people involved in this effort. We infer from the report that, in discussing parts of the total goals group, the sub-groups involved reached decisions by some mild form of consensus without voting. An occasional unanimous conclusion is noted. Further, the group of representatives describes itself as an advocacy body rather than a representative one, with an interesting definition of advocacy: that of advocating their goals to the general public in order to gain wider approval. Yet there is a disclaimer that the statement "in no way implies that it represents the official position of any or all of the various professional organizations."

At a later stage in this procedure, the original group of professional societies was expanded to include representatives of art, political and social sciences, public administration, economics, law, geography, real estate, systems technology, management consultancy, and social welfare. This is

[9] Department of Development and Planning, City of Chicago. *The Comprehensive Plan of Chicago*. Chicago: City of Chicago, December 1966.

[10] Environmental Goals Committee, Los Angeles Region Goals Project. *Environmental Goals for the Los Angeles Region*. Los Angeles: City of Los Angeles, Spring 1967.

still a professionally oriented group, not a politically oriented one, therefore the group as a whole is presumed to have some special knowledge of the public interest in order to be qualified for participation.

In 1966 and 1967, the city of Dallas promoted an effort to define goals for Dallas, actually sponsored by two apparently nongovernmental agencies, the American Assembly and the Southwest Center for Advanced Studies.[11] This interesting effort combined several different techniques for evoking expressions of preference. First, thirteen writers drafted essays on problems facing Dallas. Second, a Dallas assembly, consisting of eighty-seven residents of Dallas and near-by areas, "chosen to represent a diversity of citizens—in backgrounds, creeds, races, viewpoints, interest, occupations, and geographical residences"—met to discuss and formulate goals in a first conference. The recommended goals of this meeting were printed, going through two editions and a total of 17,000 copies, and distributed to citizens and local groups. Then neighborhood meetings were held, thirty-three in all, to discuss the twelve sets of goals, and at which "*votes* were taken and recorded on changes or additions recommended." These were in turn returned to the Dallas assembly for a second conference, at which the *Goals for Dallas* were given their final formulation. It is noteworthy that such a diversity of techniques for soliciting public opinions were used. This is a most ambitious effort to elicit wider public participation in formulating social choice, yet it still stops short. There is no indication that these goals have been officially presented to or adopted by the elected politicians for the city; thus, final accountability is absent.

All three attempts at goal formulation by widely separated governmental entities included some measure of citizen participation, which means that other than the planners were involved. Further, the recognition that some kind of "public discussion" was necessary was a basic part of the efforts, whether this meant discussion by citizens or nongovernmental professionals with some responsibility for the citizen interests. Lastly, though the final decision mechanism is unclear, the effort to reach a social consensus is clearly a part of each of the procedures. This is some advance over past goal formulation efforts.

The substance of the public interest may vitiate even the most apparently democratic of processes. What is actually said and done may fall considerably short of our professional pretensions. In these cases both internal and external evidence suggests that the selection of people to be

[11] Goals for Dallas. Southwest Center for Advanced Studies, Dallas, Texas, May 1967.

involved, the selection of subject matter to which their attention was directed, and the methods for achieving consensus, all contributed to final goal statements which are fairly abstract, synthetic, or restricted as compared with known priorities of at least some sections of the population.

For comparative purposes, the actual content of goals on two subjects—housing and employment—still the most critical in most modern cities, will be examined in each of the cities. In Chicago, the Comprehensive Plan seems to have a most ambitious and enlightened set of housing goals. The report states that it is the objective of the city of Chicago "to improve . . . the housing quality of all existing residential areas . . . [and] to meet the needs of moderate- and low-income families. . . ." The report does not say that the city *will help* to achieve this end, it says that the city *will act* to achieve it. Yet when the policies for achieving these basic objectives are examined, they are less than bold. The policies are "to undertake programs of code enforcement, spot clearance, . . . to encourage the maintenance of these areas . . . to strengthen or accelerate programs . . . building on projects *already under way or completed.*" There is certainly little new here.

To meet the needs of moderate- and low-income families, the city proposes "to encourage banks and savings and loan associations to make mortgage loans more readily available in older communities . . . [and] to expand [public housing] through purchase and rehabilitation of existing structures, leasing units in private buildings, and construction on scattered sites." But when the actual improvement plan is analyzed, the city plans to expand the public housing units from an existing supply of 35,000 to a possible upper estimate of 70,000 in a fifteen-year effort. This would fall woefully short of the actual needs, which by the report's estimate is "250,000 households with annual incomes under the 'poverty line' of $3,000 in 1959." Furthermore, there is not even any estimate made of the need for expanding the housing units needed by moderate-income families, i.e., those "who are above the limits for [public housing] units yet find the housing supply within their means limited."

The report commits the city firmly to equality of housing opportunity. The city encourages this "fair housing" objective for the whole metropolitan area, yet stops short of positive action recommendations. In another arena, region-wide opportunities for recreation, the city actively proposes that the state of Illinois take the initiative in purchasing open space for metropolitan recreation opportunities for all to use. There is no comparable recommendation that the state purchase land, even "vacant land," for metropolitan public or open housing opportunities. We may be permitted to wonder about a concept of the public interest which implies that it is more important for the state to support equality in exercise than in housing.

In Los Angeles, the actual programs to achieve the goals and objectives are not available to test their real meaning. However, as in Chicago, there is an objective to achieve " 'open housing' . . . throughout all portions of the metropolitan region" though there is no way to check on the way in which this is to be achieved. In contrast to Chicago, the Los Angeles goals do not even mention any intention of providing public housing for those who need it, however need might be determined.

Dallas expresses even less concern for housing its people properly. Its general goal is to assure "its indigent and needy at least minimum requirements for . . . housing—with reasonable access thereto—" and its specific goal is "to strengthen the Community Council of Greater Dallas . . . to assure provision of needed services . . . ." Dallas neither clearly backs "fair housing" nor expresses any real public intent to provide housing for "its indigent." Indeed, following immediately on even this equivocal goal, there is the statement: "Recipients of these services should be required to pay for them in whole or in part as financial circumstances permit." Evidently if you are poor you are not going to get much out of Dallas, and, if you do, you had better be able to pay for it.

In employment, the outlook is even bleaker. In Chicago, the only goal related to employment mentions the necessity of job training and "merit employment." Job training includes "vocational training and adult education courses in public schools, as well as in service training by industries," but merit employment is not elucidated further.

In Los Angeles, one bold goal statement proposes "maximum employment opportunities and choices" and goes on to specify this by an objective to "utilize in full our productive potentials by restoring full employment in a decade . . . [and to] synchronize effective training programs with job creation."

In Dallas, the employment goal says that "human energies and skills . . ." should be intelligently, imaginatively, and boldly employed, an undoubtable consensual statement. Its more specific objective includes "educational and special training programs" to develop human resources, not for the purpose of individual support and dignity, but to assure "adequate manpower." Furthermore, the following objective is "to *change* the under-educated and undermotivated into contributors to the total economic well-being," (our italics) as if the full cause of unemployment lay in the inherent nature of those unemployed!

We might try to rank these efforts at goal definition on these scales: credibility as goals of the population of the city, explicitness of statement of goal, explicitness of means for achieving the goals, and degree of effort to involve the population in goal definition. On the first three scales we would roughly rank the Chicago report first, the Los Angeles report second, and the Dallas report third. That is, the Chicago report's goals are more credible as expressing the desires of its people, more explicit as goal statements, and contain numerous (though wholly inadequate) statements of means for their accomplishment. The Los Angeles report is clearly second on these over-all measures, though it would score better on some details. The Dallas report would be clearly third.

On the other hand, procedurally the Dallas effort appears to score highest; Los Angeles again is in the middle, and Chicago lowest. While this demonstrates nothing, it at least forces us to ask whether a more "democratic" procedure may not often produce a narrower, more restrictive set of goals, or even one which deliberately ignores the most urgent desires of some fraction of the population.

We can go further and assert that some other recent planning documents which did not lay so much stress on consultative procedure appear to have done a more satisfactory job of trying to reflect the diverse aspirations of our people. Both the Philadelphia Plan and the New York City Community Renewal Program Report, for instance, make very explicit statements regarding quantitative needs for housing, by price class, tenure, and location. These plans provide the public with some explicit statements of what must be done to achieve a certain goal, and at what rate. Further, they implicitly weigh the disparate need of some for housing and jobs, against the less intensive desires of a larger number of others for better transportation, more parks, and better schools. But even here, in the very best of our reports, it is impossible for even the best-informed citizen to weigh the choices and register his preferences, as he can in the market place, or as political leadership must do in the haggling over public policy decisions.

Planning faces a dual problem. The first is to devise measures which can make choices relevant and meaningful. The second is to devise procedures for consultation which are meaningful. As Friedman has noted, the present state of a city or region is measured by a set of social accounts, and these are so poorly developed that it is often difficult to ascertain where we are going, much less how rapidly we are getting there.[12] We face formidable professional tasks in developing these measures, in establishing them as normal parts of the process of planning and administration, in devising measures of the effects of different policies on different sub-sets of the population, or upon different preferences. The present state of the practice is very poor. It is very indifferent in the best cases.

We face similar, and perhaps worse obstacles in developing procedures for consultation. As Altshuler has observed, though the theoretical problem is the legitimation of goals by public discussion, the practical problem is finding the discussants.[13] Too often, too few have either the interest or the knowledge required for effective participation. Advocacy planning may be helpful in politicizing those who are not concerned and raising their voices to the level of audibility.[14] But when universal voices are heard, the higher level of cacophony is unlikely to make the task of political leadership much easier, or political office more attractive to the wise. We must go back to the social sciences and develop far more systematic procedures for sampling the desires of the population; not with simple questions, "Do you want more parks?" but with forced choices: "How many parks would you trade for how many jobs?" We must elaborate the popular use of gaming techniques, of scaling techniques such as those devised by Lamanna,[15] and of other measures of the intensity of preference, suggested by Tullock and Coleman, so that political leadership can better balance the claims of different sections of the population, different areas of the city, and the different preferences of us all.

But there is a further problem. At present it appears clear that much of the time, political leadership does not want an explicit statement of issues, or measures of progress, or wider public involvement. When power and resources to affect improvements are pitiably weak, this reluctance to face issues is understandable, and the propensity to paper them over with motherhood statements and the appearance of consensus is strong. In the long run we must strengthen the ability of political leadership to respond, before we will have warm support for effective efforts to measure preferences or poll people. In the meantime, we must fortify those planning

[12] Friedman, John. "A Response to Altshuler: Comprehensive Planning as a Process," JAIP, 31:3, August 1965.

[13] Altshuler, Alan. *The City Planning Process.* Ithaca, N.Y.: Cornell University Press, 1965.

[14] Davidoff, Paul. "Advocacy and Pluralism in Planning," JAIP, 31:4, November 1965.

[15] Lamanna, Richard A. "Value Consensus among Urban Residents," JAIP, 30:4, November 1964.

officials who try, by making such procedures a mandatory part of professional standards, and by public criticism of those who fail to adhere to them.

Planners can no longer rely upon either simple goal statements or simple consultation procedures. As a profession, we must devise new ways of measuring choice alternatives and new means for reaching the people.

C. DAVID LOEKS

President, Mid-Hudson Patterns for Progress, Inc. Former director, Twin-Cities Metropolitan Planning Commission. Formerly lecturer, consultant, and professor of regional planning, University of Minnesota; Special Advisor to Secretary of the Department of Housing and Urban Development on Demonstration Cities and Metropolitan Development. Member, Urban Goals Committee of the Committee on Economic Development.

The Individual's Identification of Self-Interest

A COMMENT ON THE WHEATONS' PAPER

The Wheatons' paper presents us with three things: a premise-forming analysis of the state of the art as it pertains to the identification of the public interest in the context of values and goals; a basic conclusion concerning the nature of the problem; and some prescriptions as to what should be done in response.

The basic premise, as I understand it, is that there is, in fact, no "general public interest" that exists in more or less continuing state, about which consensual goals can be articulated in a meaningful way. Rather, the public interest is to be regarded as a highly dynamic equilibrium of various interests resulting from their bargaining about specific issues in either the market place or the political arena. Consensual goals addressed to the achievement of an impossible-to-define "general public interest" are meaningless as instruments of policy decision-making, because they fail to make explicit the choices that are inherent in their pursuit.

The central conclusion: In the real world, "Policy is not planned, it accumulates." Planners miss the opportunity to influence the manner in which it accumulates, because we have been distracted by the pursuit of consensual goals that would maximize the illusive general public interest. As a result, goals defined by this process are so broad that they are of almost no use in making day-to-day decisions about development.

165

The prescriptions:

1. Make explicit the choices implicit in our consensual goals, particularly how they affect groups within society;

2. Make the relationship between ends and means explicit. This would not, to use a phrase of the authors, "relieve us of controversy." Indeed, it might require an independent nongovernmental agency for its discharge;

3. Rather than search for consensual goals, analyze the goals of the constituent groups within society, clarifying the consequences of the ends-imposed burdens on one group on the satisfaction of the ends of another group, thus facilitating the debate and bargaining process.

Assuming, for the purposes of this discussion, that this is an acceptable summary of the authors' views, I offer the following general comments.

In my view, the Wheatons have made a significant contribution to the way we think about this subject. I am referring specifically to the stress which they place on the basic importance of focusing on the identification of the interests of the component groups within a society. I would note, however, that this approach raises further questions which in turn lead to additional conclusions and prescriptions. For example, for this approach to work, one must make the assumption that the representatives of the interest groups involved in the bargaining have the talent and the knowledge to accurately identify and reflect this interest. One must deal with the likelihood that in many situations, the interest being articulated may not, in fact, be optimal from the standpoint of the group it relates to. Given the imperfect knowledge and imperfect process within which the groups define their interest, we must confront the fact that *individuals* within a group often have a dimly perceived or erroneous notion of where their interests lie. Given more adequate information, there is a real likelihood that this interest would be defined and represented in significantly different ways.

This contingency is, of course, one of the problems to which the Wheaton prescriptions are addressed. However, the above suggests that if we really mean business in our quest for the definition of public interest, we should properly begin with the question of values and goals—not at the level of society, or at the level of the groups within society, but rather at the level of the individual. The plot thickens when one considers the fact that most of us as individuals labor with hidden fallacies which becloud our personal value and goal preferences. Individual nonrationalities are reinforced and amplified by the group. Small wonder, then, that the "public interest," when thought of as the accommodation reached by inter-group bargaining, is so resistant of definition.

I would suggest that the hidden fallacies which plague the identification of individual and group interest can be minimized in two ways: better information; and better ways of thinking about this information. The Wheatons make a plea for both, but further probing is needed about the second. Some preliminary work done on this in the joint program for Land Use and Transportation Planning in Minneapolis/St. Paul yielded the beginning of a framework within which an individual could think about his underlying value system as it affects his choices and trade-offs in making decisions about the environment. Although these results are highly tentative, they indicate an avenue of inquiry which could yield further results that would advance this long neglected aspect of the "state of the art."

The analytical approach used was built on a defined relationship among values, goals, policies, and programs.

For the purposes of this discussion, a "value" is a characteristic which individuals or society consider worth acquiring, protecting, or conserving. A "goal" may be defined as an object or end that one strives to attain. A "policy" is a settled course of action toward a stated objective; and a "program" is defined as an allocation of resource in time and space by agent for the consummation of specified results.

In a sense, a value—which is simply something somebody thinks is worth acquiring, protecting, or conserving—is transformed into a goal when the individual makes an actual commitment to do just that. The idea of policy, a settled course of action, suggests the notion of alternative courses of action, and the relationship between ends and means is generally defined. The idea of program, which specifies exactly what is to be done, is the point at which the relationship of ends and means can be made very explicit. In real life, of course, it does not work out as a neat hierarchy of progression, beginning with values and ending with programs. It plays back and forth, and often can be just as usefully worked in reverse. For example, one can infer policy by examination of programs, and goals can be made explicit by looking at the objectives that policies are directed toward. I submit that this analytical framework has general utility in defining the public interest.

From this it can be seen that the "motherhood" criticism of consensual goals simply does not take us very far. There is, of course, validity to the criticism that consensual goals which have been generalized to avoid controversy, are meaningless as an instrument for political decision-making. However, goals are by definition of no direct use in making day-to-day decisions, nor should they be required to be. Their principal use is to illuminate and constrain the examination of the policy and programs. These, not goals, are the things on which day-to-day decisions are actually made. The assertion that in significant cases goals have not in fact been used for that purpose may be more of a commentary on the state of the art than proof of intrinsic nonutility. I submit that they can be made—indeed, are being made—to serve to illuminate and constrain the examination of policy and program. Not with the *élan* and precision and relevance which most professionals would aspire to, perhaps. But that is why we are considering the state of the art and examining ways to advance it.

Getting back to values, the analytical framework suggested is based on the notion that values exist in couplets; that for every value there is a reciprocal and competing value; that one pursued to the maximum would operate to the exclusion of the other. For example, everyone values security; we also value freedom. We know that maximum freedom would produce minimum security; and that maximum security exists in prison, which is, of course, a complete negation of freedom. In real life situations, we consciously or unconsciously make value judgments somewhere along a spectrum between the poles defined by value couplets which exist in tension with one another.

To illustrate the application of this idea to an urban development situation involving alternatives, let's take the question of goals and policies for the size and distribution of commercial centers. Here we see the value couplet of convenience and choice operating to constrain the selection of alternative policies. If one were to place great value on maximum convenience of access, he would have commercial centers within walking distance of residences. But the small tributary market resulting would produce relatively small establishments with a narrow range of consumer choice of commodity, supply, quality, and price. On the other hand, if one valued maximum consumer choice, a large, diversified regional shopping center would be just the ticket. Because of tributary market area considerations, these must, of course, be widely separated in space, with a consequent diminution of convenience of access.

People vary greatly in their personal value systems as to where they would choose to compromise these two values-in-tension. Moreover, their choice will vary over time. The point is, that when a person is unaware of the implications of the partial trade-offs in values that underlie the definition of his personal interest and the selection of alternatives, he may develop considerably different conclusions concerning where his interests lie than he would if he were aware of these considerations.

Thus we can visualize the spectacle of a downtown merchant working by day to promote a high concentration of activity in center city, a pattern which can be best served by mass transit. In the evening, after returning to his home in the suburbs, he serves on his local planning board, which is zealously striving to perpetuate the kind of low-density rationalized sprawl that requires the use of a car, and cannot effectively be serviced by transit. This is the way metropolitan America is being built. It is the job of the planner to diagnose this kind of schizophrenia and assist in its treatment. An honest examination of the value system affecting alternative environmental choices would be a place to begin the search for the accommodation of these kind of competing, sometimes reciprocally negating goals.

The fact is that this kind of colloquy between the planner and the community is beginning to take place in some areas. Consistently and thoroughly pursued, it could have three results of profound significance to the success with which the public interest is identified and pursued.

It would significantly improve the validity of the reasoning process whereby the individual defines his personal interest. This, in turn, would in many cases significantly alter the view of competing groups within society concerning where their interests lie. The kind of meaningful debate and bargaining among competing interest groups which the Wheatons' advocate could then ensue. It is quite likely that such debate would destroy any superficially perceived consensus that might exist in a given situation. However, it can be anticipated that in due course this kind of "well-informed public haggling" would produce a third result; namely, a much deeper awareness of the very real interdependencies of competing interest groups within society. It would help clarify the fact that groups within society exist in such a delicate and complex equilibrium that relatively small minorities can unilaterally pre-empt the interests of the rest of society.

Thus, by this process of social facilitation, individuals are constrained in their own self-interest—if not by the ethics of the situation—to begin to pay some attention to the interests of the other fellow. Groups comprising society will rediscover that they really do need each other's cooperation, and a more relevant definition of the public interest based on a renewed sense of community, will emerge. When this happens, we will then be able to talk sensibly about consensual goals for the community at large, a concept which, I submit, should not be abandoned. It will prove to be of fundamental importance if the retreat from social progress, resulting from confrontation and conflict among competing interest groups, is to be avoided.

Thus we see the values-and-goals game in the identification of the public interest as looming large on the agenda of things to do in improving the state of the art of planning. The success with which we pursue the basic prescription advocated in the Wheaton paper ("We must devise new ways of measuring choice alternatives and new ways for reaching the people.") may very well determine the outcome of the larger question of whether American society can resuscitate and extend its belief in a changeable future.

CHARLES R. ROSS

Attorney; entered private law practice in Vermont in 1954. Served as Commissioner, Federal Power Commission, Washington, D.C. 1961–68. President, New England Conference of Public Utility Commissioners in 1960. A.B., M.B.A., and LL.B., University of Michigan.

Public Participation and Decision-Making

A COMMENT ON THE WHEATONS' PAPER

The Wheatons' paper reminds me of the dilemma facing the economics profession in its search for an equitable method for quantifying benefits and costs for the decision-maker in the case of public expenditure, involving social goods. The Wheatons recognize that the planning profession cannot rely upon the market place as the sole means of allocating natural resources when nonmarket factors are present. However, I would have been much happier had the Wheatons spent more time on guidelines to aid all of us, planners in particular, as to the necessary and proper weight and recognition to be given to social goods which are becoming a more important part of the average citizen's concept of the public interest.

The Wheatons acknowledge that the planning profession has advanced from a stage reflecting "the narrow class bias and values characteristic of their social origins." It is a relief to this nonplanner that the typical planner no longer considers himself "God." However, I am at loss to understand the Wheatons' solution. They apparently believe that better sampling and polling are the principal means of defining what the general public desires. This would be satisfactory, in their opinion, if the profession could "devise measures which can make choices relevant and meaningful."

Yet, in the various examples cited, it is apparent that there is more to it than that.

Though in fact Dallas has a very representative procedure, it is criticized as being the worst of a bad lot. The Wheatons really are criticizing the goals adopted by Dallas because they do not reflect their own. I happen to disagree with Dallas as to its goals for housing and employment, and its methods for achieving them. However, it is not the first time that I have disagreed with the residents of the state of Texas. The point is that the planners got a representative view, distasteful as it was. Though it does not agree with mine as a decision-maker, it is invaluable information. Any final decision will be that much better.

If we are going to seek a realistic expression by the general public of their concept of the public interest, let us understand our reasons for so doing. We are not always doing it for the purpose of being able to tell the politician that this is the answer. We are doing it, rather, so that when the politician makes his decision, he will have as much data before him as possible, including the results of informed public discussion. Remember, it is up to the decision-maker, the politician, and not the planner, to make the value judgment as to the objectives.

As one who has served for ten years as a regulator, mostly at the Federal Power Commission, I do subscribe to the concept that greater participation by the average citizen should be sought in government. Procedure sounds like dull stuff, but it is what can make the difference between a good and a bad government. To determine what the general public considers important, we must translate the technological language of today into the language of the common man if we are to expect an informed discussion. In this consultative process, the planner must not allow himself to become an advocate for his usual clients, big government and big business, so that he seeks to advance their interests. He has a higher professional duty to the helpless, frustrated, and alienated common citizen whose well-being depends on his plans. The planner must be increasingly concerned with pre-crises problems, not post-crises ones. One of the great values to the consultative procedure is that it may surface, under expert questioning, some of the basic problems bothering the people. This, in turn, usually makes a suggested solution easier to sell.

A more understanding consultative process between the planning profession and the black community, as a matter of hindsight, might have avoided some of the conflicts arising from programs established for ghetto areas. We all had a tendency to project plans which we thought best, and failed to give due consideration to the black community's concept of what it considered to be the public interest.

Thus, I feel that the planning profession must continue to be on guard that its ultimate plan does not necessarily represent its own biases, as the Wheatons have so correctly pointed out. This does not mean that the profession no longer has a responsibility to define our goals for a good and full life, one that seeks to maintain the quality of life which we all dream of for ourselves and our children. The planner must dream. He must be the bridge between the scientist and the humanist. He must emphasize the importance of the intangible and should recognize that the market process cannot give proper weight to such intangibles, though dollars must pay for them. Such goals and plans for implementing them must then be translated into understandable language so that the average man can understand the issues involved. Too much stress on consultative procedures is hard to imagine. I recognize, though, that if carried to an extreme, it could mean nothing gets done. We must localize it as much as possible. Let us not editorialize the answers.

Finally, the planner has to be extremely responsive to criticism, whether initially it seems legitimate or not. That is why flexibility must be built into a plan; changes can always be made in case a better way is found to achieve the desired result. Above all, the planner must refrain from decision-making that can, or should, be arrived at politically.

The Wheatons testify to the progress the planning profession has made. Their emphasis on the need to find new ways to measure choice alternatives is valid. But we should avoid relying upon a too-mechanical method of determing the public interest. In view of the complexity of value judgments in such choices, and the techniques available for their evaluation, it will not be possible to arrive at unambiguous answers.

HENRY COHEN

Director of the Center for New York City Affairs, and Professor of Urban Affairs at the New School for Social Research. Former First Deputy Administrator of the Human Resources Administration of New York City Department of Planning. Lecturer at Columbia University, and Visiting Professor in the College of Architecture and the Graduate School of Business and Public Administration at Cornell. B.S.S., City College of New York; M.C.P., M.I.T.

The Changing Role of the Planner in the Decision-Making Process

Let me begin with a broad assertion. The placement of the planning function in the decision-making system is determined largely by forces outside of the planning field.

The character of professional planning activity may influence the placement decisions in small ways. The development of new skills and new applications of planning may set the stage for increased utilization of the planning activity. Planners may define some of the details of placement and the resulting relationship. More rarely, individual planners may, by sheer brilliance, strength of character, charismatic quality, or through some special set of circumstances in a particular community at a given time, have an extraordinary influence in the decision-making system. Other than in such exceptional cases, the profession itself has only a marginal impact on its place in the scheme of things.

Far more controlling are the social, economic, and political forces which shape the structure and role of government; which define the system of checks and balances; which momentarily resolve the balance of powers among the several levels of government, among the regions of the country, and of competing interest groups. Far more important is the impact of emerging ideas, conflicting aspirations, and the perception or the lack thereof with respect to city development, current needs, and future prospects. The weight given different ideas, values, and aspirations is more likely to determine at any given time how strongly the planner fits into the decision-making system. Figuratively, the planner is like the girl with a big bust when Twiggy is in style. She has a lot to offer, and can even be well used; but she's not favored with Saturday night dates, and she goes to the movies with her girl friends.

A scanning of John Reps' excellent volume on *The Making of Urban America* gives some insights into the place of planning in the United States. Much of the early town and community design was performed by surveyors and geographers, and was based largely on the concepts prevailing in their countries of origin. Occasionally, a key explorer or political leader had technical design skills; in these instances, planning was centrally involved in the decision-making process. Champlain, explorer and planner of Quebec, was a skilled geographer. George Washington was the assistant surveyor in the laying-out of Alexandria, Virginia, though there is little indication that he distinguished himself in this occupation. William Penn, the founder of Philadelphia, was a developer.

The planning of Washington, D.C. is the most exceptional case in early American planning. The circumstances were right: a new nation; a new capital; a President who had been a surveyor; and Thomas Jefferson, a rare combination of visionary and pragmatist.

But let's bring it closer to home. The evolution of the planning commission offers a useful illustration of my general thesis about the relatively low level of influence of planners in shaping their placement and role. Beginning in the latter half of the nineteenth century, the good government movement was born in response to the emergence of the big city political machines, the spoils system, and extensive graft and corruption. A stream of muckraking literature publicized this venality. The reformers promoted the merit system, contract bidding systems, the auditing and budgeting functions, the machine ballot, and many other changes.

Most relevant for our purposes was the notion that became extant in the land that political officials were venal and corrupt and could not be trusted with the public business. Among the reforms made in one city after another was the creation of boards and commissions to supervise different sectors of public activity and to provide these activities with some insulation or protection from public officials. Cities created, for example, recreation commissions, health boards, transportation boards, and child welfare boards. (The public authority is a second-generation product of the reform movement, though many reformers now oppose authorities. The authorities were frequently set up to escape the impediments to management and the raising and use of public funds that the reformers had built into the basic system of municipal government.)

Given the reform mentality and mood, it could only follow that the function of planning would also be insulated from the greasy palms of elected officials. Political leaders who could not be trusted with the present could hardly be trusted with the future.

My point, however, is not to argue whether they could or could not be trusted. Rather, it is to indicate that planners did not create the national mood about political leadership; planners did not create the mood which led to the insulation of public functions from politically elected officials. If they did not create this mood, neither did they move against this current of thought. They followed the mood; they helped spell out the detailed application of this conventional wisdom in their specific area of concern. Few planners had any awareness of the implications of denuding municipal government and elected officials of their responsibility for vital local functions. It would take a considerable research effort to arrive at a full, fair, and definitive assessment of the contribution of the planning commission form to the cities of America. My quick, superficial judgment is that we bought a stalemate. Elected officials, since they were not charged with responsibility for planning physical development, could not be held accountable. Planning commissions, without being accountable to the voting public, were not under electoral pressure, and therefore did not produce "doable" plans. They enjoyed the luxury of being righteous, if not relevant.

Beginning in the Thirties, a major shift in national direction with regard to the role of the political executive was beginning. The election of Franklin Roosevelt ignited a new appreciation of the vital energy that a strong political executive could bring to managing complex affairs in a period of deep national crisis. Under his stimulus and that of a group of public administration experts he brought together, national thinking turned to means of strengthening the executive. These movements and shifts are rarely clear, direct, or obvious; nor is their application to all situations immediately apparent. So perhaps it is not surprising that, at the local level, municipal reformers and planners were still creating new planning commissions, oblivious to the new currents. The zenith of this dying movement occurred in New York City in 1938 when, following La Guardia's second victory over Tammany, a City Planning Commission was created. Its powers were greater than had been endowed or were to be endowed on any other American planning commission. And for some twenty years, the planning function as professionally defined languished in New York City.

Finally, the new notions about the political executive began to seep down to the cities and to the professional groups working at the municipal level. The manifestations took different forms. In Newark and several other places, the planning officer was made a staff officer to the mayor; in New York, the Commission chairman, heretofore serving a fixed term of eight years, now serves at the pleasure of the mayor. Can city planning catch up? Can it begin to anticipate the emerging national tendencies which will delineate the parameters within which it functions?

I should like now to turn to two current thrusts which will affect the placement of planning, and attempt to review their relation to and significance for developments in the field of planning as it relates to decision-making. The first cluster of issues relates to the competitive systems of planning, particularly program budgeting and functional planning. The second cluster of issues relates to the tendencies toward the localization of planning at the neighborhood level and the infusion of the participatory democracy issue.

Probably no staff agency has served the political executive as loyally as the budget or finance officer. I remember a budget officer, in stressing that relationship to the executive, once telling me that if the mayor asked him to run the subways vertically, he would run them vertically.

Municipal budget staffs are frequently troublesome for planners. Their training is not as broad, and their outlook is more parochial, rooted in the present and short-run. Their practical concerns with nuts and bolts create problems for broad-brush temperaments, who frequently fail to cross t's and to dot i's. They are less concerned with the needs side of the equation, and more concerned with the difficulties in raising taxes. They are more concerned with artifact than with art; less concerned with secondary and tertiary effects than with what they can directly hear, see, smell, feel. While not often inventive about programs, virtually all programs go through their sieve. Above all, however, serving the executive is a quality deeply rooted in their bones and in their profession. There are no advocacy planners among budget officers. To summarize in somewhat oversimplified fashion, municipal budget officers have narrower perspectives than planners, are closer to most emerging program developments, and are embedded close to the heart of the decision-making process. Planning officers tend to have greater breadth of vision, are much less involved in most emerging program developments, and suffer or enjoy (depending on your view) a degree of insulation from the decision-making process.

The emergence of Program Planning Budgeting Systems (PPBS) provides an historic opportunity to develop a general policy planning or program development, and review function in city government to overcome some of the existing deficiencies of budget offices by infusing new types of personnel, and by giving budget offices an opportunity to provide leadership to departments in strengthening functional planning. While debate goes on among planners about the scope of planning, the PPBS development, if it persists, will begin to make municipal budget offices the mayor's general planning instrument. The real power with regard to capital budgeting and programming will shift to the budget office, even if the activity remains administratively with the planning agency.

Spatial and physical resources, requirements, and relationships remain a vital organizing focus, and will, I believe, continue as a separate activity, but more closely tied in with the executive and the budget office (which will become a program and budget planning office). The commission as a body of lay citizens will disappear or decline in importance. The commission form, as we have known it, limits the planning function in two ways. It serves as a partial barrier to the development of the confidential relationships needed between the mayor and the chief planning officer. Secondly, the commission membership has traditionally been drawn in part from architects, engineers, and men in the real estate and construction fields. This bias in selection serves as a limit to the broadening of the planning function. Even if the selection bias could be overcome, the commission as a barrier to the development of a close working relationship between mayor and staff planner would remain. If the commission becomes innocuous, then it no longer serves as a barrier. The legislative body with its provision for public hearings is a sufficient substitute for the commission with regard to the quasi-legislative planning activities such as zoning.

Current interest in the localization of planning and service activities with the involvement of affected citizens is not entirely new, but it has some new features. The exhortations to involve people in the affairs that affect their lives are more intense than ever, and less yielding. Action along some of the lines proposed would certainly change the character of the decision-making process (quite another issue from the quality of the decisions), and the role of the planner in relation to the process. In order to understand what is being sought, let us first examine what we have.

The basic model of public macro-decision-making flows from the country's early notions of representative democracy:

1. Elected officials;
2. Functional agencies headed by appointed officials reporting to elected officials;
3. Systems of formal consent, advice, and consultation:
   a. Elections
   b. Public hearings
   c. Commissions and boards
   d. P-TA's (semi-formal);
4. Systems of informal consultation and advice:
   a. Private meetings with civic organizations
   b. Contributions, endorsements, other support in election campaigns
   c. Complaints and requests through the local clubhouse
   d. Newspaper, radio, and TV coverage, exposure, and editorials
   e. Letters to city hall or agencies
   f. Letters to the editor.

Big city government in the United States has provided services through units of centrally run agencies. We have not chosen to break out these activities and delegate their operation to independent political powers at the neighborhood level. The historical trend has actually been toward centralization. Consolidation and annexation have wiped out many local government units in order to achieve the benefits of economies of scale, high quality management, and improved planning and coordination. Suburbia alone has retained the small government unit by resisting efforts to metropolitanize certain public activities, and also by resisting efforts to consolidate power and responsibility at the county level.

At the big city level, even though a multitude of decisions are made by staff working in the field, basic allocation decisions are settled centrally. In addition, since many service activities are relatively standardized, the opportunities for local administrative discretion are small. Therefore, local community efforts to modify the priorities or the service arrangements frequently must go to central offices. With the exception of opposition to physical improvements, most local efforts are directed at receiving additional, not fewer, resources. Rarely does the local community offer a trade-off. Instruments for weighing alternatives and trade-offs will be as essential in the future as in the past, even if we delegate certain responsibilities to independent neighborhood groups.

What is now proposed are different schemes for decentralization of planning and service operations. The Model Cities program would decentralize planning. Proposals to decentralize school operations under community control would decentralize planning and operations in that sector of activity. The student movement within the university structure also wishes to enlarge the student role in planning and decision-making.

Underlying these proposals is a significant change in perception. The client, the student, the receiver of services is saying that until now his relations to the service system have been defined by the system. He feels that the relationship has been paternalistic, with him as a supplicant seeking something from a sometimes benevolent and sometimes not so benevolent establishment. Now wishing to be accepted with full citizenship, he says that what he receives is not charity, but a right, and he demands a key role in defining what those rights are and how he will exercise them.

With regard to public sector programs, the decentralization proposals would have community representatives selected by some agreed-on process; would determine priorities for the use of certain funds; and would be empowered to retain staff to develop and carry out programs. It is not clear under many of these proposals what would remain of the powers, rights, and responsibilities of central political, planning, or administrative bodies.

As always when dealing with problems where justice and equity have been long deferred, the arguments for equal rights and dignity on the part of the injured party are very appealing and even compelling. But no rights are absolute; no individual or groups can act without some constraints in a free society.

Let us review some of the considerations that prevent the large community from fully yielding to the decentralization proposals:

1. There are general laws, rights, and practices which we apply to all, hopefully, without prejudice. Even where the application is prejudiced, we regard that as an aberration in the working of the general system. To accept the uneven application of rules as normal would upset the system as a whole. For to overlook the even application of the rules in one instance threatens their application in other instances. If the Ocean Hill-Brownsville Community School Board in Brooklyn asserts that the local schools belong to the people of the community, that and no one outside can tell them how to run them, regardless of applicable laws and rules; and if that is not contested, then in principle it undermines the enforcement of Supreme Court decisions, say in Little Rock.

2. One of the major functions of government is income distribution through tax policy and budget allocation decisions. Therefore, there can be

no divorcement of the person taxed from programs which are supported by public funds. Each public dollar has a string, and the political process balances the equities between the person taxed and the person benefitting from public expenditures. The interest of the taxpayer is reflected in rules and conditions which the beneficiary cannot entirely avoid. Typically, communities and the nation at large go through cycles, as the pendulum swings from coalitions in which the taxpayer interest is a dominant element, to coalitions in which people interested in the enrichment of programs and services are the dominant element. Out of the sets of pressures involving taxes and budget allocation decisions, arises the necessity to define the relations between group and group, between local and higher jurisdictions, between the three major levels of government, and between local government and any local entities it delegates authority to.

3. The affairs of one area may seriously impinge on the affairs of other areas. Therefore, absolute authority within one's own area is limited. We have developed and are continually evolving systems of redressing grievances and minimizing injury to one party by another. An imperfect system, yes, but we cannot abandon the responsibility of central agencies to mediate conflicting interests.

4. The development of broad solutions to large problems may affect many localities. While the interests of localities have to be considered, local community groups cannot be given an absolute veto power over programs, services, or projects they object to.

If I have mixed feelings about the issues involved here, it is because, like all complex questions in human affairs, there are equities on each side. Let us support efforts at securing greater community involvement and participation. Let us delegate some planning and operational decisions to duly constituted local bodies. However, let us do this only within a framework of carefully defined powers, rights, and responsibilities, and with systems of consultation, review, and appeal.

Within a framework that permits enlargement of local involvement and responsibility, central planning agencies are and remain part of the mayor's decision-making and mediation nexus. They continue to have central planning responsibilities; they continue to have the right, yes, the responsibility, for planning and development initiatives on a large scale; they have a right and responsibility to set standards, review plans and proposals, and to evaluate the performance of the neighborhood agencies. The advocacy planner may not have the taste for the type of balancing and weighing that is a function of central staff agencies. Let him not disparage the function, however. Let him instead go out and work with the local groups. Increasingly, funds are being made available to enable local groups to retain professional support. The advocacy planner role is essential. But so is that of the central staff planner.

The planning function is moving closer to the center of macro-decision-making in municipal government. But this has not happened fast enough because of the ambivalence which exists among planners about relating to the political executive. The budget offices, with new tools developing out of PPBS and systems analysis, are likely to emerge as the central planning agency. Since they have none of the ambivalence about relating to the political executive, mayors are more likely to look to budget offices for general planning and programming assistance. The physical planning focus remains a vital organizing focus, but will have to be related to general planning through budget offices. Undoubtedly in some areas where budget offices are very limited, where planning agencies can grab the initiative with respect to PPBS, and where the planning leadership is not ambivalent about relating to the executive, the planning agency may emerge as a general planning instrument. It will be useful to encourage such variations, to be better able to evaluate different conditions and relationships.

In order for planning to relate more effectively to the political executive, the commission as a distinctive structure will have to be abolished, or made innocuous.

The growth of local neighborhood bodies for neighborhood planning will not eliminate the need for central planning. It may make it more difficult, but it will also make it more essential.

ALAN ALTSHULER

Associate Professor of Political Science, M.I.T. Former visiting professor, Makerere College, Kampala, Uganda; and Assistant Professor, Cornell University. B.A., Cornell University; M.A. and Ph.D., University of Chicago. Author: *The City Planning Process: A Political Analysis,* and other publications on the political, social, and public policy aspects of planning goals; the politics of urban mass transportation; and policies and programs for the human environment.

Decision-Making and the Trend Toward Pluralistic Planning

A C O M M E N T O N T H E C O H E N P A P E R

Henry Cohen has written an extremely perceptive paper, with which I find myself in virtually full agreement. Let us explore a few of its implications.

Cohen's theme is that the place of planning in the governmental structure, and the organization of the planning function itself, are determined mainly by forces external to the planning profession. I would state the thesis a bit more comprehensively, and in three parts: (1) planners have negligible influence on the universe in which they operate; (2) this universe tends to determine their substantive preoccupations at any time in addition to their administrative roles; and (3) if the universe is conceived as a spectrum of respectable political ideas, planners have a strong tendency to cluster at any time near its left (humanitarian, reform-oriented) edge.

With respect to administrative ideas, the case is fairly clear. As Cohen notes, the planning commission is a product of the Progressive era. The idea of abolishing the commission, and making the planning agency a staff arm of the chief executive, is a product of the New Deal. Robert Walker, who carried this proposal to the planning profession, freely acknowledged his debt to the President's Committee on Administrative Management (which had reported in 1937) as he did so.[1]

---

[1] Walker's book, *The Planning Function in Urban Government* (University of Chicago Press) was first published in 1941. On page 168 he cited the following words of

A similar point can be made with respect to the planning profession's view of its clients and how they should be served. True to their Progressive origins, planners till recently have assumed that their client was the total public, and that its interests could best be discovered by analysis of the hard facts (geographic, demographic, economic). Explicit recognition of group conflict within the "public," and consultation with special interest spokesmen, had no place in this schema. As poverty and race have become central issues of American domestic politics, however, and as the idea that administration can be value-neutral has lost credence among thoughtful men; planners—particularly the young ones—have suddenly discovered the concepts of advocacy, pluralism, and responsiveness. Today the whole profession is in headlong shift from an emphasis on planning *for* the people to planning *with* them. It is also in movement from a preoccupation with the need for larger scale in governmental institutions (metropolitan, federal) to a tempering of this concern with a companion stress on the need for decentralization, community control (in neighborhood-sized units), and participatory democracy. These shifts owe far more to the civil rights revolution and the New Left than to any developments within the planning profession itself.

Likewise with respect to the profession's guiding conception of the role of government in American society. The Progressive emphasis was on economy, efficiency, the regulation of obvious and extreme nuisances, and (during periods of prosperity, as an investment in amenity that was probably also good for business) a modicum of civic symbolism. This emphasis, it bears repeating, was national, not just local. To consider the regulatory function alone: planners tend to associate this era with the rise of zoning, but on the national scene the Progressive era witnessed major innovations in railroad, pure food and drug, antitrust, and credit regulation. From the Thirties through the Fifties, emphasis shifted to the role of government as master regulator (of the nation's economic life, of each urban area's development pattern), stimulator of innovation, and builder. All of these themes survive, but in the Sixties we have experienced a revival of interest in the classic functions of politics: declaring principles of justice and maintaining social peace. Again, and to their credit, with alacrity, planners have followed suit.

---

the President's Committee: "The President must be given direct control over and be charged with immediate responsibility for the great managerial functions of the Government which affect all of the administrative departments . . . These functions are personnel management, fiscal and organizational management, and planning management."

It would be excessive to suggest that in any of the above instances planners led the way. But then, as a profession composed mainly of civil servants, how could they have? The serious question is not whether planners should be further out front. It is how, within the confines of the roles society is prepared to let them play, planners can maximize their relevance to (and consequently, their impact upon) the changing scene. Some of the answers that thoughtful planners have come up with in recent years are the following:

Do not fall prey to the beguiling idea that everything can be planned, or that anyone can achieve a comprehensive perspective. Recognize that decision-making in American government is essentially a process of what Charles Lindblom has labelled "disjointed incrementalism," and that the most that "comprehensive" planners can do is tinker with the framework of pluralism. This, at least, is the most their recommendations can do at the "comprehensive" level. But it is far from clear that planners have their greatest impact when working at this level. The case for "comprehensive" plans tends to be so problematic that, even when they are implemented, their consequences are bound to be quite different from those anticipated by the planners.

Do not seek salvation in what Philip Selznick has called "the retreat to technology." Planners can indeed find a place for themselves as specialists in economic and aesthetic issues of physical development. But they can hardly maximize their relevance, in this era of growing preoccupation with social and political issues, by so confining their roles.

Participate in the tremendous vitality of American pluralism (rather than simply endeavoring to regulate it). Find other employers in addition to local governments, and other roles in addition to central staff. In view of the notable movement in these directions in the past two or three years, one should add today: go beyond the simple dichotomy of central staff vs. advocate planning roles. There is no reason why planners should not be found working for all the major groups and institutions of American society. Ultimately, it might become necessary to classify planners according to such variables as the following:

1. Whom they work for: central staff agencies in government, functional agencies in government, universities, business firms, associations of low income people, etc.

2. What kind of planning they do: physical, social, economic, organizational (i.e., of political and administrative structures).

3. In what kinds of intellectual and administrative activity they typically engage: systems analysis, invention, resource allocation, coordination.

4. What the time horizons are that characteristically guide their work: 0–2 years, 2–5 years, 5–10 years, 10–20 years, longer than 20 years.

Quite obviously, these key questions and sub-categories are merely illustrative of those that may come to seem most relevant as experience with pluralistic planning accumulates. The important point is that we are moving into an age in which planning perspectives and skills will be in demand throughout the urban social system. To play with an historic analogy: we have just come through a half century in which the need for law, courts, and judges has won acceptance; we are emerging into a period in which every actor on the public stage will recognize that he needs a lawyer.

This movement toward pluralistic planning has already had a profound impact on the planning profession's view of the world and itself; and we are still in its early stages. We may expect planners to become less and less devoted to the idea of centralizing power. We may expect an accentuation of the drift in planning education toward focusing on modes of analysis rather than a specific subject matter competence. We may also expect an intensification of interest in mid-career planning education, the purpose of which will be to provide men who have emerged as potentially important decision-makers with some broad planning perspectives and a capacity for systematic analysis of policy options.

Planners will continue to be in short supply, of course; and thus they will have to decide in each time period which of their many potential employers are likely to prove most rewarding to work for. But here again—to close the circle of this comment—their range and direction of choice will primarily be determined by forces external to the planning profession. By and large, planners will want to work in those issue areas that have come generally to be recognized as the most vital of the era, and for those employers who are widely considered innovative—whether because of their advanced methods, their original ideas, or their reform objectives. Today, moreover, those planners who wish to associate with "underdog" groups will find themselves constrained by the paucity of resources to pay their fees for such work, and by their own natural desire to earn upper middle-class incomes. Here is as good a place as any to conclude: suggesting that planning in the age of pluralism will probably still remain an instrument of the affluent and powerful, implicitly throwing out a challenge to the profession to prove the forecast wrong.

ROBERT C. EINSWEILER

Director of Planning, Metropolitan Council, St. Paul, Minnesota. Chairman of the Coordinating Committee of the Joint Program. Previously Director of Planning, Chief Metropolitan Studies Division and head of the Transportation Studies Section for the Twin-Cities Metropolitan Planning Commission. Lecturer in Urban Planning and Consultant on Planning Curricula, University of Minnesota. Visiting lecturer at University of Illinois, Brooklyn Polytechnic Institute, University of California. B.S. in Architectural Engineering, M.S. in City Planning, University of Illinois.

How Planners Shape the Role They Play

A COMMENT ON THE COHEN PAPER

More responsible roles for planners in the decision-making process will have little meaning if they are just carrying out the wishes of the elected officials. Errand boys do the same. The planner must bring solid information and advice as a basis for decisions to those who must make those decisions.

The planner's role is changing in two complementary ways. It is becoming more specialized and more comprehensive at the same time. These changes, in contrast to Henry Cohen's view, are as much at the instigation and direction of the planner as of general social, economic, and political forces.

Alan Altschuler emphasizes the increasing specialization of planners' roles and lists functional categories—transportation, health, open space; and geographic ones—state, region, municipality, neighborhood. This trend is to be expected, since specialization is needed in order to deal adequately with the complex problems before us. "Renaissance men" would be useful, if possible, but there is now too much knowledge for any one individual to absorb and retain. Specialization should be looked upon as an opportunity, not a problem, for the planning profession.

187

The significance of specialization is that it should cause us to speak of the changing *roles*—plural not singular—of the planner.

The map-oriented plans of the civic design stage of the profession showed what the city should look like twenty or more years in the future. The plans were static and frequently bore little relation to what was possible or desirable. However, these plans did provide a goal. The map-type plan was given stronger underpinnings by use of the techniques of the social scientists, through mathematical models and other means, and related the proposals to how people behave. The next step was the policy plan, a set of guidelines for making decisions. This reflects a growing management approach to urban problems. As with all swinging pendulums, the maps were all too frequently abolished from the policy plan. The better ones, however, appear as natural and reasonable evolutions of their forebears—plans which enable planner and elected official to play more responsible roles in urban development decisions.

The decision-making orientation has likewise unfolded in several different directions. There is a heightened interest in the plan-making process, the steps to constructing a plan, including who should participate, when, and how. AIP's Committee on Restatement of Institute Purposes, headed by Louis Wetmore, recommended competence in the three phases of the planning process as prerequisites to Institute membership: research and analysis, policy and plan formulation, implementation and administration. Finally, there is a growing concern with decision-making in the development process, how changes are brought about.

The development process is not strictly physical even though some of its products—buildings, roads, parks—are. People are involved; those who produce, and those who consume.

Planners, in concentrating on the development process, do not draw plans and capital budgets that will achieve the maximum desired development. Rather our plans often price land out of the market or allow too little return on investment for any knowledgeable entrepreneur to implement the plan.

We are not alone in ignoring process, however. Some years ago I taught a course in construction drawings to architectural students. Having been reared in building construction, having worked at several trades and also supervised construction, the process of constructing a building was very real to me. The students did not see construction details this way. They saw them only in their finished state as art—the three-dimensional appearance of the detail; or engineering—the structural integrity of the design. They did not realize that a given detail would cause a steel worker to do five minutes work every four hours and be idle in between.

The result of this approach, all too common in architectural schools, has been a credibility gap between the architect and builder. The planners have an equally severe credibility gap with developers and elected officials. This gap must be closed by greater understanding of the total development process.

The budget director, too, often has no firm basis for his recommendations. We know all too little about the incremental benefit of investing dollars in different ways. Until the planner has better knowledge of the development process, however, he will be ill-equipped to challenge any budget. With a greater knowledge of how development does occur, the planner can prepare long-range plans which can be translated into mid-range programs that in turn can be the framework for short-term budgets. The planner and budget officer can then mesh their work.

If the planners continue to focus on end-state physical plans, they will end up with the very narrow field Cohen has allotted to them—"spatial and physical resources, requirements, and relationships."

Cohen has shown quite clearly how the limits of planning were set by society. The planner participated little in this process because his training and personal outlook did not allow him to see the need.

What is advocacy planning but the advocacy of someone else's needs? Lawyers do this all the time. Planners, accustomed to pressing their own value system, find advocacy planning very uncomfortable. Until the planner can learn to climb out of himself and his own values, he will not be able to perceive the needs of others, whether the poor, elected officials, or society at large. Until he perceives the needs of others, he will not be able to provide the service that will result in a more responsible role in decision-making.

In metropolitan areas all across the country, it is quite common practice for planners to quote the statistics on the number of local units of government—municipalities, special districts, and others. The next step is to advocate structural change to centralize decision-making in order to implement centrally derived development schemes. On occasion, the planner looks at those statistics on local government and finds in them a better understanding of the metropolitan community. In the Twin Cities area, for example, the percentage of local governments that are municipalities is twice the national average, while the percentage of special districts is one-fourth the national average. While taxes and other items have an effect, the desire for local government decision-making carried over from the Populist movement is a prime factor. Since most special district boards are appointed, responsibility to the electorate is indirect. This is unacceptable to Twin Citians.

The last and most important factor affecting the future role of the planner is the planner himself.

Eldredge reminded us in the opening paper that as a people, one-half of us are below average. This ratio applies to planners as well. My concern is that too many of the approaches and techniques were designed by and for that upper one-half or even upper one-fourth. How are the rest of the planners to ply their trade and improve the lot of man?

The Wetmore Committee debated the degree of comprehensiveness which could be practiced with competence. Was the planner to be tested for competence in physical development, social development, economic development, or the sum of the tree? Each planner's competence has its own set of limitations. This limit to individual intellectual capacity and the differences among individuals must be borne in mind when defining a more responsible role in decision-making. Some people are constituted to play very active roles in decision-making while others are most comfortable with passive roles. Some can be advocate planners, some cannot. Some will be able to relate well to decision-makers, some will not.

The role of the planning school at this point is not clear. Planning specialization—functional or geographical—is recognized and taught. The tailoring of programs to an individual's personality is more difficult. Training all planners to be directors seems to have its faults, too.

In defining a more responsible role in decision-making for professional planners, we should remember that they will have to be carried out by those planners on hand today. For the future, however, better selection of students could occur if we can decide what traits are needed or desired for various roles. Not all chemists end up in research. Some are in engineering and others in sales. The personality of a salesman is usually quite different from that of a basic research person.

What role the planner ultimately plays will depend to a large degree on personal philosophy about the relationship of man to society and how that view "squares" with the community for which he works.

Those who hold to the end of the spectrum calling for individual initiative and freedom to solve urban problems are likely to be frustrated in working for a client committed to a policy of collectivist solutions and vice versa. This factor should not affect the role of the profession in the future unless there are too many mismatches between people and jobs. Each professional must continually ask himself: What are my personal values? What is the client's attitude? Are we properly matched?

We must define roles which are more responsive to both the needs of society at large and its various sub-groups as they see current problems. This must be done without abandoning the value of long-range planning. The new roles, however defined, must be capable of being carried out in the near term by the mortals who have signed up to do the job today.

BRITTON HARRIS

Professor, Institute for Environmental Studies and Department of City and Regional Planning, University of Pennsylvania, and member of the staff of the Institute for Environmental Studies. Formerly planning consultant to the Economic Development Administration of the Government of Puerto Rico; the Ford Foundation Team for the Metropolitan Plan for Delhi, India; the Philadelphia City Planning Commission; the Pittsburgh, New York, and San Francisco CRP Studies; the California State Office of Planning; the United Nations planning program of the Government of Singapore; and many others. B.A. (mathematics), Wesleyan University; M.A. (planning), University of Chicago.

New Tools for Research and Analysis in Urban Planning

It frequently occurs in the development of disciplines and professions that the impetus for development arises not only out of the challenges of the social environment which we are considering, but also out of the competitive success and analogous ideas which arise in other fields parallel or related to the one in question. Techniques, ideas, and tools which may arise under these circumstances and which can be to a greater or less extent immediately assimilated by a given profession, such as planning, might be called "found tools." No special effort or exertion is necessary to create them or even, in some cases, to adopt them for use. Planning, although it is falling behind the rate of advancement of many other professions, has at least the potential advantage of access to many tools from other fields.

The outstanding new tool of modern civilization is the computer. Considering that commercial computers are only twenty years old, and to a certain extent extrapolating present trends, it is patently obvious that their influence on all phases of human activity, including planning, will be enormous. Not only will the development of computers proceed quite independently of the attitude of planners, but it is predictable that the *use* of computers in planning will also proceed independently of these attitudes.

Planners who oppose the use of computers will be pushed to one side and ultimately replaced. This raises many serious moral, professional, and operational problems, since the use of the computer is not always well conceived. It is, however, quite clear that a planning influence on the development of the uses of this tool must proceed from within, rather than from without, and that planners who are themselves unable (directly or indirectly) to use computers wisely and inventively will be unable strongly to influence the directions of its development in this field.

There are many sources of tools in the intellectual rather than the technological sphere, and these are, of course, of intrinsically more interest than the computer itself. From the point of view of intellectual content, the computer at first glance appears unimportant. Its principal role is that of an amplifier of power, of ideas, and of ideologists. I might suggest that there are some aspects of processing by computer which are of interest in their own right insofar as they parallel processes of thought or processes of development, but this idea is tangential.

Planning deals with the world to a very considerable extent through the use of found tools, which are intellectual borrowings. This fact arises to a considerable extent, in a very natural and unobjectionable way, out of the synthetic nature of planning and out of the analytic nature of the academic disciplines in which the found theoretical tools of planning must frequently originate.

It is interesting to note, as we survey methods and theories used in planning, that economics, sociology, demography, biology, hydrology, and a whole spectrum of disciplines, severally contribute in ways both extensive and profound to our understanding of cities, of people's use of cities, and of the interaction of cities with the natural ecosystem. Yet none of these disciplines deals holistically with people, with metropolitan systems, and with the total environment. One of the great problems facing the planning profession is to make adequate use of these individual and specialized tools in the context of such understanding as exists of these total systems and their needs.

In the general area of academic disciplines and found theoretical tools, mathematics and logic play a special role. These disciplines are not only, and not even primarily, a source of manipulative techniques relating data to theories, and both to the computer. They are much more significantly a field in which forms of relationships are systematically developed and their implications explored. Planners and urbanists are strongly interested in forms and in relationships, and it is interesting to note that they are given to borrowing ideas about these from other fields. This is done by reasoning by analogy. Thus the morphological discoveries of other disciplines become found tools for planning. With the increasing mathematization not only of the physical sciences, but of the biological and social sciences as well, these analogies increasingly are to be found in the mathematical rather than in literary, descriptive, or visual forms. A trained capability for making use of these found tools implies at the same time a capability for rejecting them when their use is improper or inadequate. Such a capability in the field of mathematics requires more training and insight than many practicing planners possess; and to this extent, mathematical tools may be a source of confusion rather than of insight.

A judicious combination of the theoretical insights of various disciplines, of the formalisms and manipulative techniques of mathematics, and of a holistic view of people, cities, and environment can, in principle, lead to functional methods for drawing conclusions about the state of the world and the effect of proposed new policies. This possibility in principle cannot be realized in practice without adequate information or without adequate operating methods, including the use of the computer. In both of these fields, some found tools are beginning to become available to the urban planner.

With respect to data, we have a possible paradox. At the moment, it appears to me that urban planners are generally in profound ignorance about the state of their cities. They do not have any adequate information as to the location of employment; the location, size, and condition of structures and dwelling units; or the location, needs, and dynamic qualities of the resident population. Momentarily, however, the spread of computer-based administrative systems will lead to the availability for planning purposes of immense quantities of administrative data in machine-processable form. At this point, planners will have more accessible knowledge than they are prepared to use, and severe problems of reducing the extent of these data may arise. Despite the multifarious difficulties, the spread of modern administrative methods in municipal matters will provide planners with a found tool in the form of data.

The development of manipulative methods, which made possible predictions about the consequences of changes of policies, has not proceeded very rapidly in the urban field, so that in this important area, the availability of found tools is severely limited. Quite clearly, as planners are widely aware, the greatest contribution in this area comes from transportation engineering, which has contributed a whole kit of found tools to the planning profession. The virtue of transportation planning methods—by contrast with, for example, econometric models, demographic models, and other products of specific disciplines—is that these methods deal in some sense holistically with the city. This has proved to be possible only on the basis of widespread data collection, computer technology, and a vigorous interchange of knowledge and methods within the transportation engineering profession. When planners quite justifiably find fault with the limitations of the transportation engineering approach, they are sometimes inclined to throw the baby out with the bath water. A resolute rejection of all the works of transportation planning implies an unnecessary rejection of the useful aspects of transportation engineering methods. What is perhaps even more important is that it also implies a rejection of the most useful and productive aspects of the over-all approach, on which the invention of these useful methods was based. The appropriate environment for this inventive activity is the subject of the next section of this discussion.

Let us recall for the moment that the new tools which we are talking about are primarily to be used for research and analysis. Insofar as analysis refers to the analysis of plans or to the analysis of planning needs, then quite obviously analysis includes some sort of predictions or projections. At the same time, however, it is also plain that research and analysis does not include the preparation of plans. This, insofar as I can justifiably discuss it, is a question which will arise in the last section of this paper. At this point, let me simply note, however, that only in very highly constrained situations can research or analysis actually *find* a solution to problems; and even in such situations, the solution may indeed remain hidden. I am not, therefore, a devotee of the view that research and analysis will themselves substitute for planning and problem-solving, and I hold that the invention of new tools is not the same as the invention of new plans.

In discussing the invention of new tools, it would not be amiss to draw our typology from the preceding list of found tools which I have just discussed. Quite apparently, there may be many additional types of tools which could be invented for planning research and analysis, but I cannot predict what they are, since in the main their invention lies in the future. I think that an adequate agenda can be based on what is already known. However, a more vigorous pursuit of the targets on that agenda will probably result in a more rapid extension of the agenda itself as new ideas and new directions will be uncovered by actual work.

It is quite plain that the planning profession, in inventing new tools, will probably not invent and design new computers. A more experienced and computer-oriented profession, however, might very well be able to contribute directly and indirectly to computer design. Parallel processing computers are now being designed and developed in prototypical form. They can, in a sense, reproduce areal arrangements by the internal computer configuration, and reproduce interactions across areas such as might be anticipated in meterology or hydrology. The needs of these disciplines and others dealing with spatial arrangements could easily exert a direct influence on future computer development. This influence, however, can only be exerted through an intimate acquaintance with both the problems and the potentials in both fields.

Similar brief remarks might be made with respect to inventions in the field of data. It is not immediately apparent that good data can indeed be invented. The planner probably has a substantial contribution to make not only to the specification of need, but also to suggestions as to methods of data collection and methods of measurement of collected variables which he is likely to consider very important in the planning process. Once again, tedious though the whole process of data collection and data management may be, the intimate involvement of the planner in this process is certainly a requisite for progress.

It seems unlikely that planners will make very much direct contribution to the invention either of new theories in the substantive academic disciplines or of new forms and formalisms (in mathematics and logic. Nevertheless, they can provide a great stimulus to inventors in these fields in at least two different directions. First, they can suggest to any discipline or engineering profession, as may be necessary, the profound importance of spatial relations—proximity, separation, and interaction—in urban research and analysis. This consideration is almost ingrained in the planning profession and in many branches of engineering, and it is sadly lacking in many other places. Second, the planning profession can remind each academic field and each discipline concerned with sub-system planning and problem solving of the connections which the particular discipline or sub-system has with the totality. For purposes of research and analysis, this second emphasis on the holistic approach to new methods cannot be discussed in a vacuum. It is not sufficient to engage in exhortations as to the interactions between parts of the system and aspects of behavior. The intelligent, perceptive, and operationally-minded planning researcher will attempt to specify the ways in which these interactions work in the real world, their relative strengths, and the means by which they may be represented and put to work in the process of research and analysis. In following the somewhat arduous paths suggested by this requirement, the planning analyst will find himself engaged in a whole related set of activities which in many ways will precisely parallel the developmental experience of transportation systems planning. Because, however, the deficiencies of that development are well recognized, and because the land planner and the social planner both aspire to deal with larger and more complicated systems, the inventive task which I have outlined is, in fact, more difficult than that which was faced by the early transportation systems planners in the middle 1950's. The developing planning analyst in this field will have to have a similar but wider command over data sources, social theory, system interactions, computer methods for simulation, and the like.

When we examine the actual content of what will be done in the way of invention by the planning analyst and research workers, we see in fact that he will be primarily engaged in inventing models of various parts of the processes of urban functioning, urban development, and urban decision-making. The reason for this is quite simple. A model is a synopsis of the analyst's view of the world, which can also be explained to others and systematically manipulated to explore its consequences. Increasingly, the planning profession, in order to meet its democratic responsibilities, will have to share its methodology with other disciplines, other professions, and the public. Fortunately, the invention of methods to make this possible coincides in general direction with many other needs of modern research.

To a considerable extent, I have assumed up to this point that the activity of analysis and research in planning was, if not self-justifying, at least to some extent justified by the assignment of this topic for detailed discussion. Perhaps, however, it might pay to take a somewhat deeper view of this justification, especially in order to see how analysis and research are appropriately used in the planning process.

Planning is essentially anticipatory decision-making. Men and governments engage in planning because they want to change the future. Disagreements, uncertainties, and conflicts may arise in the course of planning, out of a number of sources. Groups may disagree as to the desired future toward which society should bend its efforts. They may disagree as to the resources which must be allocated, the sacrifices which should be made, or the constraints on individual behavior which should be borne. Finally, they may disagree as to the predicted effects of public measures, including failure to act. The disagreements of the first two types, which have to do with desirable futures and the resources needed to achieve them, fall into the realm of value judgments. They can only be resolved through various aspects of the political process, but this is not to say that better planning and better understanding cannot facilitate this resolution. On the other hand, disagreements as to what will happen, what will be affected, and what measures are needed to accomplish agreed-upon objectives can, to a considerable extent, be scientifically tested and weighed. The extent to which this is possible depends on the degree of our understanding of natural processes, social processes, and economic processes. The resolution of disagreement in this field rests upon the extent to which this understanding is widely shared and generally understood to be scientifically correct.

Up to the present, individual planners have been the repository of much of this knowledge and understanding. Their use of it has been confounded with the value judgments which they have personally and professionally made with regard to the first two areas of dispute. To the extent that this situation persists, the process of planning and of choosing between plans is more a private than a public process, and depends more upon the charisma and the leadership role of individual planners than upon any wide public understanding.

The first and most important way in which we can therefore use some of the new tools which I have discussed is through a two-pronged extension of our understanding of the urban system. In the first instance, this extension of our understanding must broaden the extent to which that understanding is widely shared in the population as a whole. In the second place, it must deepen our understanding in many ways by refining our knowledge in detail, by revealing the wellsprings of behavior, by lengthening our view into the future, and even in some cases by correcting or contradicting mistakes and misconceptions in the minds of people, politicians, or planners.

There is, however, another and much richer way in which the tools of planning research and analysis can be fruitfully used. I have implied strongly that planning is directed for action, and I should like to reiterate my belief that the correct course of action is rarely discovered through purely analytic and research methods. On the contrary, as I have repeatedly suggested elsewhere, the design professions, including planning, have an essential and irreducible core of creativity. But it would be my further contention that, in certain important respects, analysis and research can interact strongly with creative planning and greatly enhance its capabilities.

The essential issue at this point is the cumulative nature of some human creative activities, coupled with the great resources which must be devoted to urban development and improvement. If Urban reconstruction did not involve very great expenditures and bring about changes which will last for many years and influence the enjoyment of the urban environment for generations, there would not be very much point in belaboring the creative problems of the planner and decision-maker. They could indulge in whatever creations they liked, and we could judge the results as we judge books and paintings. Unfortunately, we must face up to more serious responsibilities. In the second place, however, if the experience of planning and designing cities is not a cumulative part of human knowledge, then we have to adopt still a different attitude from the one which I am urging. There is something to be said in humanistic creation for the idea that experience is not cumulative and that, despite the intervening centuries of bitter human experience, it would be foolish to expect Tolstoi's insights to be much richer than those of Sophocles, or Bertrand Russell's politics more universal than Aristotle's. If planning falls in such a category of creative activity, then not only are we always to some extent dependent on identifying, cultivating, and preserving genius, but we must also somehow arrange for a more fully developed, persistent, and vigilant public criticism. In the light of the widespread disagreement of the critics and the public with regard to contemporary art, architecture, and literature, the prospects of obtaining consensus in support of genius by this route seem very poor.

Fortunately, in my view, the art of inventing future cities is not just the work of isolated genius, but a part of a cumulative social exercise, like science. Past experience in engineering and technology, in social organization, and in human behavior provide a substratum of materials within which the designer works and upon which he builds. This is not to suggest that through some process of accretion each new stage in urban planning embodies the actual physical results of all previous stages. Frequently the creative act will consist in simplifying, inverting, or transforming previous concepts and old approaches. The essence of the matter is that this simplification is in large measure impossible without the preceding complication and accretion of knowledge and practice. As in science, therefore, the experience of the past is a platform from which the inventor can project himself into the future. The higher and firmer that platform is, the greater the leap which is possible.

The creative planner needs a better platform and better signposts pointing to possible directions for change and invention. These can both be provided in considerable measure by a judicious use of the tools of research and analysis to explore the nature of urban affairs, to understand the curiosities and anomalies of individual behavior, and to provide insight into the ways in which things might fruitfully be changed as well as into the limits of feasible change.

The use of planning research and analysis is thus closely related to the ultimate goals of planning and is not an end in itself—regardless of the appearance which may sometimes be conveyed by some research efforts. Undoubtedly, a substantial proportion of the need for planning research currently arises out of previous neglect by the planning profession as well as out of the dramatic acceleration of an approaching urban crisis. In this situation, the planner needs to find out (and these jobs are listed in order of increasing difficulty) what are the things to be done, how they can be done, and how they can be done at a cost which we can afford. In an increasingly complex world, these jobs are not as simple as we are sometimes told.

Consider, for example, the question of what should be done. Perhaps the broad outlines of an appropriate metropolitan development program for the United States are clear. Certainly we must respect the environment and provide adequate living, working, and transportation conditions for all. But let me suggest two or three important subsidiary questions: how much urban sprawl will we permit? And do we propose to desegregate or to improve the ghettos? And in what proportions? I very much doubt that we could get much agreement within the profession on these issues or that we could find much scientific enlightenment which would help us decide them.

Next, consider how things should be done. We are surely agreed on the desirability of good housing, but I doubt very much that we know what to do about the very substantial old and deteriorating housing stock in our existing cities. Do we redevelop or rehabilitate it? Do we convert it to smaller units or deconvert it to larger units? How much parking, transportation, and open space do we provide? Here, in a sense, our situation is worse because we do not know in fact the condition and character of large parts of this housing stock and the neighborhoods in which it is to be found, let alone its current economic condition and social occupancy. We are therefore a long way from proposing how our actual objectives should be accomplished.

Consider, finally, the very real constraints of resources which make it necessary for us to undertake many of these jobs at a cost which, if not minimal, is at least less than would be required for a perfect solution. Here the planner ought to become skilled in a kind of socio-economic jujitsu, where he exerts minimum effort, and the exertion and momentum of his "opponent," or the members of the community, actually does the job which is most needed. Solving this problem requires a detailed understanding of behavior and an innovative attitude toward social and economic rules and incentives. Here indeed the planner is furthest from a complete understanding of the needs and potentialities of the situation.

I have concluded my discussion of using new tools with a series of brief illustrations intended to suggest that our knowledge is less than complete in the face of a very substantial set of problems. I am aware that there are many members of the profession who do not agree in general that their insights or knowledge are inadequate to deal with these problems. These planners have a very different definition of the kinds and amounts of research which are necessary and desirable. In general, and in consequence of their attitude toward research, some of these planners tend to claim that excessive resources are devoted to study, and that this study takes the place of action. In general, they step forward as more modest in their requests for public support and more active in their defense of the public interest. Insofar as I believe that these claims are wrong, I must confess that I feel that a part of our challenge comes from within the profession.

The claim that planning research makes exorbitant demands on resources is wholly unrealistic and is quite the reverse of modest. The planner who claims to be able to solve large problems and supervise huge programs of expenditure with very limited research expenditures is arrogating to himself powers and abilities which in my view he does not possess. He is likewise contradicting the experience of many fields of human endeavor where substantial progress has seldom been made without adequate investment in new knowledge. Planners who refuse to participate in the design and development of an effective research program might be called twentieth-century Know-Nothings, did they not profess to know everything.

A slightly different view of the same problem leads to similar conclusions. The present, most unsatisfactory urban situation has quite clearly not arisen from the application of the findings of urban research or from delays imposed by the process of conducting such research. We already know that political fragmentation, the interposition of special interests, public apathy and lack of resources, inadequate means of planning effectuation, and lack of agreement among members of the planning profession have all contributed to the present unsatisfactory state of affairs. It is impossible to anticipate that this very real combination of causes plus many others not here enumerated will simply disappear in the face of either universal good will or planning exhortation. It is quite plain that research and analysis leading to a widely shared understanding can be a most powerful means of doing a large job with the best achievable allocation of resources. This is an important aspect of the challenge facing the planning profession today.

GEORGE M. RAYMOND

Partner, Raymond & May Associates, Urban and Regional
Planning, Development, Design, and Renewal Consultants.
Founder and director, Pratt Center for Community Improvement. Professor of Planning and Chairman of the Department of City and Regional Planning, School of Architecture, Pratt Institute. B.A. from Columbia University;
AIA Medal, Sherman Prize. Editor: *Pratt Guide to Housing, Planning and Urban Renewal for New Yorkers.*

Simulation vs. Reality

A COMMENT ON THE HARRIS PAPER

Britton Harris' paper discusses not one but two loosely related subjects.
The first is the development and use of new *tools* for research and analysis
in urban planning; the second is the need for greater *knowledge* regarding
various aspects of the urban field in order to improve our performance, and
the need for the profession to develop a receptive attitude to the formulation of a research program designed to produce the necessary data. It is
essential that we keep these two strands clearly separate if we are to
comment on his presentation intelligently.

Let me start with the need for more knowledge. It would, indeed, take a
Know-Nothing to claim that we know enough about any subject to the
point of refusing to know more. I can only agree with Harris when he
berates planners who "profess to know everything" and who "refuse to
participate in the design and development of an effective research program." I hope, however, that he will permit me to draw a distinction
between effective research programs and wasteful boondoggles, which,
unfortunately, so many major planning research programs have been to
date. It is, of course, only the latter that I have consistently deplored, and it
is only in relation to the latter that I have objected to the expenditure of an
enormous proportion of all funds allocated to planning.

No research program can be justified if it merely attempts to prove the
obvious, at great expense to the public. Nor can a research program be
deemed effective if it delves into areas where additional data can make no

difference in policy formulation. Too often these days, one reads news-paper editorials complaining that a planning study proved that the rich have more money than the poor, or that they live in better housing. This is how the *New York Herald Tribune* reacted upon reviewing the results of one such study, which lasted five years and cost $3¼ million: "The sum and substance [of the report] is that things are bad, and that the right place to start with correction is the worst spots. This would seem indis-putable, and it shouldn't have required all that money and time to discover what everybody knew already." I submit to you that the profession can ill afford many such reviews of its efforts.

A valid publicly-supported research program must be one whose findings will help remove doubt or clarify public issues, and thus facilitate the formulation of policy and the making of decisions. It is difficult for me to conceive a research program which could possibly *prove* the desirability of helping improve the housing conditions of the poor ahead of those of the not-so-poor. It seems to me that a thorough indoctrination in Isaiah and the New Testament would predispose members of the public in favor of the poor more than any of the figures and elegant mathematical manipulations in the most sophisticated, electronically processed housing reports.

Harris himself cites another area in which more knowledge, as such, would, it seems to me, be of questionable worth under the conditions prevailing today. "Do we propose to desegregate or to improve the ghettos? And in what proportions?," he asks. Anyone who has worked with the problem knows that the answers to these questions are basically political. No amount of anything that goes by the name of "research" will help us resolve them. I would go so far as to claim that anyone who asks such questions in terms of ultimately applying abstract reasoning to their solu-tion simply does not understand the context in which the problem must be resolved.

What are the facts? The key one is that, regardless of what data or machines might tell us, we cannot now integrate the ghetto residents be-cause of the white community's totally irrational resistance to the spread of black residents into its folds. The solution that I and others who share my views have advanced over the years, is that we keep pushing open housing throughout the community and its metropolitan area, and that we simul-taneously improve standards in the ghetto through its rebuilding to the fullest extent of available resources.

If this country will someday wake up from its racial nightmare, and blacks and whites will find it possible to peacefully co-exist in the same neighborhoods, rebuilt ghettos, which usually lie near the hearts of our major cities, will attract whites to replace those blacks who will by then have moved to the suburbs to be nearer their jobs. But they will do so only if rebuilt to standards as high as those in other areas available to whites, and they will not be able to do so if we continue to rebuild to the minimum standards we have so long been satisfied to use. Therefore, I submit that we have no choice but to press for subsidies not only to maximize the amount of rebuilding but also to optimize its quality.

There is an alternative to this approach, and that is to reject integration. In addition to white racists, it is the thrust of the black power extremists, with their primarily political motivation behind the demand for total black control over the ghettos. Personally, I think this approach is wrong from the standpoint of the future of our society, and totally unrealistic in terms of accomplishing the objectives its proponents hold forth. I would consider it a major defeat were this approach the only one realistically feasible within the context of the present situation.

This is the dilemma which we face. I frankly admit that my position is not based on any research other than looking in the face of what I consider the obvious. I would be curious to hear how Harris would propose to use high-speed computers to help us resolve it, and what kind of data would help us to better understand our predicament.

Now, let us turn to his second example of areas needing research; namely, the always vexing problem of urban sprawl. Harris is looking to mathematical tools to help us decide how much sprawl we should "permit." But how can we formulate the question in terms which will be intelligible to computers? Why are we concerned with urban sprawl at all? As Henry Churchill asked at the end of a professional career almost entirely dedicated to a fight against it, "Is urban sprawl as bad as it is said to be? Bad for whom, and why?" Are we any nearer a resolution of this question? We cannot totally ignore Herbert Gans's thesis in *The Levittowners,* that the crab grass syndrome does contribute to the public happiness.

If, on the other hand, the basic objective of planning is not to follow but to lead, and what is sought is the condensation of development to create a "sense of place" or "urbanity," can these types of goals be quantified? And if one of the objectives is to preserve open space, are answers not obvious? Do we really need a computer to tell us which areas possess the more unique natural characteristics? Only if the objective is to minimize travel on highways and maximize travel by rail is it useful to resort to the computer—and this is the one area, namely, transportation planning and traffic engineering, in which computers can be immensely useful since there is no dispute as to the relative predictability of traffic movements given certain objective conditions. But even here, as Victor Fisher once cautioned, we should not "confuse research sophistication or the imaginative use of computers with the real solution of planning problems. . . . [A] good balance between transportation planning and comprehensive planning does not mean that the latter must simply be computerized to the extent that the former has been. For if planning is to be effective and have real purpose, it must take into account not only tangible data, but also the values of the community that may not be subject to quantification."

Let me repeat here my position regarding metropolitan land-use planning objectives: "In physical terms," I once wrote, "a regional environment is superior if it offers a maximum range of choice: congestion and serenity, urbanity and open country, high-rise and low-rise apartments, and one-family houses, detached and in clusters; small neighborhood shops and shopping centers; offices and factories; beauty, excitement, order, human scale—all within the physical reach and economic means of a maximum number of its inhabitants."[1] I submit to you that this does represent the kind of "holistic view of people, cities, and environment," which Harris hopes planners will adopt. And while, as he claims, it may be possible *in principle* to judiciously combine this view with "the theoretical insights of various disciplines and the formalistic and manipulative techniques of mathematics" to some higher purpose, I doubt that efforts in that direction are likely to lead anywhere, in practice.

And this brings us to a consideration of his arguments promoting the use of new tools. I do not know who are the planners who "oppose the use of computers." If any do, I fully agree that they do not belong in the profession. The desirability of using computers to simplify the task of manipulating large masses of data is incontestable. I would no more argue against the use of a computer than I would argue against the use of a slide rule, or of an abacus, for that matter. My concern is with the uses to which the computer has been put in planning research, and particularly with the claims made on behalf of the importance of the results achieved so far, or likely to be achieved in the future.

[1] "The Planning Profession: A House Divided," George M. Raymond, *Pratt Planning Papers,* Vol. 2, No. 4, February 1964.

Let me cite an example of what I mean. Over the years, the Ford Foundation has been funding a number of multi-million-dollar projects designed to sharpen our urban technology. One of its officers, William Pendleton, felt the time to be at hand to stand back and tell us what had been learned. Let me convey his thoughts to you in his own words:

> The first [lesson] is that we must take care not to exaggerate the potential contribution of technology to solving the problems of the cities. The really critical and immediately pressing problems—poverty, unemployment, crime, bad housing, poor health, and inadequate education—will persist until the nation finds the will to provide very basic economic, social, and political solutions. . . . Technological approaches . . . appear to offer promise toward solving what may be called the hardware-related problems—pollution, congestion, waste disposal and the like. They may be useful in achieving better understanding of the systems out of which the really critical problems develop, but actually solving those problems will depend upon progress in redistributing population, in tapping greater sources of financing for urban services, in restructuring our antiquated political institutions, and ultimately in a revolution in basic attitudes of both the white and Negro populations.
>
> Our second proposition—but a qualified one—is that the potential role of the systems approach to urban problems, at least as the approach has developed in the aerospace industry, is currently being oversold to a rather substantial degree. The findings from . . . [Foundation-backed] California experiments . . . revealed no spectacular successes. A recent meeting in Washington of the Operations Research Society of America heard systems analysts time and again wring their hands over the complexities, the data problems, and the political obstructions they faced as they tried to tackle some of the most pressing problems of today's cities. Those who attended that meeting heard Joseph Engel, the incoming president of O.R.S.A., say, "As we move closer and closer to human beings, human life, and to its goals, we find that we are dealing progressively with more and more difficult problems. . . . We're very good at hardware and tactical problems and starting well-defined research and development programs. We're lousy at strategic and philosophical problems."
>
> Furthermore, it is not at all obvious that the heritage of Department of Defense and National Aeronautics and Space Administration contracts prepares the aerospace companies to operate in the context of municipal problems. With those agencies, systems people worked for a single identifiable client—who was extraordinarily well-heeled and in a position to conceal from the prying eyes of the political sector many failures and false starts. Not one of these conditions is

likely to be present when and if a bigger push is made for research and development in the municipal field. That fact has led to speculation that the aerospace companies may have only a limited role in developing new municipal technology. . . .[2]

More important than the experience of the Ford Foundation with the systems analysts is the experience of the country as a whole. After all, many of the people who now flock to help us solve urban problems are the same "think-tank" people whose advice brought us to our current position in Vietnam; in escalating the war to include the large-scale employment of air power, the President followed the recommendations of a 1964 Rand Corporation study. As reported by *The New York Times,* the study suggested cynically that, since we were deeply involved and hated anyway, and since, as a consequence, "we've got the onus," we might as well "get the bonus." In figuring our chances of getting the "bonus," whatever that may have been, the Rand systems analysts were unmindful of the truths discovered by John Roche. Two years on the White House staff, "uptight with power . . . sent [him] off on a theological bent. You can't practice the exercise of power," he said, "any more than you can practice dying. The problems you see are not intellectual problems—though they have intellectual dimensions. All the history in the world doesn't make any difference if the Russians decide to bail out their clients."

Remember those who advised John Foster Dulles in the art of getting the "most bang for the buck"? Well, they are here to tell us how to house the most poor without spending money (they call it "rehabilitation"). Before we let them tinker with our domestic life with consequences similar to those which have fouled up our foreign policy, I suggest that we would do well to check their credentials a little more closely.

I can well understand Harris's yearning for a formula which would reduce everything "to the comforting specificity of manageable numbers," in Edmund Bacon's felicitous phrase. Confronted on all sides by resistance and complexity, many planners seem to prefer to spend their time with numbers rather than people, hoping to find a miraculous method which will produce only incontrovertible evidence. We might look to Princeton's Professor F. Ashley Montagu for a clear statement of the ultimate meaning of this search. "It is understandable," he said, "that . . . men will readily embrace an explanation having the appearance of plausibility, especially

---

[2] "Technology and Cities, a Foundation Viewpoint," by William C. Pendleton, Address before the *Conference on Impending Technology—Its Challenge to Livable Cities,* Georgia Institute of Technology, Atlanta, May 9, 1968.

when that explanation is offered pretentiously, with at least the appearance of support from the apparatus of scientific learning." Thus, Harris and many others like him provide us not with real answers, but with formulas and jargon which are perhaps complex enough to make it *seem* "that a highly scientific decision-making process is at work . . . that [political leaders and the general public] need entertain no doubts or misgivings . . . and that the job is getting done."[3] This type of presentation may fool some of the people some of the time; unfortunately, it is now fooling too many people too much of the time. In the end, however, it is bound to be rejected as the hollow and basically useless instrument that it is.

But then, in fairness to Harris, he has never said that the new tools are now ready to produce usable results. Throughout his long and distinguished career, he has only claimed that general systems theory with respect to the total urban, metropolitan, or regional system will *ultimately* play a direct role in decision models. He has only suggested that a systematic and better informed approach *might* provide some surprises . . . and that general systems theory *may* well contribute to our understanding. He has acknowledged that "there are certain deficiencies in present knowledge and concepts regarding systems in their application to the problems of a metropolitan community," but he has reassured us by his promise that *"there is every reason to believe* that these shortcomings can be remedied and that more fully developed methods of systems analysis *may* be most fruitful in planning."

And so it goes, year after year. "In principle," all these claims sound plausible; in practice, the promised results seem always to loom just over the horizon, just beyond man's reach. In Kierkegaard's words,

> . . . I am willing to fall down adoringly before the System, if only I can catch sight of it. Until now I have not succeeded in so doing. . . . Several times I have been quite near to adoration; but lo, at the moment when I had already spread out my handkerchief in order not to soil my trousers in kneeling; when for the last time I guilelessly said to one of the initiate, "Now tell me honestly, is it really quite finished? For in that case I shall prostrate myself, even though I should ruin a pair of trousers"—for by reason of the heavy traffic to and from the System the path is not a little soiled—I always got the answer: "No, as yet it is, in fact, not quite completed." And so it was postponed again —both the System and the kneeling. . . .

[3] Testimony by Admiral Hyman G. Rickover before the Congressional Joint Committee on Atomic Energy, July 25, 1968.

The real problem is not, as Harris claims, that planners who suggest that we devote more resources to applied research and less to excursions into the wild-blue of so-called "pure research," arrogate unto themselves powers and abilities which they do not possess. The problem lies rather in the fact that people who suggest that we will ever be able to reduce infinitely complex entities, such as a metropolitan region, for instance, to finite, manipulatable models, are simply misleading the public. They know that computers have limitations, that they cannot cope with simulations which involve an excessive number of variables. Three years ago, John Campbell, editor of *Analog* magazine, pointed out that "no computer can solve the simple, perfectly logical game of chess" with its mere thirty-two pieces and sixty-four squares. He went on to point out that "even when calculating in fractional millionths of a second, the number of possible situations that can arise in so limited a game as chess entails more computations than the greatest computer can manage in the next 10,000 years." If this is so, then I suggest that it is nothing short of fraudulent to claim that the complexities of a metropolitan region can be neatly laid out and "resolved," whatever that may mean. Just think of the "systems" that would have to be quantified and the relationships that would have to be identified and understood in, say, the New York Metroplitan Region, with its 1400 governments spread over 7000 square miles, containing 16 million independent decision-making citizens and hundreds of thousands of businesses, with its roots in Albany, Trenton, Hartford, and Washington, and its branches in San Francisco, Buenos Aires, Europe, and Vietnam!

The fact is that the devotees of the scientific approach to comprehensive planning merely abstract and use in their models only a few of the more easily quantifiable aspects of the world. They thus deal with abstractions rather than reality. As Aldous Huxley put it, "However elegant and memorable, brevity can never, in the nature of things, do justice to all the facts of a complex situation. . . . Omission and simplification help us to understand—but help us, in many cases, to understand the wrong thing; for our comprehension may be only of the abbreviator's neatly formulated notions, not of the vast, ramifying reality from which these notions have been so arbitrarily abstracted."

One may agree with Harris that our problems may not "disappear in the face of either universal good will or planning exhortation," but neither will they, unfortunately, disappear because of facts and figures describing less than the full reality. Years of research into the cranial and other physical similarities of the races were unable to undo the misinterpretation of one sentence in the Bible which vaguely suggests that God intended races to live apart. It took Martin Luther King's Montgomery bus boycott to really make a difference. I urgently suggest to you that the challenge before the planning profession cannot be met by appeals to reason based on the narrow kind of balance sheet which computers can understand.

In conclusion, let me emphasize that my plea is not for less expenditures on research—if, by research, we mean a process which has an output as well as an input; rather, I plead for a greater allocation of resources to community education. In the last analysis, only citizens who can appreciate the end product of the planner's work will back his efforts to attain it. The end product of a physical planner's work is the environment. It seems to me that the time has come for this country to devote a lot more resources than it has in the past to the education of the public to the end of enabling it to recognize the difference between various proposals put before it and of increasing its willingness to insist upon, and, if need be, to fight for the better solution. I know of no better way in which such a policy could be implemented than by the engagement and involvement of the public first in the preparation, and second, in the implementation of a plan.

To realize to the fullest the potential inherent in this process, it is essential that the public have confidence in the professional competence of the physical planners. And so, while physical planners should not deny the validity of meaningful research in real situations and theoretical speculations in the universities, "they are fully within their rights when they show deep resentment in the face of criticism of the validity of what they want to do, based not on the results of research performed to date, but on the *possible* results of *future* research. . . ."[4]

We may not now be ready to create a perfect world, but if we allow the possible to wait on the perfect, we will never do anything at all. In the task of creating an environment fit for man in this—the wealthiest and technologically most advanced country in the world—the physical planner has a unique function which he must perform now and all the time. And, to help him perform it, I hope that Harris and those who follow his enlightened leadership will heed Edmund Bacon's advice and "stop using the term 'intuitive' [pejoratively] as a means to kill in the bud any creative thinking." If they fail to heed it, and if their converts win out in the end, it is most doubtful that we will be able to deal with many of the most basic issues of our urban crisis.

[4] "Man the Measure," George M. Raymond, *Pratt Planning Papers*, Vol. 4, No. 2, March 1966.

PAUL C. WATT

Deputy Executive Director, Tri-State Transportation Commission, New York City. Formerly Director, Metropolitan Dade County Planning Department, Miami, Florida; and Director of the National Capitol Regional Planning Council, Washington, D.C. B.A., University of Illinois in Landscape Architecture and City Planning.

The Value and Limits of Data-Processing

A COMMENT ON THE HARRIS PAPER

I compliment Britton Harris on having the ingenuity to write a paper on "New Tools for Research and Analysis in Urban Planning" when, in fact, as he so wistfully states, there have really been no "new tools" developed, at least not by the planning profession. He divides his discussion into three areas: what he calls "found tools," those adopted and adapted from other fields; the (again) wistful hope that the planning profession itself might invent some new tools; and the use of the "new borrowed" tools or the hopefully to-be-invented ones.

Under "found tools," those from other fields which can be assimilated by the planning profession, Harris rightly extols the computer as the outstanding new tool of modern civilization. I concur; its influence on planning is already enormous. However, I offer a stronger word of caution than Harris as to how the planner uses this devilish device. He states that, in effect, the planner who opposes the use of computers will be pushed aside and replaced. I would add that the planner who misuses the computer should also be pushed aside or replaced. Already we see too many instances where the computer has been used by the planner because of its tremendous manipulative capacity as a means for cranking out reams of meaningless data, the product of a passionate love affair with some process or methodology. To make things worse, the output of such a run is too often regarded as the divine answer because it comes out of the computer (Garbage in—Gospel out). I have probably overemphasized this point, but

I think the planners' predilection with process rather than using the device to assist in reaching a product must be faced squarely by the profession if this adopted tool is to be used wisely.

I would like to ease some of the harshness heaped on the poor planner striving to adapt the computer to assist him in the plan-making process. The author makes two very good points which emphasize partially why the planner will be some time in wisely using the computer. First, his point that the planning profession has a long way to go before it can properly use such a tool in relating to the needs of the total environment in terms of how metropolitan systems (economic, demographic, biologic, hydrologic, etc.) intermesh. I seriously question whether such an orchestration will ever be possible; it might be better to solve the functional elements separately with some more simplistic means of interrelating them. Second, the author's point that, at least in the present generation of planners, the lack of training and insight in the fields of mathematics and logic, which are paramount to thinking through and applying the forms of relationships, is a source of confusion rather than of clarification. It will be the job of our planning schools to prepare future planners for this new planning world. For those of us who are presently ill-prepared and are caught up in this world, it means hard work both to try to keep up and to rethink some of our "old planners tales."

As to data as a "found tool," I agree with the author that there is much we do not know about our cities and regions. I am not completely taken, however, with the vision of a tremendous quantity of data stored in the computer, readily retrievable and in the exact form that you want it so that you can plan better for your city or region. Here again, through intellectual laziness, the planner can build a mare's-nest rather than help to narrow the data gap. It is much more important to think out the data we really need for our planning purposes and then use the computer to assist us, rather than to store everything conceivable because of the voracious capacity of the machine, and experience the severe reduction and extraction problems referred to by Harris. My meager experience to date seems to cry "keep it simple."

I find myself in complete agreement with the author relating to the "found tools" emanating from the transportation engineering sector. It behooves the planners, particularly the new breed of the "mathematical-logic school," to zero in on the fruits of this work and to urge those specializing in transportation planning to join them in applying their knowledge to assist in the over-all planning process. We have much to learn from their substantial lead in thinking and doing. This is particularly true as it relates to simulating the over-all pattern of settlement. We are just scratching the surface in this area. As we make progress in isolating the influence of accessibility, we become aware of its role as a tremendous force as between current trend and prediction.

I cannot disagree in general with Harris's philosophic approach that the invention of new tools is not the same as the invention of new plans. Nor do I believe that the planner will invent and design a new type of computer or new inventions in the data field. I rather feel, however, that he paints too dark a picture of the future as to the planner's contribution to the invention of new tools in "software" in the form of growth and sub-system models. The profession in the future should prove capable of overcoming its inhibitions and should achieve innovative breakthroughs. It almost sounds as if we must invent a new planner before we can invent new research tools. I realize the problem is not that simple. The fact that planning crosses so many disciplines makes it unlikely that such a breed is capable of excellence in all areas,—even with the computer. I would hope, however, that the planner could achieve a more primary role rather than that of assistant to the inventor, where Harris seems to relegate him.

I would argue with Harris's point that the use of new tools in influencing the decision-making aspect is to assist men and governments to adapt to future change rather than to change the future. Certainly none of us, who over the years have been applying planning judgment with great rectitude, are wont to turn down better, more credible means of bolstering and justifying those ends. Research and analysis alone cannot wholly supplant this so-called intuitive judgment. I do get nervous when Harris talks about using this device to broaden the understanding of the population as a whole or to correct or contradict mistakes and misconceptions in the minds of people, politicians, or planners, lest we are again hiding behind the computer "which says it's so." However, it is really the timing of such action, rather than whether it should be done, that is the cause of my concern. The creative spirit of the planners can and should be bolstered by research and analysis.

The use of research and analysis, as Harris describes it—in drawing on past experience to seek out the things to be done, how they can be done, presumably considering alternative means, and at what cost weighed against the many trade-offs—is the essence of the kind of planning we all seek. I do not feel that there is the strong undercurrent of opposition to this approach that Harris observes within the profession. If there is conflict in this area, I feel that it revolves more around how to do it, rather than whether it should be done.

If Harris is saying, and I must admit that this point did not come through clearly to me, that such an element of the planning process must begin as an "on line" operation, I do not agree. If, on the other hand, he is saying that this is an essential aspect of the planning process but will be pursued "off line" while being developed and tested as a means of influencing planning decisions, then I am with him all the way. It will be made operational in part or totally as it justifies its use in the planning process.

In the end, the proper use of research and analysis within the context of functional resource allocation is what planning is all about, and until we can get such an approach operational we are only going to be making and talking about plans instead of implementing plans and being a participant in getting things done.

ISADORE CANDEUB

President and Planning Director of Candeub, Fleissig and Associates. Previous to 1953 on staff of Housing and Home Finance Agency. B.A., City College of New York; M.C.P., M.I.T.

New Techniques in Making the General Plan

A thorough review of this subject would include new techniques in data collection and storage, new methods in introducing social and economic analyses into the planning process, new methods of graphic presentation, and new procedures in plan formulation to relate to programming requirements. In fact, the list could be so extensive as to suggest that our present techniques are now totally different from those of the past. However, with regard to one of the most fundamental elements of planning, the general or comprehensive plan, we are still bound to a set of techniques that largely originated around the beginning of this century. As planners, we have been trying very diligently and with considerable ingenuity to apply the techniques of 1910 to the problems of the 1960's and 1970's and, incidentally, finding it increasingly difficult to do so in a meaningful fashion.

In order to fully establish the degree of change in techniques that is needed, let us first review some of the principles out of which the general or comprehensive plan originated.

1. *Long-Range Plan:* It was considered that most of the problems of the city could have been anticipated if there had been some prior study of needs; and the proper application of foresight could have reduced or eliminated the problems. In effect, with due regard for growth, streets would have been wider, park lands reserved, utility systems provided for, and other measures would have been taken that would have contributed to a healthy growth pattern. The fact that such measures had not been taken pointed to the need for a long-range plan.

2. *Comprehensive Plan:* Urban problems were in large measure due to lack of proper recognition of related needs. Residential areas had been

developed far from places of employment, shopping areas without regard to parking needs, and new subdivisions with no provision for school needs. Therefore, proper planning had to be comprehensive in nature and should cover every aspect of community development so that improvements could be carried out in a properly balanced fashion.

3. *Coordination:* With a projection of future needs and a plan to meet those needs, coordination between various governmental as well as private groups could be in everyone's interest. Through this coordination of effort, the plan could be realized. (It was essential that the plan be truly comprehensive in scope, since it should be a guide for all groups involved in the improvement and development of the city.)

4. *Citizen Education:* In view of the fact that politicians were subject to immediate, rather than long-range, pressures and self-interest, it was important to place the responsibility for the comprehensive plan in the hands of the "people" both in its making and in safeguarding it in the future. This required the education of the "people" to the importance of planning and the plan.

These four concepts—long-range planning, comprehensive planning, planning as an instrument for coordination and the role of citizen education—have been drummed into every student who ever took a course in planning and every planning board member who was ever subjected to indoctrination lectures on the role of the planning board. They are such obvious common sense doctrines that questioning them is akin to questioning the institution of motherhood.

However, it is essential that we investigate whether these concepts should still continue to serve as basic doctrine in the light of changed conditions and new insights into the process of environmental and social change itself.

Our traditional emphasis on the long-range plan has some implications that bear careful review. Despite all claims to "flexibility," long-range plans seem invariably to take on fixed, physical features. This inflexibility becomes an obstacle to programs that may follow at a later date.

In an age of rapid and massive development with continuing change in living patterns, industrial technology, financing methods, and the role of government in urban development, our ability to correctly predict and to specifically anticipate the needs of the future appears to be actually less than in any other era in history.

The long-range plan invariably has its focus on the distant future. In a built-up, older city, however, the urgent problems are the problems of today. The misplaced emphasis on the future frequently leads to planning that has so little relevance to the problems at hand that the plan presented is deemed by the local citizenry as nothing more than a technical exercise.

We cannot preach a doctrine that planning should reflect social and economic needs if we are bound by physical plans that do not permit us to respond to shifts in those needs over short-term intervals.

Our public and private programs of development and improvement are geared to the fiscal and administrative capabilities and motivations of corporate and governmental organizations. The relevancy of extensive and detailed physical planning in advance of even the creation of some of these instruments for change is more and more open to question.

A plan should be "comprehensive," at least in the sense that it should cover all of the elements that properly belong in it. The question is, where should the line be drawn? In recent years, we have been running the danger that no line is drawn. There is now considerable confusion with regard to the proper limits of the comprehensive plan.

Rather than get into the details of what does or does not belong in the comprehensive plan, let us consider some of the results of this pursuit of comprehensiveness:

1. the confusion as to coverage generates additional confusion as to function;

2. the all-encompassing plan places unrealistic demands on the time and attention of the members of a planning board or governing body in their efforts to review in detail;

3. focus on key elements is lost in the overburden of documents and maps;

4. the preparation of the comprehensive plan is frequently a mammoth task that takes from two to three years;

5. its complexity and bulk and the cumbersome procedures involved in its preparation rule out any simple process for modifying it or bringing it up to date.

The plan is still largely a "coordinating" document rather than an "action" document. Even where separate departmental review has been made of its various provisions, the long-range nature of the plan usually rules out any commitments on the part of operating agencies.

The concept that the plan would serve a coordinating function was always better in theory than in fact. During an earlier period, this was of little importance since there were relatively few operating agencies on the local scene, and at any given time no more than a few public improvement projects were in effect. This is no longer the case. With a wide number of agencies, programs, and sources of funds, casual coordination does not serve the public interest. Neither is the public interest served by the general plan functioning as a catchall of programs, short-range and long-range operational, and those not even funded. This generates public confusion and, in many instances, an unwarranted assumption that something effective is under way when, in fact, no action is in sight.

Emphasis is still being placed on public education, but the previous relevancy has long been lost. Instead of distrusting the "politicians," planners increasingly view their role and that of the general plan as an aid to decision-making on the part of government and as an important function of government.

While planning reports are no longer written as preachments to the laymen, the traditions of the past continue to linger on in reports that are ostensibly devoted to technical presentations or policy statements. The planner continues to be more desirous of educating the public than to be educated by the public. A continued posture that "people don't know what's good for them," unless they are told by the planner or the planning board, is not compatible with the principle of public involvement and participation.

These inherent weaknesses in our general plan procedures, as well as other reasons, have created the need for a number of supplementary types of planning activities:

1. the capital improvement program, separate from but related to the general plan, became the chief action instrument serving to "implement" the general plan;

2. the Federal Workable Program requirements have served to furnish commitments to an active improvement program in the absence of such commitments in the general plan;

3. the Community Renewal Plans, where formulated, have been largely directed to the framing of neighborhood improvement programs;

4. Community Action Plans, where formulated, have been for the purpose of providing comprehensive programs serving social and economic needs;

5. the Model Cities program is a new attempt to deal intensively with local problems on a short-range basis.

Some techniques that have been introduced, or are being considered for application, to the development or utilization of the general plan are the following:

1. the policy plan, expressing broad policy considerations rather than detailed planning specifications;

2. the concept plan, providing simplified graphic expression to the major land-use and development features of a community or region;

3. planned unit development (PUD), establishing only generalized controls over large land areas subject primarily to three-dimensional design review;

4. open-ended planning designations such as "redevelopment areas," providing that a detailed development plan will be furnished at a later date;

5. planning, programming, and budgeting system (PPBS), establishing a functional schedule for the sequential carrying out of stipulated plans and programs and providing feedback or monitoring provisions.

As new types of planning programs proliferate, and as successive additions are made to the planning and zoning procedures available to us, it is obvious that we are now reaching a point where either the general plan as we have known it will be allowed to fade into the background as a largely ceremonial type of report that will be refurbished every ten years, and then brought out for periodic viewing on special occasions, such as a new request for federal grants; or it will be radically reconstructed to take into account urgent present needs and to serve to meet those needs.

We are beyond the point where the general plan can be made more relevant by adding or subtracting items in the laundry list that has now become its typical burden of content. Nor do we add substantial substance to it by requiring that it "be fully responsive to social and economic needs," "project a higher level of urban design" and "incorporate procedures for feasible effectuation." These continuing amendments to the basic set of requirements, made without due consideration to whether or not their application can be meaningfully incorporated into the total structure, are creating a potpourri of scrambled data gathering, objectives, and bits and pieces of plans that are an increasingly incompatible mixture. If the old-fashioned comprehensive physical plan tried to cover too much ground, its latter day version, which is much more global in nature, must obviously fall on its face as an effective instrument with which to control change.

The general plan as we know it is urgently in need of complete restructuring to respond to a different set of purposes and related to the new technology available to us. I suggest that to be relevant the general plan should be a meaningful commitment to public action directed to meeting the social, economic, and physical needs of the present as well as the future population within its given locality or region. Furthermore, it should take form through a process that permits and provides for direct citizen involvement and participation in its planning.

Not one of these objectives is very startling, radical, or original. However, let us give some careful attention to some of the new directions in which these objectives can take us if we free ourselves from some of our old thinking.

To begin with, we can start with the word "relevant." The dictionary definition of relevant is "to relate to the matter at hand." For planning purposes, this could be translated to relate to the here and now, and immediately raises the question as to whether *any* fifteen-year or twenty-five-year target plan can be truly considered "relevant" to the public at large. It suggests that to be relevant we focus on the immediate and the five-year period, keeping the long-range plan as part of our perspective but not as the central focus of the general plan. If this single step were taken, it would represent a major change in technique.

Moving to the much used and abused phrases "social and economic needs," it should be pointed out that if these are to be construed as of only limited importance, we can be content "to relate" to them in the design of our cities. If we consider them to be truly important, it is necessary to go beyond "relating" to them and start responding to them. But this means that they must be clearly identified, objectives must be spelled out, and planning must be directed toward the achieving of those stipulated objectives.

It should be recognized that social and economic needs are generally expressed at a regional level. Without appropriate directives established for a region, with some binding control over the planning at a local level, we will not be able to properly respond to social and economic needs in most of our general plans. In the absence of such directives, our central cities are becoming increasingly concentrated holding areas for the poor, the elderly, and the black. Under the auspices of planning, we have allowed the creation of barricades to free movement from these older cities in the form of restrictive general plans and zoning ordinances in our suburban belts.

If we truly want to stress the importance of responsiveness to social and economic needs, we must further stress the factor of time. During a period of rapid change, the general plan that is redone at ten-, twelve- or fifteen-year intervals cannot be considered as "responsive." We should move to a procedure under which a five-year review and modification and a ten-year complete reconsideration would be mandatory. However, as our data banks become more adequate, we may be able to provide a yearly review of critical social and economic indices, and have this feedback generate priority shifts and other changes in the general plan.

Having touched on the question of "needs" and "time," let us now consider the question of "commitment to public action." All of us who have had to face the public are thoroughly tired of having to go through the ritual of explaining, "Yes, the plan is supposed to guide development but, no, it is not a plan that will be carried out as shown." If we find ourselves getting tongue-tied in our endless explanations of a plan that is not a plan, what can be expected of the people at the other end who will presumably be directly affected by it?

The way out of this dilemma is really absurdly simple. Those elements of the plan that are to be considered a general guide should be placed within covers called "a General Guide Plan." Those elements that are commitments to action of any type should be identified as "Actions to be Taken to Improve our Community." If the second document is embarrassingly slim in content, at least all concerned will have a fairly good idea of what actions are being proposed.

Since the value of these two documents will probably be in direct ratio to their clarity and simplicity, it should be a requirement that they be stripped down to a minimum text and to simple, easily understood maps. We should not confuse the technical work in developing a plan with the plan itself. We should once and for all stop parading all of our technical work between covers on the principle that the public should be given everything that we do because ostensibly it has value.

Even more important than this principle is the level of detail to be incorporated in these documents. If we are dealing with a general guide, let us keep within the limits of what is properly general in nature. A land-use breakdown in twelve to fifteen categories is hardly "general." Specific locations for fire stations and libraries are hardly "general." The temptation to overplan within the framework of the general plan has been responsible in the past for much of the confusion as to function of the plan, and has been one of the factors in making such plans obsolescent within a one- or two-year period.

Excessive detailing should also be avoided in the action plan. This should be organized around separate functions with clearly identified objectives, the plan to accomplish these objectives within a limited time period, and a general schedule identifying target points for initiation and completion. This need not be to the level of detail of the capital improvement budget, but should be prepared to sufficient detail to generally indicate the commitment for action represented by the adoption of the plan.

There are two additional points to be stressed in regard to the action plan.

1. Some of the action categories might well include such elements as are not now commonly included, such as:

a. specific commitments for the development of a given amount of housing units, both private and public;

b. specific commitments toward the improvement of given neighborhoods through extensive code enforcement and rehabilitation efforts;

c. specific commitments for increasing the level of social services, such as day care centers, family counseling, and teenage recreation programs.

2. Approval and adoption of an action program plan by a planning board should be recognized for what it is—a no-commitment plan. An action plan must be approved by the governing body, and either concurred in by such other bodies as school and recreation boards, or else act as a binding control over them as a result of legislative changes. We should stop playing games with the public. If the plan is to represent a public commitment to action, it should not be in a form where it can be waived as the occasion warrants.

In the planning system that has been outlined, we started with the regional level and moved to the city-wide guide plan and then a city-wide action plan. A third level of planning that should be maintained separate from the general program, but related to it, should be the sector or development area plan. The sector plans should be program-oriented plans identifying the specific measures needed to improve or properly develop the area under study, and should furnish design suggestions based on the city-wide guide plan. The development area studies prepared under John Duba in Chicago are good examples of the type of planning that should be carried out for small areas.

In this paper I have sought to suggest, in a very rudimentary fashion, only the direction that we should take in restructuring the general plan. It is clear that we have to make a break with the patterns of the past, that we will have to depart from the monolithic plan to a plan with discreet parts which have separate functions, and that the elements of the plan will have to focus more specifically on the needs of the present. The development of a methodological system of this type would not only prove to be technically more functional, but would also make it possible to achieve true public involvement and active participation at every level. It should not be our function to educate the public. If we are dealing with their problems and if we present our recommendations in a form that permits intelligent review on their part, we will find that they will be educating us. In the process, our planning will become more, rather than less, relevant.

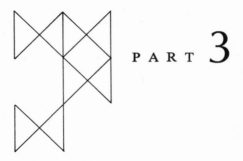

PART 3

THE PROFESSIONAL
PLANNER'S ROLE

LOUIS B. WETMORE

Professor, Urban and Regional Planning, University of Illinois. Deputy Commissioner of the Chicago Department of Development and Planning; Director of the Tri-Cities Planning Project of TVA; Director of the Providence Redevelopment Agency; Consultant to the Chicago City Planning Department, the Rhode Island Development Council, the Housing and Home Finance Agency and the São Paulo, Brazil, Basic Urban Plan.

Preparing the Profession for Its Changing Role

The American Institute of Planners held a series of conferences during the late 1960's aimed at determining the nature of national development goals, and the appropriate response of the profession. As a result, the members of the Institute have achieved a consensus on the need for an expanded scope of professional practice.

Once before, the Institute reviewed its position and made a long-range commitment. This was in 1936–37–38 when the Institute, under Russell Black, determined to change its name and recognize a broader scale of concern. In changing its name from the American City Planning Institute to the American Institute of Planners, the profession made more than a symbolic gesture. The constitution was drafted to indicate a concern for comprehensive planning of city, state, region, and the nation.

In the years that followed, members of the profession provided leadership in the embryonic field of state planning, in the pioneer work of the National Resources Planning Board, and in the effective regional approach of the Tennessee Valley Authority. From these experiences the Institute derived many broader-based professionals as well as an expansion of membership. These new members provided an essential cadre for the rapid expansion of scope in the planning schools and professional practice in the 1940's and 1950's.

The Institute has acted to broaden its commitments again. By revision of the constitutional section on Purposes of the Institute, the membership has renewed its commitment to the full range of city, regional, state, and national planning and made clear that its scope of concern also includes *social* and *economic,* as well as physical, development.

In 1938 the scope of commitment was expanded to cover the full range from neighborhood to nation. Professional competence in the planning process, especially synthesis of plan and program, was adapted to respect the differences of content and of governmental organization involved in state or regional planning. New procedures and new professional roles were developed.

Today, the commitment is again expanded to apply planning and programming competence to a wider agenda. Issues which cities, states, and the nation did not recognize, or ignored, are now being acted upon under national commitments to resolve them. Racial discrimination, air pollution, higher education and anti-poverty programs are illustrative of this broader agenda. Again we need to adapt the planning process, to innovate new procedures, to add specialist competences, and to define new roles.

Through the 1965, 1966 and, 1967 national conferences, the directions of choice have been made by the American Institute of Planners. It is moving to execute that commitment for expanded professional contribution.

This paper asserts that the central question for the next five to ten years is: How can planners move rapidly toward a broad application of effective professional practice? What we know how to do in university theoretical models, and what we have demonstrated through a limited number of innovative cases, must be converted to application over the full range of states, regions, cities, and neighborhoods.

This paper further asserts that the most effective strategy of approach would be to focus on developing operational procedures for professional practice and on communicating this know-how through continuing education.

Those who are now experienced and practicing must provide the leadership in professional practice over the next five to ten years. Within this time span, the future graduates of planning schools will begin to play a responsible role only to a limited extent. Continuing education must be focused on equipping professionals to do their jobs better. It must also be directed to assuring effective participation in planning programs by those who join the team without previous practice or formal education in comprehensive planning.

The definition of roles to be performed is an effective approach to clarifying and specifying the profession's response to new demands. A broad framework is suggested which encompasses the full scope of activity to which the profession aspires. The framework—a cube diagram—can facilitate comparability in role definition.

This paper is written with a built-in split "personality." The paper is structured around an objective statement of the steps this profession can and should take to meet the demands for a vastly broadened practice of urban and regional planning.

Paralleling this relatively dispassionate statement of what we want to be able to do and how do we get there, is an undertone of personal concern. This personal concern may sound a series of gloomy notes which could be misinterpreted as the chorus of a Greek tragedy. "A voyage into the future is being planned but it can only end in disaster."

Such a deeply pessimistic view is not intended. What is intended by these "footnotes" is a constant reminder that all is not well with the profession. Why this emphasis? Because I sense a complacency within the profession. It lacks a sense of urgency in response to the urgent issues faced by our cities and our nation. There is not enough evidence of cooperative and concerted programming by the professional associations or the professional schools.

The main structure of this paper proposes an orderly approach to preparing the members of the profession for their many new roles. The undertone says "with deliberate speed" in thoughtfulness, but "with urgent haste" in action.

The main structure of the paper accepts the desirability of a pluralistic approach in professional education and in professional practice. But this profession must chart a course and not just accept a broad statement of goals. The conclusion contains a recommendation for a strategy of emphasis and direction that would focus major attention in education and practice on two vital program areas symbolized by the terms "model neighborhoods" and "urban regions."

In each profession, basic research and innovative professional activity lead to refinement or expansion of professional practice capabilities. There is an urgent need for a parallel emphasis on extending this new knowledge into the field of practice in comprehensive planning.

There are compelling reasons for continued basic research essential to improving professional practice, and this paper does not call for reducing these efforts, symbolized by the doctoral programs and urban studies centers. However, the professional field of comprehensive development planning needs a major expansion of continuing education aimed at disseminating knowledge so that the general level of practice can be strengthened. Continuing education means formal programs of instruction for practicing professionals which are intended to up-date or supplement professional knowledge and skills.

In all professions, continuing education is essential. Some programs of continuing education bring newly developed understanding or procedures to the practitioner. Some programs offer the opportunity to supplement the limited range of the course work which can be fitted into any degree program.

In comprehensive development planning, the formal programs of continuing education are so limited that we have few examples to build upon. Workshops at national conferences cannot meet the needs, and the professional schools have been concentrating on building degree programs. Funding is only now becoming available through Title VIII of the Housing Act of 1965.

Effective programs of continuing education aimed at widespread improvement in practice will require texts and manuals directed to professional practice. We need an expanded emphasis on applied materials in the form of procedural guides or manuals for professional practice.

These procedural guides will be varied in their level of complexity or the professional competence required to make appropriate use of the procedure. This is true of all professions. In medicine, for example, the treatment of a cut with a few stitches is not in the same category with an appendectomy, but procedures have been spelled out for both applications of professional skill. In engineering, there are established professional procedures for the design of a twenty-foot culvert or the design of a mile-long suspension bridge.

Some manuals or guides to professional procedure may be complex and require professional experience for their proper use. Other manuals may be simple in structure and usable by professionals with limited experience or may define sub-tasks which can be carried out by technicians under professional direction.

The term "professional operating procedure" can be defined by illustration:

Stuart Chapin spells out a professional operating procedure for comprehensive urban planning in his book *Urban Land Use Planning*.

The National Resources Planning Board devised an operating procedure for capital improvement programming.

The International City Managers Association has sponsored a series of Local Planning Administration which culminated in the 1968 edition, *Principles and Practice of Urban Planning.*

The Model Neighborhoods demonstration program is aimed at devising operational procedures for coordinating social and physical programming for a district of a city.

The terms "operational guide" or "professional procedure" are used in this paper to emphasize the application to practice. In no way is this intended to indicate a diminution of professional responsibility to exercise judgment or be innovative in practice.

It is also recognized that there is a tendency for professional procedures to be restrictive of flexibility where bureaucratically administered. Advocacy planning implies professional services for a client with legitimate but special interests. Guiding policy for this area of planning practice is needed, but it could be organized in a useful form which need not be a rigid set of rules.

We need a systematic approach to the provision of effective procedures for planning practice. We have useful models in many areas of survey, of plan formulation, and of program. There are important gaps, however, which can only be filled by pioneering efforts in the professional offices or in the professional schools.

One of the most demanding tasks is the challenge to develop more effective procedures for synthesis at those points in the planning process to which this profession makes a unique contribution. The Model Neighborhoods program calls for the formulation of a neighborhood plan and a neighborhood development program which integrates social and physical objectives and activities. It is difficult to think of a more important responsibility of the profession in meeting the crisis in our cities.

In relation to urban expansion, which we all know is of crisis dimensions, there is a similar challenge to devise politically feasible and administratively effective urban regional plans and programs. These cannot be procedures for city planning at large nor can they be plans whose goals aim at a better suburbia.

A related area of need is concerned with more effective allocation of responsibilities among the levels of planning. We need to sort out the kinds of decisions which should be made at a state level from those which are national or regional. Similarly, we need to differentiate the decisions which should be made at a local neighborhood scale from those appropriate at a city-wide or county scale.

A current study at the University of Arkansas is devising a professional procedure manual adapted to the smaller municipality (under 2500 population). This study recognizes the specialized needs for an effective procedure growing out of the limited scope of local decision-making and the increased dependence on relationship to a regional plan.

Another kind of approach to procedures which is needed relates to more efficient use of limited professional planning personnel. This would be directed to devising ways for greater use of technicians and para-professionals, especially where the time and specialized competence of senior professionals can be released from routine tasks.

One of our critical restraints is limitations as to the number of trained and experienced professional practitioners. Over the next five to ten years we cannot foresee any way in which the tremendous need for large numbers of experienced professionals can be met. Therefore, procedures which would expand the supporting usefulness of nonprofessionals can have major value.

To develop procedures for practice where there are presently gaps, we need teamwork between the pioneering professional offices and the professional schools. Such teamwork should make it possible to close the gap in know-how, and to communicate the results so that innovative techniques can be applied widely as soon as their usefulness has been demonstrated.

The successful efforts of a few cities or states is not an adequate response to the urgent problems of urban America. Widespread improvement of professional practice in support of programs across the nation is the essential goal for the profession.

We are faced with a more complex challenge than we were thirty years ago, but we start from a very different base.

The number of professional planners has grown at least ten-fold, and knowledge at the disposal of the practitioner has grown in depth and scope. The number of professionally-staffed agencies with a depth of experience is numerous at the city, county, regional, state, and national levels. There are more than twenty well-established professional planning programs at public and private universities across the nation. The national organizations cooperating with the profession are stronger in staffing and in financial resources.

This change in scale also creates problems. Because of the rapid increase in activity, there are problems of communications and problems of agreement on relative responsibilities. Because of the change in scale of membership, there are problems of complacency or lack of recognition of our limited resources in relation to the task we have assumed.

We need to set goals precisely if we are to move forward effectively. The American Institute of Planning, a professional development program, like any other program, needs a strategy which sets priorities and allocates resources.

Clarity as to the roles to be played and definition of the competences required to play each role, is the first step in programming.

This paper recommends that the profession's discussions focus on the urgent need for widespread expansion and improvement in professional practice. The need for expansion in scope arises from the decision of the profession to accept the challenge of a broader agenda. The need for improvement in the general level of practice arises from the fact that the number of experienced and well-trained professionals is so limited in relation to demand.

Where are the critical gaps in professional practice? How can professional resources be adapted or expanded to fill these gaps? It should be possible to identify the more urgent needs, and also to suggest where the responsibility for action might be placed—with the schools? the professional offices? with AIP? with HUD? with the American Society of Planning Officials?

We know that the members of the profession do not have the full range of capabilities required to carry forward at every level of government a successful comprehensive planning program. We know also that the set of interests held by the various members of the profession ranges widely. The 1966 report of the Committee on Restatement of Institute Purposes made the following findings about practice:

> While, in the past, planners have been primarily engaged in the preparation of plans for the physical development of urban areas, there is a definite trend toward involvement of increasing numbers of planners in planning programs for larger areal units (counties, regions, states).
>
> There is a clear trend toward emergence of comprehensive planning which includes social and economic development as activities integral with planning for the physical development of areas. A significant number of Institute members are engaged in these activities.

Relatively speaking, the number of individuals practicing the full range of the planning process is declining. Increasing numbers of those engaged in the practice of planning are becoming specialists in various areas of planning work such as: economic studies, transportation planning, or urban renewal; municipal, state or regional jurisdictions; and physical, social or economic development.

In approaching the definition of roles, a useful focus would be the question of clients. Which clients require what services through what professional competences? If the profession is to serve the whole society and not just segments of it, the needs of all clients must be considered.

The *client approach* also raises more sharply some of the ethical questions which the profession must recognize and resolve. Clarity of lines of responsibility between a professional office and various governmental agencies and interest groups is essential to integrity in practice.

With *increased state, county, and regional planning activity,* the relative roles of professionals at various levels require consistency of definition. The system of planning activity may vary by state or region, but it should be defined and not left ambiguous.

Within the planning team, the *generalist role* and responsibility must be recognized for its critical contribution to the unique synthesis functions of comprehensive planning. The trend toward specialization is logical and appropriate so long as professional leadership and teamwork continue to focus on comprehensive development planning and programming.

There has been a strong tendency in the past to think of the professional planner in one role only: the director of the city planning agency. With the emergence of large offices, the need to recognize and define the other professional roles in the planning team is vital to success of their programs. With differences of scale and scope (urban regional planning or model cities), there is an equally important need to redefine the membership of the teams and the professional roles of these team members.

New terms emerge—state planner, transportation planner, renewal planner, social planner, advocate planner. What are the professional roles identified by these terms? How does a planner become qualified to fill such roles? Are these areas of specialization in the graduate schools of planning?

In the course of discussions leading to the report of the Committee on Restatement of Institute Purposes, several diagrams were drafted to supplement written statements in description of professional practice. The Committee members found a particular diagram, a cube, especially helpful in describing the scope of comprehensive planning. The cube diagram projects the planning process on one axis. On another axis is the hierarchy of area jurisdictions and scales. On the third axis of the cube is the scope of subject matter or content.

In 1938 the American Institute of Planners expanded the scope along the scale axis to move from neighborhood and city to include region, state, and nation. In 1968 the Institute committed itself to expand the scope of content beyond the physical environment to include social and economic development planning.

The cube diagram makes it possible to see the place of varied roles which may be appropriately chosen by different members of the Institute. It is also possible to visualize the range of capabilities which must be brought together in relation to any specific planning assignment. The cube diagram provides an over-all framework, a way of describing the whole of professional practice.

The particular usefulness of the cube diagram is, then, as one form of framework encompassing the full scope of activity which the various members of this profession now practice or may reach for. It is a diagram which permits us to place in context the activities of any member or of any professional program.

Comprehensive planning should be defined as the work of those who engage in efforts, within a delimited geographic area ranging from a neighborhood to an international region, to identify and order the physical, social, and economic relationships implicit in development programs. Comprehensive planning may be for a government, a group of governments, or private organizations; the essence is that it have an area dimension; be directed toward determination and achievement of goals; and formulate a development plan which orders effectively the physical, social, and economic relationships.

Sector One is the planning process. In application, the process may be structured with three to eight or more steps. A four-step sequence is stated because the last three of these steps identify synthesis activities, which is the unique professional contribution of comprehensive planning.

Sector Two is the hierarchy of scale. These units also might be structured differently, but the series used is representative.

Sector Three is the subject matter or substantive scope. This is stated in

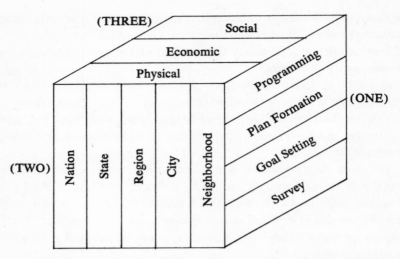

the terms physical, social, economic. It can also be stated in systems, such as transportation, residence, industry, education, health, welfare, etc.

This paper recommends a strategy of approach to meet the need for a rapidly expanded range and volume of professional practice.

This strategy calls for allocation of resources to a two-fold program which would coordinate development of professional procedural guides and manuals with continuing education for practicing professionals.

Such a program can use existing know-how to improve and extend current practice. Such a program will depend upon innovative work to devise procedures which will expand the scope of professional competence.

The essential first step to such a program is the definition of roles—roles which indicate clearly the professional services to be provided and the professional competences required. This paper suggests that reference to a common framework, the "cube diagram," would facilitate a series of related and comparable definitions of role for the professional planner in physical design, in social planning, in economic planning, in transportation, in health, in multi-professional firms, at various levels of government.

This paper recommends that attention be given to the need for continuing education and professional procedures to raise the planner's capability in each role.

The following questions will prove useful in guiding the profession toward improved professional practice procedures:

1. What illustrations do we have of operational professional practice procedures which could and should be more widely used?

2. What gaps in professional procedure should be given priority by devising operational guides from present innovative cases?

3. Where should innovative case efforts be focused to develop professional procedures needed for specific purposes?

4. What roles are being defined for professional planners which will require complex client relationships, interprofessional activity or otherwise raise questions of ethics, and therefore questions of procedure in professional practice?

5. What approaches to continuing education can be most effective for the agency directors, for generalists, for specialists, and for other professional roles?

6. What responsibilities should be assumed by HUD, by state planning agencies, by professional offices, and by the professional schools?

7. What cooperative efforts should be considered or expanded with other professions and disciplines?

The findings and recommendations which come from efforts to answer these questions should make a significant start toward an inventory of urgent needs and rewarding projects leading to more effective practice.

A strategy of emphasis and direction, explicitly stated, should be devised to answer two urgent needs for professional role definition and for expansion of professional competence and professional practice:

1. The Model Neighborhoods demonstration program requires determination of concepts and procedures of approach to social development planning. Adaptations of planning process and definition of new professional roles are essential to the success of this vital program.

2. Development planning for the urban region requires the sorting of responsibilities and roles of professionals in federal, state, and local governments. Concepts and procedures for multi-level planning systems are essential to effective regional development.

Both challenges are central to resolving urgent national problems associated with human needs and expectations. Both call for expansion of traditional city physical development planning: Model Neighborhoods programs require innovations in scope for use on the *content* sector of practice; urban region programs require innovations in scope focused on the *scale* sector or practice.

The results of the current discussions of planning's changing roles may expand these two critical areas to three, four, or five areas of practice requiring priority attention by the profession.

These discussions may also urge priority changes and additions to basic research and professional degree programs, as well as to applied procedures and continuing education.

If so, this paper will have served its purpose: to define a strategy of approach, emphasis, and direction for professional development for the decade of the Seventies.

HERBERT J. GANS

Center for Urban Education, Columbia University. Formerly assistant planner of Chicago Housing Authority and Professor of City Planning at the University of Pennsylvania. Consultant to HUD, the National Advisory Commission on Civil Disorders, and many other public and private agencies. M.A. and Ph.D., University of Chicago; Ph.D. in City Planning, University of Pennsylvania. Author: *People and Plans; Essays on Urban Problems and Solutions; The Levittowners: Ways of Life and Politics in a New Suburban Community; The Urban Villagers: Group and Class in the Life of Italian-Americans.*

The Need for Planners Trained in Policy Formulation

A COMMENT ON THE WETMORE PAPER

Any discussion of how the planning profession can be prepared for its changing role must be based on an analysis of how that role is changing. Louis Wetmore's analysis has described the change largely as it is perceived by the American Institute of Planners and its Committee on Restatement of Institute Purposes. He stresses two major components: the addition of social and economic development to the traditional concern with physical development; and the creation of planning specialties, for example, transportation planning and social planning.

Although no one can predict accurately how the role of the planner will change in the future, I believe that the AIP's redefinition is not far-reaching enough, and that it may even be obsolescent in a few years. Actually, a professional organization, regardless of what profession it represents, is rarely a viable source of professional redefinition, and for three reasons. First, professional organizations must limit themselves to highly general role statements because they represent many different practitioners whom they must place under the definitional umbrella. Second, such organizations are almost by nature conservative. They are dominated by the senior members of the profession who scarcely look with favor on role redefinitions that would make them appear old-fashioned. This is as true of the American Medical Association and the American Sociological Association as of the AIP. Third, and more important, a professional association rarely plays an important part in determining the professional roles of its members. These roles are determined primarily by the clients of the professional, or in the case of the bureaucratic professional, by his employer. In other words, the future role of planners is going to be determined largely by the cities and other political bodies which hire them as employees or consultants.

These political bodies, particularly the large cities which are most influential in shaping the role of the profession, are now beginning to demand, and will demand much more insistently in the future, a role change by the planner that is considerably more radical than that suggested by AIP or set forth in the Wetmore paper. What some cities are already saying is that the condition of the city is becoming so critical that neither their traditional methods of political decision-making nor planners' traditional techniques of comprehensive planning will be sufficient. Instead of making comprehensive physical plans or comprehensive plans or physical plans, planners must develop a method of planning that will provide the cities with rational but politically relevant advice on how to solve the problems of the city.

To put it another way, what the cities are asking is that the city planner become a *planner* who deals with the current and urgent problems of the city, and cease being an *urbanist,* a professional concerned with the physical city and an advocate of the ideal (or comprehensively planned) city.

Let me spell out what I mean. By planning, I mean a method and process of decision-making which includes the proper formulation of the problems which the city needs to solve (or of the goals it wishes to achieve); the determination of the causes of these problems; and the formulation of those policies, action programs, and decisions which will deal with the causes to solve the problem, and will do so democratically and without undesirable financial, political, social or other consequences. This conception of planning embraces rationality insofar as it calls for a causal analysis of the problem, and for the choice of those policies and programs which can be shown, empirically and logically, to deal with the causes and solve the problem.

Planning as I have defined it can be applied to the problems of cities, business firms, political institutions, or any other social body which has problems (or seeks to achieve goals). This conception of planning is, of course, totally different from either traditional comprehensive physical planning or the AIP's new definition of comprehensive planning.

Traditional comprehensive planning was (and is) neither comprehensive nor planning, as I define it. It was not comprehensive because it dealt only with certain spatial aspects of the city (as if a city were mainly a set of land uses), and ignored many of the economic processes of community life, and almost all of the social, cultural, and political processes. It concerned itself with space but not with people and their social groupings; with the location of facilities but not with what went on inside these facilities; and with land values but not with social values.

More important, comprehensive planning was not planning, because it did not involve the formulation of problems and goals and the determination of policies and programs that would solve problems or achieve goals. Instead, it was an attempt to create an ideal urban environment through the advocacy of a set of preordained solutions which, put together, made up the master plan. Among the most important of these preordained solutions were the separation of land uses by zoning; the mixing of house types and densities in residential areas; the creation of physically bounded and school-centered neighborhoods; the development in large numbers of a few favored public facilities, including parks, playgrounds, libraries, civic centers, and marinas; the establishment of large amounts of open space; the control and delimitation of city growth; the development of efficient central business districts and transportation systems to reach it; and the creation of an economic base which would maximize land values and tax receipts.

These solutions were preordained because the planner accepted them unquestioningly as proper professional practice, without ever asking what goals these solutions were supposed to achieve, whether they actually achieved them, or what consequences they would have for the city and for the many economically and socially important, but spatially unimportant, urban functions, institutions, and social groupings. And because they were preordained, they were proposed in master plan after master plan, with little variation between plans, regardless of the distinctive characteristics of the city being planned. Because these solutions were intended to bring about an ideal urban environment, the professional who formulated them was an urbanist rather than a planner. And because he was striving after an ideal, he was also an advocate rather than a planner. Ironic as it may seem, although the term advocacy planning is less than five years old, the planner has always been primarily an advocate, explicitly of his own vision of the city, but implicitly also of certain special economic and political interests.

Modern city planning began as one of a number of late nineteenth-century reform movements, headed by upper- and upper-middle class native Americans who were disturbed about the urbanization of their previously agrarian nation, about the coming of the poor European immigrants, and about the slums, high crime rates, and socialist movements that appeared after their arrival. The first planners were hoping that by physical planning, they could eliminate the slums and break up the ethnic ghettoes, creating middle-class urban neighborhoods as substitutes for the rural towns they loved, with parks as substitutes for the open space of the farmland. In these neighborhoods, the immigrants would be mixed with native middle-class neighbors and would thus stop behaving like poor people or demanding more radical change in the American economy and political structure. What the early planners sought, often quite unconsciously, was the City Orderly. Later, as planning became a profession dominated by architects, they also stressed the City Beautiful, and when planning became a commission in, but not of, city government, headed by business leaders, the professionals also emphasized the City Efficient. Again largely unconsciously, they advocated the goals of the business community: for example, zoning to protect the central business districts and residential areas, their concern with land value maximization to increase the profitability of property, and their emphasis on efficiency, to keep taxes minimal.

In short, the master planners were advocates for themselves, for the city's business interests, and for the upper- and upper middle-class residents of the community. Indeed, modern advocacy planning, which seeks to represent the interests of the poor and the black community in the planning process, has developed precisely because comprehensive planning has largely ignored their problems, goals, or needs.

Whether or not AIP's redefinition of comprehensive planning will bring about any significant change in the method, solutions, and explicit as well as implicit advocacy of planning, remains to be seen. Insofar as the redefinition retains the basic emphasis on "a delimited geographic area," it seems to suggest that physical planning will be of prime importance, with social and economic development programs as an appendage.

As noted previously, however, the planner's future role will not be determined by AIP definitions, but by the cities and other political bodies which employ him. These will increasingly be asking the planner to concern himself not with urbanist solutions but with plans to resolve the crucial problems of the urban crisis.

The most crucial problems fall into two categories: how to eliminate poverty and segregation, and how to cope with the city's own municipal poverty. More specifically, planning is needed to help do away with unemployment and under-employment, particularly among the ghetto youth; to create income maintenance programs for those who cannot work; to educate the children of the poor and to alter the structure of the school and teaching profession to achieve this goal; to build housing that the poor can afford; to deal with crime, delinquency, drug addiction, and mental illness; to resolve the conflict between the police and those residents who are protesting the *status quo;* and to incorporate the poor and, particularly the black poor, into the social, economic, and political structure of the community—to mention just a few problems.

In addition, planning is needed to find ways to resolve the city's financial crisis at a time when the large tax payers, residential and nonresidential, are leaving the city. Other problems include how to get the suburbs to bear their share of financing city services and dealing with urban poverty and segregation; how to cope with the increasing centralization of the urban bureaucracy at a time when many residents demand political and administrative decentralization; and how to restructure the decision-making apparatus so that citizen participation can be increased without leading to a total breakdown in decision-making.

Of course, cities will continue to ask the planner to deal with the space-related problems with which traditional physical planning has concerned itself, especially since some of the crucial urban problems cited above have spatial implications as well. Spatial considerations will remain important for two other reasons: urban jurisdictions are delimited spatially; and the federal government is still encouraging physical planning, so that cities must participate in the 701 program in order to obtain federal funds for capital investment. But cities will no longer be satisfied with the pre-ordained physical solutions that do not work; for example, urban renewal programs that require large scale relocation, especially of Negroes, even when such programs are proposed as part of the Model Cities package.

In order to deal with their crucial problems, the cities will need not physical plans or comprehensive plans but plans that deal with specific problems and their causes, and that result in policies, or policy guidelines, action programs, and even individual decisions. For this type of planning, the cities will need not physical planners or social planners or economic planners, but planners per se—professionals who can analyze problems and their causes and can develop policies and programs to deal with these problems. This requires planning analysts trained in the new policy-oriented kinds of economics, political science, and sociology; and planners trained in policy formulation, program development, systems analysis and cost-benefit analysis.

In addition, the cities will ask planners not to hide themselves in planning commissions which exist independently of city hall—often as ivory towers erected by civic leaders who consider themselves above politics. They will demand that the planners become advisors to city hall, so that they can participate in the day-to-day decision-making process. As a result, planners will have to deal with the political aspects of planning; for example, in framing goals, considering the political consequences of policies and programs, encouraging citizen participation—and not just citizen consent to preordained solutions—and working with advocate planners, whether they represent the poor or the Chamber of Commerce.

Many traditionally inclined planners will undoubtedly oppose the demands for role change asked of them by the cities. Some will argue that if the city fathers only permitted them to do old-style comprehensive planning, the problems of the city would be resolved. That argument will not be persuasive anymore. Others will argue that neither their professional ideology nor their training equips them to deal with the social-economic-political problems of the city. That argument will only result in their being replaced by new professionals, trained in social science, policy formulation, and systems analysis. Indeed, such new professionals will be the planners in the future, for only they can offer the kind of advice that their clients and employers need.

Eventually, then, the profession and the AIP will have to make a choice between becoming planners or remaining urbanists. If they choose the former, they will undoubtedly play a major role in the future of the city; if they choose the latter, they will perform some useful functions but will play only a minor role in solving America's urban problems.

If the profession decides to opt for planning, it can prepare itself by changing the focus of AIP, by reaching out to the policy-oriented social scientists, systems analysts, and other new specialists dealing with urban problems; and by supporting the new forms of planning education now emerging in some university schools of planning, departments of urban affairs, and the even newer schools of policy study that are just beginning. But such forms of preparation are ancillary; the main task is on the job itself, to turn away from the preordained solutions and their new social and economic development appendages, and to apply and perfect the methods of planning I have described.

If we choose, as a profession, to transform ourselves from urbanists into planners, I can predict that in a generation or so, there will be an AIP which will include all planners, whether they work for cities, other governmental levels, anti-poverty organizations, school systems, medical services, manufacturing firms; in short, all organizations, public and private, who need to plan for their futures. At its annual meetings, such an institute will concern itself with the theoretical, practical, and methodological issues of planning and the planning process, while sub-groups hold special sessions devoted to the different substantive specialties, whether problems of city government, poverty, peace, TV programming, or automobile production. But if AIP remains a profession representing urbanists, then I can envisage, someday, a court battle in which a much larger and more powerful organization of planners will sue to demand the exclusive right to the term "planner."

PATRICK J. CUSICK, JR.

Vice President and General Manager, Litchfield Park Properties. In charge of the planning and development of the new town of Litchfield Park, Arizona, near Phoenix. Previously construction engineer, assistant city manager, and Executive Director of Pittsburgh Regional Planning Association and the Southwestern Pennsylvania Regional Planning Commission. B.S.C.E., University of Pittsburgh; M.C.P., Harvard University.

Extending the Public's Acceptance of Planning

A COMMENT ON THE WETMORE PAPER

Few planners have been attracted to the profession merely to prepare plans, but because the profession was viewed as a sort of "thinking man's" way to influence, for the better, the environment of this country. Certainly the opportunities to plan at every governmental level have proliferated almost beyond planners' wildest dreams during this past decade, resulting in the need for better prepared planners of many varieties, with concomitant increases in income and social acceptance. Sophisticated and expensive planning techniques and equipment have become accepted as necessary. All of this has resulted in a veritable deluge of plans.

Here I pose a crucial question: To what extent have plans had any substantial impact in bringing about a better environment? However uneasy it may make planners to consider this question objectively, it deserves a very high priority on the profession's agenda—before some less understanding individual or agency undertakes to answer it for us.

How would I propose going about this? First I would embark on a pilot project covering planning in a city of less than 50,000, a city over 50,000, a metropolitan-regional agency, and a state agency where, in each instance, there has existed for some years—not less than three nor more than ten—a reasonably competent, published comprehensive plan or significant parts of such a plan. The principal thrust of the project would be to study every conceivable aspect of the area covered by each plan in an attempt to learn how much of it has been implemented; what the prospects seem to be for implementation in the near future; and the main factors for the successes (or lack thereof) achieved or likely to be achieved—quality of plans, continuity, finances, personalities, etc.

The goal of the undertaking should not be either praise or condemnation of the planning agencies studied—indeed, their identity might well be kept confidential—but the development of a standardized approach and measurement criteria that could be employed, with appropriate improvements during the years ahead, to measure with reasonable objectivity the effectiveness of the planning function. I will leave it to you to imagine the value of this type to planning, planners, and AIP—not to mention the clients—all the people of our urban areas. It is the people, of course, who cast the final vote for or against the comprehensive, planned renewal and development of our environment.

A German planner who visited the United States was quoted in the April 1965 *ASPO Newsletter* as follows: "In the course of my trip [to the US], the impression ripened that the crisis of planning is a crisis of society, of which the planners, in spite of honest self-criticism, are not yet conscious: they are looking for the shortcomings in their own ranks while in fact they often seem to be the scapegoats of a society which cries out for planning and yet repels it as uncompatible with its tradition and the sacred principles of unlimited individual freedom and opportunity."

Because my experiences and my observations of the activities of the planning profession indicate that, as a general rule, our German colleague's remark is uncomfortably true, it has occurred many times to me that we ought to react to the implications it contains—at the very least to the extent of developing and carrying out a carefully-conceived, well-financed, continuing program designed to improve the general level of acceptance and utilization of planning in this country.

How do I suggest that AIP go about this? For a starter I would propose that it engage the services of the best available Madison Avenue public relations firm to develop both a well-rounded short- and long-range program of activities and the costs be aimed solely at overcoming this public resistance to the utilization of comprehensive planning.

While I believe that much can be accomplished in the short run by a well-considered public information program, the long-range aspect is every bit as important. In the latter context I recall a recurrent proposal that AIP take the lead, alone or in concert with others, to develop teaching materials on our cities and plan for inclusion in elementary and high school curriculums. As I have already noted, this would have a long-range pay-off; but this seems particularly appropriate for a profession whose areas of concern include the future as well as the present. The validity of this approach is found in the success reportedly achieved by the *Wacker Manual* in developing support for planning in Chicago in the early decades of the century as an outgrowth of its use as a textbook for generations of citizens during their childhood in the local public schools.

It would not overstretch the Wetmore proposals at all to include these suggestions aimed at ascertaining the effectiveness of planning and the improvement of the environment for planning. Both should be invaluable in many ways in preparing us for our changing role; they envision regular, formal, external inputs into the process which appeared to me to be the missing link in the paper under consideration.

D. Elton Trueblood, in his book *The People Called Quakers,* explains why this group has always exerted an influence beyond its numbers by saying: "But it would be a serious mistake to see the central Quaker message in purely intellectual terms. . . . It was reserved for John Hunt . . . to state the central point with a clarity which modern man has not surpassed. 'Perfection,' wrote Hunt, 'does not consist in teaching truth, but in doing it.' "

Though the planning profession has never achieved perfection—an unattainable state for mortals—by "doing" the truth for over five decades in the face of public resistance to comprehensive planning in a nation which regards as sacred the "principles of unlimited individual freedom and opportunity," as noted by our German colleague, the planning profession has made a considerable impact on public attitudes. The Wetmore approach, strengthened by my proposal for critical evaluation of the effectiveness of plans, can add greatly to the profession's ability to "do" the truth in a manner that will extend public acceptance of planning.

LAWRENCE MANN

Chairman, Department of City and Regional Planning, Rutgers, The State University, New Jersey. Former planning advisor to the Chilean Government; acting coordinator, Ford Foundation Technical Assistance Program in Community Facilities and Planning. A.B., M.C.P., and Ph.D., Harvard University. Harvard national scholar and graduate national scholar. Received the Frank Knox Memorial Fellowship (1959).

The Fuzzy Future
of Planning Education

There is an old and still not fully answered question: "Who plans the planners?" (while the planners are busy planning plans?) It is a complex question, posed, I think, first in terms of central economic planners with the suspicion that their preparation might be somehow sinisterly manipulated. In our present context, it has to do with the nature of the teachers, and with the nature of the students in educational programs that in one way or another called themselves "planning education." A sub-question that we are going to hear more and more often, is implied: "Which planning?" However, in the real world the broad question of "Who plans the planner?" can unfortunately be disposed of with much less analysis. Its answer is: "Nobody." Just as in the old saw about the personal lives of planners, few things are more planless than planning education. This is true despite the fact that most planning schools are now undergoing some kind of continuous but *ad hoc* curriculum revision. There is much imitative or traditional thinking, there are some impressionistic insights, there are clear elements of academic and other politics, and there is some public relations gimmickry; but there is hardly enough explicitness of objectives or calculation of alternatives and their probable outcomes to justify the term "planning" as it applies to curriculum requirements in planning schools.

There is another area of question concerning the appropriate identification of the products of planning schools. Years ago, Charles Abrams spoke of them as "planning clerks." Hans Blumenfeld has talked of the "universal dilettante." Norton Long has dubbed them the "intellectual gun-for-hire." Harvey Perloff has talked of the "generalist with a specialty." And most recently, Michael Brooks and Michael Stegman have written of the "generalist within a specialization." There is no end of other designations, some more conventional and some scarcely printable, but the question is whether any or all of these designations apply to the products of the planning schools now or in the future. Behind this lies the related question of whether the planning schools are preparing people for any real job market or markets. Or are they simply assuming that employers, given the recent and growing seller's market, will take anything they can get if it is appropriately labelled "planner" and certified with a postgraduate degree?

Dependent on these questions, it would seem, are the more complex questions of the kinds of training and the appropriate lengths. For example, only if the schools are preparing for explicit job markets, can questions of which skills are best learned in school (as opposed to those that are best learned on the job) be answered. The appropriate length of graduate study, it must be suggested, depends largely upon this information and decisions taken from it. Similarly, present projections on the basis of the general term "planner" must be considered highly suspect as guides to understanding the future supply and demand of faculty, students, and graduates.

The aim of this discussion, then, is to clarify some of the aspects of the situation of planning education for today. With this, and if we really want to, we may begin now to program education for planning or "plannings."

From my responsibilities in one of the country's newer and faster growing schools, I bring to this subject some of the concerns and some of the insights that my more experienced colleagues in other schools possess. Beyond this, I am bolstered in daring to discuss this subject by the following facts:

After more than three years out of the country, teaching and planning advisory work at several levels in Latin America, I have had to effect a re-entry into US planning education. This has made me particularly sensitive to how much, and yet how little, things can change in a brief span.

I have authored, given, and graded the first written examination for the registration of professional planners in the United States. The relevance of this fact is that the graduates of planning schools, including a couple of former students of mine from Harvard and Chapel Hill, did not score as well on this exam, even in the theoretical questions, as did some of the self-trained planners. This alone is enough to drive one in search of some basic answers concerning planning education.

Before further tracing the implications of current planning education and its relation to planning practice, I will set down my own version of the recent history of planning education. You are free to write it all off as value judgments if you wish. But the following is pretty much common knowledge, at least in the circles of my rotation. And the events I shall mention are ones that I think have some implication for the future.

In the beginning, of course, there was Harvard. Our saga must begin with that venerable institution's decision to offer formal postgraduate degree programs in this field through its Graduate School of Design. Had Harvard decided to offer planning as an undergraduate program, parallel to its nonprofessional liberal arts concentrations for architects or engineers, the nature of planning education during the succeeding thirty-five years would probably have been quite different. But the tenor of the times had made planning appear quite clearly as a polish to be applied primarily to such existing professionals as architects, engineers, or lawyers. And it was in this spirit that an embracive but uncertain discipline was born.

M.I.T., in her curious competition with Harvard in those times, could not long allow a new and potentially technical field to be dominated by its sibling school. Not many months had passed before that institution also had a program. M.I.T.'s program, if the truth be told, grew much more rapidly than Harvard's, while keeping on a steady, unspectacular course with fewer ups and downs. M.I.T.'s impact on the planning movement—and certainly on the planning education movement—has consequently been much greater. M.I.T. produced the carriers and the propagators of a sure and technical professional doctrine. Harvard's output was much more mixed and generally included more humanistic questioners of given truths than any real continuity from professor to practitioner. It was less "professional." I am aware of exceptions on either side, but I am also sure that the weight of the instances are on the confirming side.

Columbia and Cornell developed programs of surprisingly moderate impact, though the latter has at times turned out a middling share of key men in planning education. The later program at Penn continued the pattern in the Ivy League, while concurrent developments at Berkeley (University of California) and Chapel Hill (University of North Carolina) brought planning education into the public institutions. The latter case was particularly instructive. On the initiative of the regional sociologist, Howard Odum, the planning program was set up in the graduate school, as there was no design school in Chapel Hill. But the early faculty was heavily influenced by M.I.T. in both doctrine and in subject matter. This illustrates, I think, the way the M.I.T. viewpoint made its way into initially nontechnical liberal arts settings.

The introduction of the Ph.D. degree in planning at Harvard, and since the 1940's, at every other school that aims high, has made a major impact on planning education. Some of the reasons for this will be developed later.

There was another highly impactful event, or episode, in planning education that came from outside the mainstream of the mentioned planning schools. This, of course, was the University of Chicago's program in "Planning" (not just city planning but Planning with a capital P), which owed so much to historical accidents of the 1930's. These centered around the person of Rexford Guy Tugwell, economist and member of the New York City Planning Board before being appointed Governor of Puerto Rico, where he made a personal synthesis of urban—physical and national—economic planning. Following this, he formed the graduate program in "Planning" per se. The intellectual validity of this latter is still being debated by the faculty he formed, the students it produced, and others that both have affected. (Harvey Perloff, Martin Meyerson, Edward Banfield, and Richard Meier, as well as a number of others, were included in the faculty. Jack Dyckman, John Friedmann, and Lowdon Wingo were among the students.) It was a short-lived and probably an unstable mixture, but planning education in this country has never been the same. The impact of this innovative program is quite evident. Indeed, scarcely a year goes by without someone attempting to resurrect some aspect of the intellectual spirit that marked this venture in planning education.

The impact of the Chicago School of Planning was partly facilitated through its breaking up and the fact that this coincided roughly with an upheaval in the planning school at Harvard. Together these events started a chain of musical chairs, involving principally Penn, Harvard, a few other schools, and most lately Berkeley, that has probably not yet played itself out.

The panorama of the relative faculty strengths of the various planning schools today is not entirely clear, at least not as clear as it was a few years ago; but one point is evident. Berkeley has become predominant and shows no real signs of "peaking out." Also, North Carolina and a number of the other state universities are much stronger than they have ever been before. In this fact probably lies the next round of developments in the planning schools: the solidification of programs in the larger public institutions. The traditional growth in the major private institutions will probably come from major foundation grants, such as those recently given to Harvard, M.I.T., Columbia, and Chicago. But it is not at all clear that the net beneficiaries will be the planning schools themselves. Rather, it is probable that urban questions with policy implications will be developing in various parts of these universities. And we may expect something parallel to be happening in some of the public institutions for reasons that will be discussed below.

Throughout the early years and decades of the planning education movement, certainly up through the 1950's and through part of the 1960's, there were certain implicit principles operating. We should discuss each of these in turn.

One of the most memorable myths of the urban planning movement in the United States has been that, despite the apparent (even obvious, in retrospect) diversity of approaches, skills, and roles included, planning was really all of one piece. The clear implication was that the planning schools should be producing something of a homogeneous product. And this engendered what I have called elsewhere "the salt and pepper theory" of planning education. This means simply that, if a man comes to a planning school with design skills, you should starve these and teach him the social, economic, political, and administrative perspectives to make a complete planner. Alternatively, if a student comes in with great strength in social science research technique, you should starve this, teaching him drafting, design, aesthetics, etc., at least to the level of a highly informed consumer of such services to be provided by specialists. In no case would a man be allowed to grow further in the undergraduate specialty he brought to graduate education.

Harvey Perloff's famous proposal for the "generalist with a specialty" is really a variance of the "salt and pepper theory." Under this proposal, the student *would* be allowed to develop a specialty, which might or might not be his main undergraduate skill area. But, until recently, this has been more of a slogan than an operational principle of planning education.

An older dogma of planning education came from the view of the planner as a sort of artisan. This meant that planning education was simply relieving practitioners of the task of extensive apprenticeships. It was thus appropriate for the planning faculties to be staffed largely by experienced planners either "put out to pasture" or else leaving the workshop at more tender ages for their own good reasons. In either case, the main function of planning education was that of the "gate keeper," to assure that inferior items did not insert themselves into the chosen numbers of the guild. This attitude was most evident a few years back in the approaches of certain professors in the schools, rather than in program-wide policy, and I suppose it must still persist in some cases today. The major responsibilities recently accorded the planning schools by the American Institute of Planners (and state boards of registration where these exist) opens the door for the perpetuation and strengthening of "gate keeper" tendencies. But it is doubtful that the planning schools are internally capable of orienting themselves in this way, at least in the narrow way it has sometimes been used in the past.

A third area of traditional doctrine, partly related to the other two, has to do with the predominant importance of the studio or workshop course. Such classes were to simulate the real world and to keep training from being entirely theoretical. A very large proportion of the student's time in some programs has been devoted to such courses. But, in operation, these studio courses often tended to arrive at such unreal problems that their educational value was dubious. Moreover, they required so much student time that often students simply did not do the reading or other work for nonstudio courses. Finally, with their vast scope and compressed succession of deadlines, they often made decision-making on team proposals a caricature of the worst elements of office practice. A studio problem is usually decided by head-on collisions in which the one with the thickest skull survives, and then having the rest of the team draw up his solutions to the problem at hand. But the gravest difficulty with studio instruction in graduate planning schools has been the excessive costs in terms of necessary faculty imput, space and materials requirements, and opportunity costs for students in terms of other educational opportunities, relative to the demonstrable benefits that are obtained from such instruction.

Sometime in the early 1960's, a quiet revolution began in planning education. It is far from over today.

Due, presumably, to a combination of an improved student body and an increasingly younger faculty, the old myth of the "all purpose planner" began to break down. Efforts were made for several years to introduce options within the planning program, to little avail. Then, suddenly, the concept of separate tracks for different options within planning were independently discovered in half a dozen different schools. There is even some competition now between the planning schools to see how many different options they can offer. Concurrent with this were attacks on the old central concept of physical planning as the identifying focus of education and practice in AIP. Particularly after the "war on poverty" began, many of the brighter students and faculty came to see modifications to the physical environment as almost trivial approaches to the solution of basic urban social and economic problems. Not only did options alternative to the traditional physical planning approach come into being, they came to dominate in the planning schools. The traditional planning approach has, in some schools, become little more than residual to some of the *avant-garde* options.

Melvin Weber and some of his Berkeley colleagues have tried to pull together the sense of the newer approaches under the term "new planning." That is, a sort of combination of "new politics," "new math," and "new economics." As I have remarked elsewhere, this probably implies little more than a "new uncertainty" for the movement as a whole. For, while I have actually known one or two people who have the combination of high vocational aptitudes for both computer programming and social work, it would pretty clearly be a mistake to predicate our future programs on the existence of a large cadre of such people.

An alternative view of the emerging planning would be to admit that planning has simply become a very broad and sometimes leaky umbrella. It shelters many different kinds of people, with different kinds of skills and approaches. Nor need we assume that any kind of mythical "planning team" is implied by the kinds of people who are being trained to call themselves planners. The outlook is considerably more anarchistic with the model of "each doing his thing" probably a more accurate description than any alternative.

What have been the consequences of these abrupt changes? Specialization has certainly some positive attributes: students are probably happier and are probably being better trained for something specific that they can do. The faculty, particularly the younger faculty who have become highly specialized in one approach or another, are probably happier because they have less of a mixed bag in their classes. But there are also some questionable features of the move toward options and specialization. Separate empires, bitterly competitive, have appeared in some schools. It is widely known that students in one option are sometimes systematically harassed when they take the required course given by the faction controlling another option. And I have already seen cases of students in the same school for two years who have never met or even heard of one another.

The next stage of development in planning schools, it would seem to me, must either be a return to a neutral common core, if one can be discovered, or else an outright schism from among the separate option programs. And, as I said earlier, I believe the schools must take a new look at their offerings in terms of real job markets.

Before going any further, and certainly before starting to make recommendations, I think we must say some blunt words about the state of planning education today. I would like to make the following points:

1. While many of the good graduates of good planning schools perform well, many of the most competent people in one or more skill areas have never attended planning school. Others similarly skilled attended poor planning schools or have done very badly in planning school, or both. On the other hand, some of the best graduates (in terms of grades) from the best planning schools (in terms of general reputation and faculty) are very poorly skilled in all, or almost all, of the basic activities of planning as defined by what members of AIP do. The point is that there is no one-to-one relation between education and quality of performance, as some seem to assume. At best, success in high quality planning education is probably just one index of an ability to learn certain skills or ranges of skills, to adapt to new approaches and techniques.

2. The skills that planning students have on leaving graduate study are largely refinements of skills they had when they entered; they generally are prepared to employ these skills from a broader perspective after graduate school.

3. Evidently, many of the skills planning schools have traditionally attempted to teach are either better learned on the job or else (in some cases) simply unteachable in the classroom.

4. Where planning schools have attempted to train the all-purpose planner, they have often frustrated the full development of budding skills students already have on entering graduate school, and thus lessen the potential professional contribution of these people.

5. Where planning schools have concentrated on teaching planning as it is currently practiced, their graduates have had especially difficult times adapting to the constantly new innovations in planning activity.

6. Where planning schools have concentrated on far-out approaches and technique, with little attention to the basic intellectual disciplines or to the current state of planning practice, their graduates have become specialists who often have great difficulty in adapting to their first job in planning and, at worst, are so engrossed with a passing fad as to be obsolete before they start. That such careers are usually salvaged is a tribute, not to the schools, but to the basic quality of the human resources that are entering planning and their potential for retraining.

7. The future of planning education is probably one of increasing specialization, but a basis for switching specializations through minimal later retraining is also in prospect. Since the basic objectives of planning activity must remain social, economic, and environmental in nature, the path of least risk will probably be a solid core of socio-economic, environmental, and policy sciences plus a maximum range of possible specializations open to the student.

8. The delegation to the universities by the AIP and the profession, of quality control of new professionals will probably have a snowball effect; for universities internally are constantly trying to upgrade themselves, especially at graduate levels. Thus, over time, it may be expected that it will become about as difficult to get into and to get through graduate schools of planning as it is now to get into medical school or law school. Perhaps even harder. For the broadening of the field of urban planning education on the frontiers has tended to move it out of the professional schools. And when this happens, universities tend to treat graduate programs in planning by the same criteria as those in traditional and purely academic disciplines such as physics, philosophy, history, or economics. And these latter graduate programs are geared to the production of the Ph.D., where the Master's degree is sometimes not much more than a consolation prize for failures.

9. The trend is compounded in the most reputed graduate schools of planning by constant increase in the content and the difficulty of subject matter in planning education. Justification is found in the complexity of things in the real world and in new knowledge about these matters and relationships that is constantly being developed. Several of the top planning schools in the country now have almost three full years of quite sophisticated graduate study before a Master's in City and Regional Planning degree or its equivalent can be awarded. This requires more course work than some of the Ph.D. programs in certain traditional disciplines. As a consequence, it is likely that the leading planning schools of the country (say, the top ten schools) will produce more Ph.D.'s in planning than MCRP's at some not too distant date. From the student's point of view, there are many advantages and almost no disadvantages to working toward the more prestigious degree.

As mentioned earlier, it is now widely recognized that "urban planning" covers a number of more specific approaches, roles, and subject matters. Differing elements within the profession draw upon very distinct sets of skills and carry out quite distinct sorts of activities. The day of the "jack of all trades" planner has largely passed.

It is in response to this that the trend has set in among the leading schools of planning that allows for specialization within professional education. Options are offered so that the student may orient his graduate study along one of several main lines. Three or four such options are typically available.

An alternative approach would be somewhat different. The effort is to identify the maximum number of potential specialties under the umbrella of "city and regional planning" and then to develop curricula appropriate to as many of these as possible. Three main dimensions of possible concentration in study are used.

The first of these is the *fundamental approach* to objectives and problems and to ways of dealing with these. The physical planning orientation, the relation of environmental change proposals to social and economic aims, is traditional to city and regional planning. But basically different economic planning and social planning approaches have taken or are taking shape both in the United States and abroad. Moreover, combination approaches should be considered. Thus there may be at least the following possible concentrations with regard to fundamental approach: physical, economic, and social.

The second dimension has to do with the *functional role* of the planner. Traditionally there has been confusion about this matter in the profession, and especially in planning education. For example, planners trained to be designers were expected on the job to be skilled administrators or, more recently, researchers. At least the following possible role types suggest themselves: administrator, researcher, and designer.

The third dimension consists of topical specialties of at least two kinds. First, there are the categories of human activity such as those found in general land-use classifications or generalized input-output studies: agriculture, extraction, manufacturing, commerce, transport, utilities, education, and residential households.

The other kind of topical specialty consists of the activity-combination subjects that take on special importance in planning thought and practice at a given time. Examples are urban renewal, environmental health, resources development, underdeveloped areas or countries, and internationally comparative planning.

A distinction between city planning and regional planning might not be necessary. The latter has become, in many cases, urban development policy at another scale. (The relatively rare exceptions, we feel, can be treated in other ways according to the dimensions above. Essentially, fundamental principles will apply.) Moreover, as in state planning, such a distinction implicitly supposes that a planner will be spending his professional life working in one level of government. Given present trends, we find this assumption unrealistic. Rather, we should seek to train for planning and urban policy development at any level of government and with the flexibility to move from one level to another as necessary.

The broad range of possible concentrations and specializations according to the dimensions above seeks to provide a maximum of flexibility for the student in deciding on the role he seeks in the field of planning. At the same time, it would enable us to develop faculty and curricula in the kinds of specialties and concentrations that are most likely to be required by students' interests and by employing agencies. Finally, it enables us to correctly identify the kind of training our graduates have taken, in letters of evaluation and recommendation. The product becomes more accurately and specifically labeled.

The use of the above dimensions is not merely conceptual. All courses available to graduate students in a university could be identified as corresponding to one or more locations in the three-dimensional grid. It is thus possible to identify a student's concentrations by rapid visual examination. It would not be necessary to identify specialties on the degree itself, but rather to keep an accurate record in each student's and each graduate's permanent file.

In the "umbrella approach," just as in the option approach, the question of a possible common core in planning education is bound to arise. It seems unlikely that many schools will be ready to follow M.I.T.'s recent lead in abolishing all requirements in a planning curriculum. If the physical planning core is no longer adequate to planning education, what would be the minimum courses that all students in programs called planning should take? My own experimentation with this question over the past couple of years seems to indicate that some sort of an "orientation course" is necessary. Such a course must tell where the profession or social movement of planning has come from and what are the most probable directions of its future development. Another course, experience indicates, would be a highly intensive course to acquaint the graduate student with the several most relevant disciplines applying to urban phenomena and problem—as well as planning and policy formulation. And it may be argued that any planner, whatever be "his thing," should have a solid orientation to qualitative methods, though not necessarily one that presupposes calculus. While the question is still debatable, it also seems likely that some kind of a course in planning thought or "theory" should be required in the core course, probably including something on decision theory but brought back to some sort of a practical closure. The core of the planning program could also well include an intensive "studio," or "field," or "community-linked" problem, posed broadly enough to allow each student to make use of his skills and at the same time to become acquainted with those of other disciplines. There is one more course that belongs in the core program on graduate planning curriculum. This would be a course in program budgeting, for this subject has the potential of linking most, if not all, of the various specialties emerging in planning. Beyond these elements, I am not sure that anything else in the planning curriculum should be required.

It must be faced that the planning schools, especially the most highly reputed ones, are preparing planners for a Utopian market. Planners are not being trained for jobs that exist but rather for ones that the students and professors think it would be nice to have exist. This problem becomes more serious as planners move into areas that border the recognized territory of other professions and disciplines. As planners move from physical planning into social planning or kinds of economic policy formulation, there are legitimate questions that may be posed concerning whether they are entering these new fields for any reason other than their own whim. For there are already other people there. Unless planners entering these new fields are of indisputably high competence, the outlook for later generations of planners to enter the same field will be dark indeed. And yet planners do have things to offer in a number of these new fields. It is somewhat easier for planning schools to prepare people in a truly interdisciplinary manner than it is for other professional schools or for separate academic departments. But it is not likely that the products of the planning schools in socioeconomic areas are going to be seen as uniquely qualified as compared to the products of some other professional schools (including some of the *avant-garde* social work schools), graduates of such synthetic disciplines as operations research or administration or graduates of traditional disciplinary departments such as economics or sociology. And, with a spate of new planning programs opening yearly, the profession could not maintain quality control even if it knew it wanted to. For these reasons the profession ought to take a hard look at the dangers of overproduction in the planning schools. The annual rate of granting new Master's degrees in planning is increasing geometrically in the face of a market almost directly dependent on the political mood of the country. If the late lamented war on poverty is resurrected as a war against the poor, a job market for social planners of the various kinds is seriously going to dry up. (I *know* that that is when they will most be needed; I am simply saying that the job *market* will not reflect this need.) The same could be said for "planning system scientists." Although the most talented of these will certainly survive somehow, their great dependence on the flow of federal research funds from HUD and the somewhat dubious outcome of the highly ambitious systems studies of urban problems, should give the profession pause.

The dilemma of decision on future demands for planners lies in the problem of the generalist and the specialist. The worst dangers are for people who are over-specialized in their training, who consequently cannot adapt to changing situations. It is this that makes the rediscovery of a common core of substantial proportions so important in planning education.

Perhaps it has been too horrendous to contemplate for the professors of planning, or perhaps the immensities of the unknowable have been simply too overwhelming, but the fact is that planning education has seldom given due importance to the fact that most graduates have thirty to forty years of professional lifetime ahead of them after they leave the planning school. (The professors, of course, typically do not, and it would be less than human if there were not some sign of muted jealously for intellectual offspring.)

The parallel to the useful lifetime of building is difficult to escape. We may have some lessons to learn from our own thinking about that. For example, if we think of a useful lifetime as being roughly symmetrical, or even having calculable skew, then there comes some point in the cycle of useful lifetime that is "average" or most typical. This enables us to consider the full cycle in terms of a concrete year, which sometimes is a way of simplifying human decision-making. This key year, average for the lifetime cycle, in the case of most planning students graduating in 1970, will come shortly after the year 1984. Given this rather staggering date, we must now ask whether we are really prepared to train planners today who will reach the peak of their useful effectiveness in the post-Orwellian years.

If you put the matter in proportion, however, it is really the same question that would have had to be posed by Penn, Berkeley, and Chapel Hill had they contemplated the preparation of planners to reach their peak efficiency in 1963 or 1968. Without going into details, I think most of us would agree there has been some success in both concept and fact in preparing planners over such time span. The only alternative is to plan for obsolescence and retraining at the mid-career point or perhaps every ten years. I doubt that this is feasible or really necessary. One of the principal objectives of a programmed planning education would be to minimize the frequency of retraining. This posit has some implications.

First, as noted earlier, the quality of students entering the planning schools is probably more important than the curriculum they receive during a brief two or three years of graduate study. It may well be that we should give more attention to psychological tests showing flexibility and tolerance for new ideas than to the Graduate Record Examinations if we are to prepare a group of people capable of semi-automatic adjustment to new developments in the profession without major retraining. It is also doubtful that anyone has anything like the answer on criteria for selection of graduate students. I am sure that the traditional criteria are almost worthless in predicting useful professional performance. For example, no matter how things go, heavily pigmented skin is going to be an asset, if not a prerequisite, for the functioning planner in central cities of the United States, or for a major portion of the US job market.

A second implication of what we have suggested is the careful recognition of the limitations on what can be taught at given ages and, in particular, how little a new basic approach can be imparted to graduate students in a brief span of time. Hand in hand with this is the recognition that most of the practical skills valued by planning agencies and offices are better taught on the job than in planning school. A major exception is drafting, which is better taught in high school. The implication is that the planning schools should be concentrating on the basic disciplinary approaches that make the practical skills meaningful and enable the practitioner to adapt to changes in method and approach.

A new humility about the implicit limitations of planning education should stop the trend of ever increasing programs leading to a Master's degree. When many doctorates require less course work than the three-year Master's degree now returning to vogue, something is out of order. Now that many law schools are granting the doctorate in jurisprudence or Doctor of Laws as a professional degree, now that some schools of engineering are treating a professional doctorate as standard for high-level employment, and now that doctorates in the basic sciences such as biology, chemistry, and physics are being used merely as certificates for high-level commercial employment, somewhat less awe is called for in contemplating the future of the doctorate in the field of urban planning. Several of the planning schools in this country will reach a point where they will be granting as many doctorates as Master's degrees. There are now more than 150 doctoral students enrolled in US planning schools, nearly a quarter of them at Penn. It is not likely that all these people will be effectively employed in the planning schools, and they will enter planning offices and consulting work (as some already have). In time, they will make the doctorate not unusual for the director of a large planning agency or the head of a specialized consulting agency.

To the extent that the doctorate becomes the pattern, more time may be expected in seeking original lines of individual professional development. And there will be some added depth.

Questions of the useful professional lifetime, frequency of retraining and depth of initial training, along with appropriate curricular reforms, are relatively straightforward. There is another problem, however, that is going to make the future of planning education fuzzy no matter what we may say today. That is the emerging head-on confrontation between the two main forces in the "new planning": the planning-systems scientists and the new-politics-participatory advocates. Perhaps events in the world at large are going to give the day to one camp or the other; but, if not, it is going to be nearly impossible to program one kind of education for two very different modes of operation. This confrontation makes it doubly important that we be very specific about the activities we prepare people to carry out.

No discussion of the future of planning education could now be complete without reference to the report, "A Study of Education for Environmental Design," recently submitted to the American Institute of Architects by Robert Geddes and Bernard Spring. In a number of ways, it is an approach to professional education more easily comprehended by planners than by architects. And it has the very marked advantage of being quite specific in its main proposals. Indeed, I have never seen a proposal for such careful evaluation of the true impacts of various kinds of courses. Six different processes of design are indicated: identification, formulation, prediction, selection, management, and evaluation. These are played out in permutations and commutations with six areas of concern of different size, as well as with six different scopes: basic research, applied research, pilot study, proposal, communication, and effectuation. They thus obtain 216 different kinds of environmental design activities, or of professional education for these tasks. This report has justifiably attracted considerable attention among the engineers and, though key areas of the architectural profession, will resist it, it is especially important that it be appreciated by planners.

Two points must be made at once. First, environmental design does not encompass the whole of planning as it stands today. There are now considerable numbers of planners who would not fit into this mold, because social planning is central for them rather than supplementary to environmental planning. Geddes and Spring have not dealt with this fact. The other point is that many of the criteria for environmental design in planning are also pertinent to the planning process as it applies to social and economic means. I strongly believe that the AIP should be supporting this move on the part of the architects, as it will be very useful in programming future developments in planning. Despite the fact that some of the additional categories (the processes of design, the scales, and the scopes), seem artificially delineated (as indeed does the discovery of exactly six categories in each of the dimensions), this tool for analysis of processes of design or planning and for the training appropriate to them may be of very great usefulness. Whether or not one agrees with the dimensions and the parts thereof that Geddes and Spring have arrived at, it must be admitted that the method does give highly specific descriptions of planning or design activities. It helps distinguish, for example, "the applied researcher" who is interested in metropolitan areas and only in prediction for them, from the maker of proposals for a very local area who follows a formulation approach. And it does seem to be a useful starting point for approaches more closely oriented to planners' work. (Those who have worked most closely with the Geddes-Spring formulation insist that the various categories are quite distinguishable one from another and, in particular, that there is little confusion between dimensions. They also insist that the categories are quite exhaustive, but this is more difficult to believe.)

I have called these remarks "The Fuzzy Future of Planning Education." Despite a very clear quantitative upsurge in the planning schools, despite the increasing quality of faculty and (especially) of students, it is far from clear that the schools are going anywhere in particular. The increasing apartheid from practical considerations makes planning a quasi-discipline of the kind implied by the term "new planning." Curricular contents have depended more on intellectual whim and vogue than on any serious assessment of present or future occupational requirements. My main proposition is that we may be now moving into a phase in which the planning schools are plentiful enough and that the kinds of training should be given more careful thought.

It is possible that the "new planning" includes elements that are so different from one another that they should be quite separated. Perhaps some of what is now called "planning education" will be taught in schools of different names. On the other hand, it may be possible to discover a new communality of interests and to train for that plus the new specialties. But the latter alternative is going to require some very specific thinking and programming.

LEO JAKOBSON

A native of Finland, he received the Master's of Architecture degree from the Technical University at Helsinki in 1945. He also studied at the Royal Academy of Art in Stockholm in 1946 and at the University of Pennsylvania as a Fulbright Exchange Fellow in 1954. After professional work in architecture in urban planning in Finland, Sweden, and Israel, Professor Jakobson came to the United States in 1956 and joined the University of Wisconsin faculty in 1957. From 1964 to 1965 he served as a member of the Ford Foundation Advisory Planning Group in Calcutta, India. Professor Jakobson is the recipient of several prizes in architectural and urban design competitions in Finland and Israel. In 1966 he was among the first to receive a research grant from the new National Endowment on the Humanities. The result of this research, entitled "The Nature of Urban Form: Concepts for Design" will be published in book form in the near future.

Toward a Pluralistic Ideology in Planning Education

A COMMENT ON MANN'S PAPER

A response to Lawrence Mann's paper may well begin with an examination of the underlying reasons for his suggestion that the future of planning education is fuzzy, since, in my interpretation, most of his views on the subject appear not to be fuzzy at all. On the contrary, he is outlining a very explicit future in his well-structured, three-dimensional "umbrella" curriculum based on supply and demand analyses and calculated "useful lifetime" considerations. Also, he advocates increased specificity in the tasks people are prepared to carry out, using the excellent Geddes-Spring study of environmental design education as his springboard.

The causes of Mann's "fuzziness" are quite obvious, however. They originate in two fundamental issues affecting nearly every aspect of contemporary life: the apparent confusion about the roles and purposes of

266

higher education, per se; and the growing impact of technology on traditional ideologies and value orientations. Mann is aware of these issues, and he considers them to be serious problems. Explicitly, he identifies the latter and describes it as a central problem: "the emerging hear-on confrontation between the two main forces in the 'new planning': the planning-systems scientists and the new-politics-participatory advocates." The former, the role of education, is, implicitly, evident throughout his review of current planning education. It can be exemplified by the following statement: "It must be faced that the planning schools, especially the most highly reputed ones, are preparing planners for a Utopian market."

It is to these two basic questions that I will respond first, in order to construct a framework for a brighter future. In the latter part of my response I can then throw out the umbrella, be less calculating and less specific, and even suggest that Robert Geddes' model be replaced with Patrick Geddes' so that our generation, hopefully, may become the first to understand him, among future ones he used to address.[1]

What renders my task difficult, however, is that Mann does not clearly reveal his views on these basic issues, nor does he discuss them except for a few *passim* remarks. To me this suggests that he may not have a clear position on either one. This ambivalence is evidenced in many parts of the paper leading, in part, to contradiction, notwithstanding my previous comment regarding clarity, in many of his suggestions. But clarity on specifics does not negate confusion on the broader issues; this dichotomy contributes, however, to the over-all fuzziness of the picture he tries to paint.

First, let me suggest that the role of higher education is to advance an art or a science through improving our understanding of present knowledge and through the discovery of new knowledge. Mann's critical comment that "planners are not being trained for jobs that exist but rather for ones that the students and professors think it would be nice to have exist" can hence be construed to be a compliment, although a somewhat misleading one, because no professor should attempt to prepare a student for any particular kind of job, existing or Utopian. It is the student who has to decide what he wants to be: a protector of the *status quo* or an agent of change. The role of education is to make him aware of the choices before him, to equip him with sufficient knowledge that will enable him to choose his role intelli-

---

[1] Defries quotes a lady sitting beside him at Patrick Geddes' final lecture at Dundee as having said, "He has been talking to the next generation—it is too much for us." (A. Defries, "The Interpreter Geddes," London: Routledge, 1927.)

gently, and to allow him, over time, to make a contribution to society as an educated person.

One must admit, however, that in our present societal turmoil, the role of education is less clear and subject to great exogenous competing forces. In particular, the purposes of professional education in a critical field like planning are torn by the three main forces that participate in its goal formulation: the university, the student, and the profession. Of these constituent groups, I see the profession at the conservative end of the spectrum; eager as it is not to step out of bounds in order not to endanger its newly acquired status of acceptance, respectability, and responsibility. It expects the university to swell its ranks with well-trained, well-groomed, law-abiding junior professionals who know how to advance the art and science of planning with new skills but not necessarily to contribute to it with new thoughts. At the opposite end, the student of today is idealisic and impatient with the inherent slowness of all societal change. Hence he easily, and understandably, turns radical, militant, and most often also irrational. Historian Christopher Lasch aptly observes that "large sections of the student movement, indeed, have come to be dominated by people who, as one writer describes them, 'feel automatically excluded whenever rational debate threatens to break out.' "[2]

Pressured by these extreme positions is the university which, as an idea, is one of the most diffuse, though greatest inventions of Western culture: a community of learned men and a body of scholarly aspirations, linked to society at large by bonds that are valued, but rarely defined, ever-present but changeable. This mutability and lack of definition are a vital part of the university idea; however, they render the task of role-playing equally variable.[3] When one recognizes that this reflects a British view of the European university, what can then be said of the American multiversity, devoted to the apparently conflicting ideals of mass education and excellency; the discovery of new knowledge and direct, immediate service to the surrounding community, city, state, and nation? One of the few explicit statements on this dilemma is one by Henry Steele Commager, who a few years ago wrote that "the first responsibility of the university is not to serve its immediate community but to serve the much larger community of learning of which it is a part; not to serve its immediate generation, but future

[2] Christopher Lasch, "Where Do We Go From Here?," *The New York Review of Books,* Vol. XI, No. 6, October 10, 1968, p. 5.
[3] Adapted from an editorial comment on universities, *The Architectural Review,* London, Vol. 122, No. 728, October 1957, p. 235.

generations."[4] If we accept this premise, part of Mann's fuzziness is removed. I would like to add, though, that in serving future generations, the university cannot be a center for learning only; it must also be an agent of change. It cannot play a passive role. If it would, it would cease to be a body of scholarly aspirations, destroying thereby one of the fundamentals of its idea.

Let me now discuss the apparent confrontation between humanism and technocracy. Mann recognizes this conflict only from the point of view of the "new planning": the advocates of participatory democracy in planning and the systems-scientist planners. To this I would like to add the two dominant dimensions of the "old planning": the liberal reformer in search of social justice, and the Utopian designers who firmly believe in the superiority of their ideal community. This typology would not be complete without admitting that political expedience is an ideology in its own right, and one that commands a substantial following among the profession. Finally, one must give recognition to the few who approach planning from a philosophical perspective and question what is good and what is bad in a society's ethics, values, and norms.

These six ideological traits which Mann and I have crudely described above can be classified and systematized in several ways. In the following table an attempt is made to identify them by terms which would elicit an image, albeit interpretative, of the dominant concern in each of the six traits. These identifying terms may not be coextensive; they may refer to institutional arrangements, methods, or objectives—whichever provides the clearest and most concise ideological imageability. Each ideological trait is thereafter described by a series of predominant characteristics which will narrow margins of interpretation if one accepts them as being representative of the *modus operandi* of the typical followers of each ideology.[5]

---

[4] Henry Steele Commager, "Is Ivy Necessary?," *Saturday Review*, September 17, 1960, p. 88.

[5] Some of this discussion has been stimulated, aside from Mann's confrontation notion, by the many articles on ideological conflict in the press, in literary magazines, and in scholarly journals. Specifically, I should mention Jouko Kajanoja, "The Ideologies of City Planning," *The Finnish Architectural Review* (Helsinki, Vol. 65, No. 5, 1968) p. 51; Arthur I. Waskow, "The Future—Who Can Imagine It?," *The Wall Street Journal* (Thursday, September 12, 1968); and "The Civilization of the Dialogue," A Center Occasional Paper (Santa Barbara, California, Center for the Study of Democratic Institutions, Volume II, No. 1, December 1968). The Table is naturally incomplete. It is full of personal value judgments and arbitrary polarization. I am also aware that few, if any, individuals would consider themselves typical representatives of any one of the six traits. Most would probably combine several sets of these characteristics, and I can imagine that a few might want to identify themselves with nearly all of the enumerated ideologies. If one would be allowed to check only one square in

Central Ideological Concern	Professional Attitude	Goal of Planning	Method of Planning	Validating Measure	Method of Implementation
Utopian Conceptualization (Utopian)	dogmatic missionary	ideal society	deterministic design	uniqueness of idea	convincing proselytizing
Quantitative Determinism (Scientist)	scientific absolutist	predictable society	technological forecasting	measurable facts	scientific professionalism
Ethical Norms (Humanist)	humanist philosophical	better society	intellectual conjecture	logic of purpose	educational dialogue
Administrative Efficiency (Bureaucrat)	cautious traditional	orderly society	adaptive integration	conformity to norms	policy initiation
Participatory Democracy (Activist)	classic liberal	new society	interpretative advocacy	urgency of cause	political activism
Institutional Democracy (Liberal)	democratic reformist	just society	deliberative rationalization	majority vote	democratic process

From this table one can group the six ideologies into two sub-sets, one representing an elitist and the other a popular attitude, with respect to their role as professionals.[6] In the former are the Utopians, the scientists, and the humanists. In the latter, the liberals, the activists, and the bureaucrats. They can also be matched into pairs reflecting either a clear attitudinal conflict or concordance. Of the five possible pairings for each trait, three represent a conflict situation, and two are concordant. If one assumes that each ideology represents a terminal point on a hexagonal field, half of which represent elitist ideologies and half popular ideologies, the diagram on page 271 emerges.

The patterns of concordance in this diagram of ideologies are interesting. They suggest that the important division in reality is a conflict between those ideologies which represent the existing order—in other words, the establishment—and those which tend to question the validity of this order. The former work within the framework of existing institutions and organizations; they obey facts and measurable trends; and they observe the norms and desires of identifiable majorities. The latter, the Utopians, the

each column, it is likely that a complete set of all possible permutations would emerge. Despite its obvious limitations, I have included it in the hope that it will be useful for stimulating further discussion.

[6] The word "popular" is used herein as an antonym to "elitist."

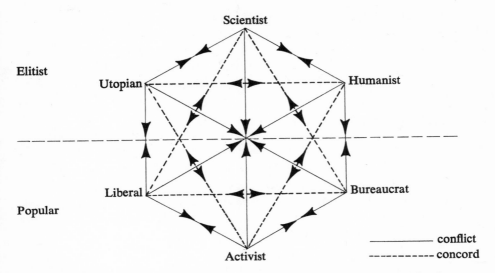

humanities and the activists, tend to establish their identities outside the establishment; they advocate change, and they rely on the exploratory and creative qualities of the human mind rather than on empirical fact.

As an individual whose views on this classification came closest to that of the humanist, I can recognize the conflicts which I have with liberals, with scientists, and with bureaucrats, and my affinity to activist causes and Utopian thought. However, I fail to see that I could have a head-on clash with the former group, nor can I imagine that I would coalesce with the latter. But I can see a mutuality of benefits emerging from the fact that all of these ideologies are represented in my field of interest. Hence I suggest that this ideological pluralism be considered a most desirable condition in a profession which, as Mann points out, operates at a multitude of organizational levels engaging in an equally complex set of activities. The task of the planning schools is to recognize the benefits of this pluralism and to staff their faculties in a manner that the student, irrespective of his particular interest, will be exposed to these ideological differences, allowing him to sort out for himself his future professional ideology.

Having removed the second of the causes of Mann's fuzziness, I will now dismiss the specifics of his paper as well. But before doing so, I would like to digress for a moment and suggest that Mann's reference to trespassing in the domain of the related disciplines being a serious problem not be taken to imply that in the more established disciplines perfection exists. From my observations as a practitioner, I tend to agree wholeheartedly with Robert Heilbroner, who, in describing the irrelevancies of much current economic theory, suggests that this is by no means accidental but rather that "it results from a fundamental failure of vision on part of the modern model-builders who do not see that the social universe that they are attempting to reproduce in a set of equations is not and cannot be adequately described by functional relationship alone, but must also and simultaneously be described as a system of privilege."[7] To describe a system of privilege is, however, a humanistic endeavor involving fundamental societal values. Heilbroner points out to that the construct of such a model is feasible, and uses Marx's economic theory as a case to demonstrate his point. But Marx, as economist, would be adjudged by most to fall into the category of a humanist and philosopher, notwithstanding the many technocratic applications of his theory.

In a different vein, but essentially addressing himself to the same problem as Heilbroner, sociologist Anselm Strauss suggests that in his field "the elements of urban theory tend merely to be refinements of common sense conceptions and urban social relations, however sophisticated the language and however 'data-based' are the supporting facts."[8] In his lucid manner Strauss then suggests strategies for discovering urban theory, many of which would provide for beneficial cross-fertilization of thought among sociologists of different ideological bent.

Often the likelihood of an ideological confrontation is argued from the point of view of the increasing demand for specialized competence in all professional activity with a concomitant emphasis on skills and with less concern for the broader issues. To know much about little is more valued than knowing little about much. What seems to have escaped our attention is the simple fact that the very quest for specialization has brought about increasing demands for coordination, correlation, conflict minimization, program evaluation, and mediation—in other words, comprehensive planning. Whether a person engaged in comprehensive activity analysis and coordination is called a planner or something else, he must possess a broad understanding of the complex sets of interrelationships that prevail within

[7] Robert L. Heilbroner, "Putting Marx to Work," *The New York Review of Books*, (Vol. XI, No. 10, December 5, 1968), p. 10.

[8] Anselm L. Strauss, "Strategies for Discovering Urban Theory," in Leo F. Schnore and Henry Fagin, editors, *Urban Research and Policy Planning* (Beverly Hills, California: Sage Publications, Inc., 1967) pp. 82–3.

his area of surveillance. He must be equipped with the unique intellectual capacities of a generalist, with skills comparable to those of the specialists, albeit of a different nature. This was recognized as early as in 1950 by the British Committee on Qualifications of Planners. The Committee, chaired by Sir George Schuster, said this about the chief planning officer: "The officer carrying the chief planning responsibility must have the capacity to organize the use of specialists of many kinds, and to see how a number of aims and activities can be fitted together in a harmonious whole.· . . . Finally, he must see all these complicated and interrelated stages as one whole and continuous process, with far-reaching social and economic aims to achieve. . . . These abilities demand a creative or imaginative faculty of mind, a power of synthesis, and a broad human understanding. It is in developing such abilities that a university education is of value. . . ."[9]

The importance of this statement lies in the notion that planning education should provide the student with such intellectual habits and qualities which would assure, over time, the unfolding of his capacities to meet the requirements for assuming the role of a chief planning officer. I must admit, however, that only a select few among our students seem to possess the attitude and the innate capacity required to become true generalists. But curricula and professors should provide the opportunity for those students who have the interest and the capacity to move in this direction. Mann's "umbrella" may be protective and may keep the rain out, but it cuts off all bright rays and also limits the horizon

In his section on "programming planning education," Mann recognizes the dangers of over-specialization and suggests that "this makes the rediscovery of a common core of substantial proportions so important in planning education." His "umbrella" approach, on the other hand, sees the core as a minimal program of four to six courses that includes an "orientation course of some sort" which makes me think of freshman English. "Beyond these elements," Mann says, "I am not sure that anything else in the planning curriculum should be required." The question of a substantive or minimal core is, however, an insignificant issue. The major objection to the umbrella should be directed at its very first step, "the fundamental approach," which suggest that economic, social, and physical planning are basically different and thus should be treated as separate concentrations.

---

[9] Ministry of Town and County Planning, Department of Health for Scotland, *Report of the Committee on Qualifications of Planners* (London: Her Majesty's Stationery Office, 1950) p. 47.

Though Mann admits that combination approaches are possible, I would like to ask: Why bother with planning schools and curricula? The separate concentration could much better be taught in the respective units of the discipline involved. And as joint or intradisciplinary degree programs are more and more frequent, the question of the combination approach can also be taken care of without a planning school.

Over a half a century ago, Patrick Geddes was already aware of the dangers of over-specialization and disciplinary fragmentation when dealing with man and his institutions. I would like to suggest that instead of examining Robert Geddes's static matrix, it may be most useful for us to go back to Patrick Geddes's dynamic matrix, "The Notations of Life." It would be sad, indeed, if Mann's viewpoint were valid and the three-way decision between physical, economic, and social planning is deepening, that we have not by now even reached Patrick Geddes's chord of the simple practical life that links geography, economics, and sociology (anthropology), or, in his terms, place, work and folk, not to speak of the more advanced chords of simple mental life, full inner life, and effective life.

If there is something unique to planning education, the fundamental approach must lead to the unification of the various disciplinary approaches that may have taken shape in recent years. Where Mann and I differ so fundamentally is that he accepts the current situation and current practice as a basis for all of his recommendations; I recognize the present but am not content to accept it as the sole determinant for the future. I am therefore not much concerned with supply and demand questions, or the useful professional lifetime of my students. I fully agree with Edmund Bacon, who, in describing the city "as an act of will," states that "with the enormous improvement in the techniques of mathematical manipulations of electronic computers applied to the problem of projecting past trends, we are in danger of surrendering to a mathematically extrapolated future which at best can be nothing more than an extension of what existed before. Thus we are in danger of losing one of the most important concepts of mankind, that the future is what we make it."[10]

If there is a dilemma in planning education, it lies in the simple fact that the planner's present is the future. Hence he has no facts to work with, only *futura*. Bertrand de Jouvenel describes the construction of a likely future as an intellectual work of art, in the best meaning of that word. In my view three basic skills are needed to accomplish this: the art of thought, the art

[10] Edmund N. Bacon, *Design of Cities* (New York, New York: The Viking Press, 1967) p. 13.

of judgment, and the art of conjecture. The teaching of these three arts should, therefore, become the core of every planning curriculum. If we can provide our students with the ability to apply these arts skillfully to whatever future tasks they may perform as followers of any professional ideology, the future of planning will be bright indeed.

SIDNEY L. WILLIS

State Planning Director, Department of Community Affairs, State of New Jersey. Formerly Director of Jersey City Community Renewal Program; Jersey City Director of Planning; Planner and Acting Chief of Community Development, New Jersey Division of State and Regional Planning; and Chief Research Planner, South East Chicago Commission. B.A., Geneva College; M.A. in Planning, University of Chicago.

Planning Education:
A Balanced Role

A COMMENT ON MANN'S PAPER

I have little basic disagreement with Lawrence Mann's proposals for planning education. The realities of planning practice and its diversity of present and reasonably possible approaches, roles, and subject matters is a welcomed jumping-off place for the design of a system of planning education. The dropping of the "jack of all trades" idea in the definition of a planner is welcomed as well. Finally, the call for a return to a solid common core in planning education, while allowing maximum room for specialization in a variety of optional areas, seems eminently sensible.

Since I am not an educator, I can only comment on the implications of these proposals from the point of view of an administrator of a planning program and as a member of a state board charged with decisions on the qualifications of persons to be licensed as professional planners.

Mann's appreciation that in many respects planners are not being trained for the jobs that exist (or even those likely to exist), and his recognition that we are going to run into increasing difficulties with other professions and disciplines is well received among those of us who do have program responsibilities which we try to pursue within the context of existing political and administrative frameworks.

By calling for university trained planners who can more appropriately fulfill the needs of today's planning agencies and, as Mann has suggested, tomorrow's as well, I agree fully that it is not the planning school's role to train people in the so-called practical skills. The agencies themselves can and should provide that training on the job. What we need from the planning schools are trained persons who in many cases will form only a small part of a total staff. These persons, by reason of having mastered basic disciplinary approaches and sharing a common core of knowledge of the progression and the current state of planning in this country, should be prepared to make a significant program contribution almost immediately. Mann's proposals seem to provide for this.

However, there are some aspects of Mann's paper with which I would like to take issue. And there are some aspects which I would more strongly underline than he did. Before doing so, a question raised by Mann should be underscored: How important is graduate study to planning practice? The experience with the New Jersey Licensing Law examination may reveal what most professional planners already know: some of our best planners never went to planning schools. Certainly most of our planners never went to planning schools. With the proliferation of planning schools and with the increasing number of graduates, we should remind ourselves that the backlog and the number of new jobs calling for planners is still not likely to be met by graduate planners, and that the main sources of personnel continue to be predominantly from outside the graduate schools. This will be particularly true in the black core of cities. If we forget for a moment the necessity to educate those who might in the future be educating more planners, and the education of certain personnel in agencies to make special kinds of program inputs, perhaps we should not be so concerned about the training offered in graduate schools. We may need, instead, to be concentrating more on providing supplementary training and orientation for persons who find themselves in planning, and on providing specialized opportunities for self-educated planners.

Mann has observed elsewhere the dangers of separate facilities and student bodies in day and evening programs, and prefers not to provide extensively for the latter if a choice between these two must be made. It is possible to conceive that the resources might all be placed in the evening program to best serve those who will actually be holding the planning jobs.

Being concerned with staff development in my own case is a matter of providing educational opportunities for people in the jobs rather than the new graduates. A perusal of the New Jersey Division of State and Regional Planning, which I believe is fairly typical, indicates that of a total of thirty-two professionals, two have undergraduate training in planning only; seven have graduate degrees in related fields only; five have graduate degrees in planning; and eighteen had no formal training other than a college degree before joining the staff. As a product of the Chicago School of Planning I fall within Harvey Perloff's classification of a generalist with a speciality.

With that background I am, of course, a great believer in the diversity of approaches which is so often pointed to as a source of great creativity in planning. But I am also very appreciative of the problems this diversity creates with other professions, particularly our sister design professions. It creates problems as well with the administrators, the budget directors, and the personnel officers with whom one must deal if planning ideas are to have program substance in real governments in the world of job titles, qualifications, salary ranges, budget positions, etc. Here the title of "Planner" must mean something reasonably specific. In some jurisdictions where it does not mean anything specific, it could very well mean political hacks and incompetents who could not find any other title to use.

The New Jersey experience in the licensing of planners and all its problems of working toward an operational definition of who is qualified to present himself to a governmental jurisdiction as a planner, is an illustration that the unlimited diversity of the "jack of all trades" is truly a thing of the past.

I take issue with any suggestion that planning is not really all of one piece. The broad umbrella which Mann describes does indeed have some perimeter, some circumference, in spite of its holes. It seems to me that there must be some essential core of knowledge, and that the planning schools should define this and expose it to all who would hold a degree in planning. While the schools should be expanding concepts and ideas to meet newly realized needs, they have an equal obligation to tie these back to some central theory. This does not mean that the schools should produce an homogenized product, but that there can be no specialization which does not relate to some common core.

As a Chicago graduate, I do not find it difficult to abandon the physical planning core. Still, I do object to the off-hand dismissal of the concept that we are basically dealing with the physical environment. The centralizing theme of man's environment should not be too lightly disregarded as not sufficiently definitive. However, I want to underscore as essential Mann's extensions of fundamental approaches to include economic planning and social planning.

I hope that the graduate schools would interpret these subjects in terms of their impact on environmental change and spell out the effects of alternative arrangements of the environment on social and economic concerns. Where the relationships are not definable, let us be sure not to pretend that any other profession may not have an equally valid basis for doing these kinds of planning.

Others in the planning profession have already pointed out that, while we have been very quick to dismiss this traditional concept of city and regional planning because the pressing problems of today in the "now communities" are so much more complicated, the physical separation of ghetto areas from employment, the effect of the environment on suburban and central city life, and the social consequences of current housing and public facility design and construction are almost certainly a part of these problems, and their physical solution most certainly a part of the solutions which will be required.

I believe a sobering thought for those of us who are concerned with these social and economic problems as citizens as well as planners might be that in the preparation of people who can adequately deal with them, the planning schools could become inhibitants to the development of needed new ideas. Indeed, so could the American Institute of Planners. I say this without being critical of either, and with full recognition that every profession must contribute its part toward the solution.

The planning profession, it seems to me, has a job to do in contributing to solutions to these problems. But to stake out a claim that we are uniquely qualified to the exclusion of any other may be a disservice. And to train people in the idea that they can be environmental planners this week and social planners next week is also a disservice.

As we extend our role into these areas, let us be sure to distinguish between our commitment to social and economic concerns and our increasing competence. Competence has to be earned, and its characteristic is often a degree of humility toward the solution one proposes. Whether in the future we will earn the title of planner, as Herbert Gans has defined it, rather than urbanist will depend on performance.

There are two points I would like to advance for consideration:

First, I am very sympathetic to the planning schools' problems of often being asked to perform the function of gate keeper.

The New Jersey Planning Licensing Law does rely on educational qualifications as well as experience, character reference, and examination. We have moved through the difficult period of the "grandfathers." We are still not out of the woods on the problem that at present architects and engineers are automatically qualified. At the present time there are some compromise amendments being discussed which would result in eventually requiring formal training in planning for a minimum of twenty-one credit hours of all applicants for licenses. I personally would have hoped that we could rely more heavily on the examination than on any of the other qualifications, including the educational requirement. To the extent, however, that we insist that planning is a separate profession, we find it necessary to indicate that specialized training in a field called planning must make a difference.

Second, I was disappointed that Mann did not discuss one of the implications of the Geddes-Spring Study, and an implication of his own proposals for providing a variety of specialized planning training. This implication points to a number of planning schools ultimately agreeing on a planning core and offering a variety of special tracks. This would enable a student to move from one school to another, to pursue his special interests and to exchange credits. In this manner the best faculty for each specialty could offer courses wherever it is located. A degree could then be granted from one of a number of cooperative graduating schools, or jointly by them.

Another implication of a system of specialty or concentration offerings is that, at least in the area of environmental design, it might ultimately be possible for the architectural, engineering, and planning schools to cooperate through a similar exchange to produce persons specializing in environmental planning. Here the AIA study's implications that the architects must share the over-all task with others in the environmental design professions would seem to be an opening to more mature resolution of some of our interprofessional problems.

Finally, the subject of the education of planners must include some discussion of the necessity to educate persons who have not had educational advantages sufficient to enter or successfully complete college. A subprofessional or pre-professional program to enable persons with high school or less formal training to take positions within urban planning programs should be developed jointly by the planning agencies and the educators. Only by establishing such an intermediate education program are sufficient personnel acceptable to the cities likely to be ready in the forseeable future.

BERNARD J. FRIEDEN

Associate Professor of City Planning, M.I.T. and Research
Member M.I.T.–Harvard Joint Center for Urban Studies.
Staff member of President Johnson's Task Force on Urban
Problems (1965–66) which developed the Model Cities
program. Consultant to Department of Housing and Urban
Development and the Massachusetts Division of Urban Re-
newal. Member of the Task Force on the Organization of
Social Services of the US Department of Health, Education
and Welfare. B.A., Cornell University; M.A., Pennsylvania
State University; Ph.D. in City Planning, M.I.T. Author:
*The Future of Old Neighborhoods; Metropolitan America;
Challenge to Federalism; Urban Planning and Social Policy*
(with Robert Morris).

New Roles in Social Policy Planning

Can planners, traditionally trained to plan the urban physical environment,
play major roles in planning urban social policy? If social policy deals with
increasing opportunities for disadvantaged people, providing social services, and promoting social and economic mobility, then a great many
activities today come under this heading. Planners with a social orientation
are very much in demand to staff anti-poverty agencies, Model Cities
boards, and neighborhood development organizations. Current planning
graduates who want to work in social action programs seem to have little
difficulty finding jobs. Yet there is a widespread impression that the agencies operating socially-oriented programs in fact do very little systematic
planning, and it is not at all clear how planners can help them.

While the various community development programs focusing on poverty areas are intensely involved in social and political action with little
attention to planning, the traditional city and metropolitan agencies that do
prepare urban development plans give low priority to social policy issues.
Changes under way will probably lead urban planners to increase their
involvement in social policy, but meanwhile the physical environment
continues to dominate their work. Thus a membership survey conducted by

the American Institute of Planners in 1965 showed very few planners working primarily on social issues. Of 361 planners who estimated the proportion of their professional time oriented to physical, economic, and social factors, only eighteen spent more than 40 per cent of their time on social factors, compared to 262 spending more than half their time on physical factors.

In defining appropriate roles for planners in the development of urban social policy, we need to look at both the traditional urban planning agencies and the new community action programs. Traditional forms of planning do have important impacts on social policy, despite their lack of explicit consideration of social issues. They need to be strengthened by introducing social issues more deliberately into the formulation of urban development policy. Community action programs, on the other hand, are directly and primarily concerned with social issues. Here the question is how to introduce an appropriate planning function, so that goals can be clarified, alternative choices weighed, and program effectiveness gauged.

This paper will therefore begin by considering ways of building social components into urban development planning. I shall then review recent planning experience with joint social-environmental programs, and then propose a new social policy planning function to support and strengthen the social action programs that are now under way. To illustrate specifically how urban planners can contribute to social policy planning, I shall also draw on the experience of one area of social policy for which an explicit planning function has already been organized: health service planning.

Much of the conventional content of city and metropolitan planning—housing, transportation, recreation, public facilities—can contribute directly to such social policy goals as equality of opportunity, participation in community life, and access to jobs and services. But traditional comprehensive planning does not analyze these elements of the physical environment in a social policy perspective. Typically, environmental components are seen within a conceptual framework that stresses land-use patterns, physical development standards, and the coordination of public services with land development. A new perspective is needed if urban development planning is to be sensitive to social policy issues.

The physical development of American urban areas has fallen far short of its potential for meeting the material needs of the poor and of minority groups. We are building communities with a high degree of social and economic segregation, and with dramatic inequalities in housing and environmental conditions, public facilities, and access to jobs and services. Where development programs involve public land-takings and the displacement of people and businesses, we have imposed disproportionate costs on poor families and small firms—without assuring equitable forms of compensation. We have not yet created effective channels for relatively powerless minorities to have a voice in shaping and managing urban development programs that affect them.

The Advisory Commission on Civil Disorders (Kerner Commission) discovered the effects of these shortcomings in its investigation of grievances in ghetto communities. Inadequate housing was among the three most intense grievances; poor recreation facilities and programs were among those at the second level of intensity. Planning and decision-making processes of local government were also among second and third level grievances. Specific criticism was directed at the lack of adequate representation of Negroes in the political structure, the failure of local political structures to respond to legitimate complaints, urban renewal, and insufficient community participation in planning and decision-making.[1]

The Kerner Commission report is salutary reading for urban planners in still another respect. The Commission staff reviewed low-income housing programs in three cities that have been widely praised for their extensive rebuilding efforts: Detroit, Newark, and New Haven. In Detroit, 758 low-income housing units were added through federal programs since 1956, while 8000 low-income units were demolished for urban renewal. Newark build 3760 low-income units since 1959, while displacing 12,000 families for renewal, public housing, and highways. In New Haven, since 1952, 951 low-income units were subsidized, while 6500 housing units were demolished.[2]

To cite these findings of the Kerner Commission is not to say that they result from the special conceptual or professional limitations of planners. The same report finds equally serious shortcomings in other areas of public responsibility, such as education, manpower training, and welfare. More important than any professional insensitivity has been the lack of political commitment to meet the needs of the poor and of minority groups. City development programs in particular have reflected a policy of making the central city more attractive to middle-income groups, in an effort to per-

[1] US Office of the President, *Report of the National Advisory Commission on Civil Disorders* (Washington: Government Printing Office, 1968), pp. 80–83.
[2] *Ibid.,* p. 80.

suade some of them to return from the suburbs and others not to leave. Programs for the poor have received lower priority.

Although this political orientation has been much more significant than any planning bias in explaining recent urban policies, it is nevertheless true that many socially objectionable projects have been carried out according to comprehensive plans. And it is also true that some of the same city programs that were criticized by the Kerner Commission have been highly regarded in professional planning circles. More to the point for the future, however, is that traditional planning concepts and methods may prevent planners from contributing fully to the development of socially sensitive programs even when the political climate is favorable.

Signs of change are evident in several of the major federal aid programs with which urban planners work. Low-income housing programs in the past have been far too small to make substantial additions to the supply of sound housing that poor families can afford. The 1968 housing act marks the start of a vastly expanded federal housing commitment, aimed at providing six million low- and moderate-cost units in the next ten years. (In comparison, the last thirty years of public housing have produced fewer than 700,000 units.) The projected volume of the new housing amounts to a redefinition of housing priorities. If Congressional appropriations are consistent with the new legislation, federal aid programs will, for the first time, be commensurate with the number of low-income families living in slum housing.

In addition to this increase in volume, low-income housing programs have begun to offer many options as alternatives to the traditional large housing projects. New public housing options include small projects, units leased in existing buildings, "turnkey" developments purchased from private builders, and other variations. Aside from public housing, the new possibilities include rent supplements and, under 1968 legislation, low-income home ownership as well as rental housing.

Urban renewal is also being reoriented to give higher priority to the needs of the poor. As a result of legislative changes in 1966, the Department of Housing and Urban Development has put local renewal agencies on notice that it intends to give priority to projects that conserve and expand the housing supply for low- and moderate-income families or that develop new employment opportunities.[3]

[3] US Department of Housing and Urban Development, Office of the Assistant Secretary for Renewal and Housing Assistance, Local Public Agency Letter No. 418, "National Goals and Urban Renewal Priorities," May 19, 1967.

Another federal aid program, planning assistance for metropolitan planning agencies (section 701), has also been amended to define new social priorities. Agencies receiving metropolitan planning funds are now required to develop policies, plans, and programs "to ameliorate the transportation, housing, and recreation deficiencies of low-income and minority groups." An additional requirement calls on the metropolitan agency to solicit and recognize the views of low-income and minority groups in preparing its plans.[4]

These shifts in priority so far say nothing about broadening urban planning to encompass social as well as environmental components. They deal with the physical environment, but they are addressed to meeting the environmental needs of low-income groups more adequately. This is the first and most direct way for urban planners to contribute to social policy planning. It is entirely consistent with the traditional focus of planning on the physical environment, but it calls for explicit recognition of the distribution of physical facilities to different social groups. Since the needs of these groups may not be reflected in usual planning standards, however, planners will have to give special attention to identifying the needs of low-income and minority groups for housing, transportation, recreation, and public facilities. Further, planning studies ought to be explicit in recognizing who will benefit from physical development programs, in framing these programs so that they reach low-income groups, and in monitoring the results to insure that they help narrow environmental gaps between the poor and the rest of urban society.

This reorientation of physical planning calls for changes in both the substance of plans and the process of planning. Changes in plan priorities can take the form of different program proposals, different schedules, and shifts in budgets to favor poverty and ghetto areas. Changes in the planning process are equally important, and may represent greater departures from traditional practice. These changes should include provision for more direct and greater participation of the poor and of minority groups in plan-making and in program operations. Possible steps include review of plan proposals by citizen organizations, the funding of advocacy planning to allow local groups to prepare their own proposals, public opinion research and surveys, local referenda on plans, more extensive employment and training of neighborhood aides and sub-professional personnel from pov-

---

[4] US Department of Housing and Urban Development, Office of the Assistant Secretary for Metropolitan Development, Circular MD 6011.1, "Requirements for Metropolitan Planning Assistance," July 1, 1968.

erty and ghetto areas, and the implementation of plan elements by community organizations. These extensions of present planning processes offer ways to discover minority needs more effectively, to build coalitions of minority groups that will support plans, and to overcome some of the alienation that now exists between minorities and city government.

A second step which follows logically upon these changes involves a reconsideration of physical development programs in the light of needs and priorities that go beyond the physical environment. This extension of urban planning requires a careful rethinking of individual programs as new knowledge emerges about the values and wishes of the people for whom they are intendeed. It may mean altering the content of programs to take advantage of complementarities between environmental goals and other aims of urban policy.

This second approach can be illustrated by examples from housing policy. It has been clear for some time that decent physical shelter is an inadequate housing goal. Many potential tenants have been rejecting decent shelter in public housing projects. Further, good housing is not the only high-priority goal of low-income families; employment and several other issues usually outrank housing. If we consider housing programs as a way of enhancing individual opportunities, bringing people more fully into the urban economy, and encouraging the development of local competence and managerial skills in poverty areas, we may be led in several new directions. (Note that these goals differ from such formulations as improving land use or eliminating blight.)

This view of housing would argue for greater emphasis on diversifying the housing choices open to individuals; offering low-income housing in a variety of locations—including locations near job centers, which are increasingly in the suburbs; making construction jobs and job training on new housing developments available to low-income people; encouraging the creation of small contracting firms for construction and maintenance; encouraging community development corporations to sponsor new housing; providing for tenant management of projects; and offering home ownership to low-income families. A parallel rethinking of urban transportation, recreation, and other elements of the physical environment would undoubtedly lead to innovations in these fields as well. This reconsideration of environmental programs depends upon increasing our understanding of the needs and priorities of client groups and clearly must involve the participation of these groups.

These opportunities for contributing to urban social policy are still within the bounds of programs that operate on the physical environment. Questions of how to link these programs to others that operate more directly through social service systems—such as health care or legal aid—will be considered as part of the problem of developing new institutions for social policy planning.

Physical planning cannot be reoriented significantly, however, without political support. Most planners work as agents of city governments. Where mayors and city councils continue to give low priority to the environmental needs of the poor and of Negroes, planners will have only limited opportunities to build city development programs more favorable to these disadvantaged groups. They can, in any case, pose social policy issues within city government by advancing plan alternatives based on different priorities. And just as other city officials cultivate direct political support from their clients among the public, planners can work closely with minorities to marshal their support for physical development programs. Further, planners can exploit the opportunities generated by unpredictable crises that occur in city affairs as well as those generated by gradual shifts in public opinion. The release of the Kerner Commission report, for example, might have been an opportune time to advance new approaches to physical development.

In contrast to the traditional urban development programs, several new approaches to community development are attempting to blend environmental and social elements. The Community Action Program, started in 1965, aimed ambitiously at mobilizing a wide variety of resources in a concerted attack on poverty. The Community Action Program Guide, issued by OEO, urged local agencies to develop programs that would include the following systems: education, employment, family welfare, health service, housing, economic development, consumer information and credit, and legal services. A number of city planners joined the staffs of community action agencies, where their skills in neighborhood analysis and program development seemed reasonably transferable to the unfamiliar ground of planning programs of manpower training, youth employment, and health services. But the planning function in these programs generally has been very limited. Although the evidence is fragmentary and impressionistic, it suggests very strongly that the main planning input has been in the initial application for federal funds, where relatively simple information is presented on community characteristics and program proposals. Little attention seems to have been given to advance planning, to evaluation and testing of alternative strategies and components, or to monitoring program results and adjusting operations in the light of results.

There are many reasons why the planning function in community action has been abbreviated. First, the time horizon is very short. While the OEO guide urged careful attention to program planning, buried in its financial provisions was a revealing comment on the probable life span of community action agencies: "When there is a question as to whether it is cheaper to rent or purchase property or equipment, a comparison of relative costs shall be made on the assumption that the project will continue for three years."[5]

In addition to the precarious life of the community action agency, uncertainty over the availability of funds—especially unearmarked funds that could be used for a variety of programs—further discouraged long- or even middle-range planning and planning that would weigh and evaluate program alternatives. As Congressional appropriations fluctuated from year to year, they also came to allocate program funds to certain standardized components such as Head Start.

Still another factor that worked against systematic planning was the emphasis on strong neighborhood participation in poverty areas, which turned out to be highly divided into conflicting groups. The intense political atmosphere surrounding these programs made it all the more difficult to base decisions on planning analysis and consistent social strategies. Peter Marris and Martin Rein, in their incisive review of the predecessors of the Community Action Program (Ford Foundation "gray areas" programs and programs sponsored by the President's Committee on Juvenile Delinquency and Youth Crime) have shown how local agencies took on the character of social reform movements more than centralized planning operations.[6] The same tendency seems to have emerged in Community Action Programs.

Program decisions appear to have consisted of seizing opportunities rather than implementing careful plans. Program components were included because funds were readily available, because some projects offered more opportunities for local control than others, or simply because it was possible to get conflicting local groups to agree on a particular component.

In 1966, the Model Cities program came upon the scene as a deliberate attempt to combine environmental and social programs, with greater

[5] US Office of Economic Opportunity, *Community Action Program Guide*, Vol. I, Instructions for Applicants, February 1965, p. 8.

[6] Peter Marris and Martin Rein, *Dilemmas of Social Reform* (New York: Atherton Press, 1967), Chapters iv and x.

emphasis on the physical environment than in the Community Action Program. Again, the program was directed toward poverty areas, with an explicit mandate to reduce social and educational disadvantages, expand personal opportunities, and improve living conditions. The federal program guide called for attention to education, health, housing, income maintenance and social services, employment and economic development, crime and delinquency, transportation, the physical environment, design, historic preservation, and new technology. Again, city planners helped staff the new agencies.

Early and informal returns suggest that the Model Cities program, too, is surrounded by institutional uncertainty, local conflicts for control of the program, disagreement on priorities, and doubts about the availability of funds. Systematic planning does not seem to be flourishing. Planners seem to be working as negotiators, community organizers, and proposal writers. But my impression is that the potential strengths of planning as a way of matching programs to local needs and maximizing the return from expenditures are not yet being tapped.

If these impressions are reliable, planners involved in anti-poverty and model cities programs have only limited opportunities to practice their craft or to make the contributions that they are best equipped to make. And the obstacles to systematic planning are rooted in the very nature of these programs—in their stress on local participation, militancy, and challenge to stable institutions. The political base of these programs in the poverty areas and ghettos of cities makes them useful instruments of social policy, in that they supply belated attention to the needs of disadvantaged groups. At the same time, however, it cuts them off from the potential benefits of systematic planning and from many of the resources allocated from city hall through more conventional bureaucratic and planning structures.

In the present circumstances, it is probably unrealistic to expect these social action programs to incorporate well-developed planning functions. But they could be strengthened by developing an appropriate city-wide planning function. If recent experience is a guide, a certain amount of chaos and conflict seem inevitable in programs that try to bring about social change. Innovative organizations draw their political support from interest groups dissatisfied with the present system, and they challenge established institutions. The role I propose for city-wide social policy planning is not one of imposing order on social action agencies, but one of making the inevitable disorder more productive.

What might a more central social policy planning function do? And what are the obstacles to establishing one?

There are many ways in which a well-established central planning function can assist neighborhood action programs and make them more effective. It can supply the technical and informational background that will make more reasoned choices possible—background on anticipated changes in job opportunities, municipal budgets, and the movement of people from one neighborhood to another. Whether better information will affect major decisions in social action programs remains to be seen, but current proposals are sometimes shaped by inaccurate perceptions of forces in the community at large.

More significantly, a central planning function can link neighborhood programs to one another, and to existing service systems. There are many potential complementarities in community action programs. Two neighborhoods may be able to share staffs and facilities for manpower training, for example. New elements in community action programs may also create special needs for supporting services that can be met through regular community channels. Thus a program to promote tenant management of low-income housing developments may create new demands for legal and technical aid to tenant groups, which could be supplied through the city's urban renewal agency. The special support of a central social planning agency could help neighborhood groups press their claims for supporting city services.

Program evaluation is an important but neglected element of neighborhood action. When anti-poverty agencies take on the character of social reform movements, they cannot easily take a detached and objective view of their own programs. Without such a view, however, the cost and effectiveness of program elements are difficult to establish, and local groups may become committed to unproductive efforts. A central agency that monitors local programs could become a repository of information for the evaluation of program alternatives.

Monitoring the results of programs and compiling them on a city-wide basis is another function that a central social planning agency can appropriately perform. This idea is by no means new, it has been suggested in several forms, including Harvey Perloff's proposal for an annual state-of-the-region report charting progress toward social goals.[7] As we attempt to deal with the problems of poverty and unequal opportunity, such a

---

[7] Harvey Perloff, "New Directions in Social Planning," *Journal of the American Institute of Planners,* XXXI (November 1965), pp. 297–304.

report takes on new significance. Out of the confusion and conflict that surround community action, city officials and the public will need to know what is being achieved. How many new jobs are actually being created in the ghetto? Are children in poverty areas performing better in school? Are health conditions improving where neighborhood clinics have been established?

The pressure to discover this information will be a reflection of the seriousness of our commitment to new social goals. If we are concerned with improvements in opportunities and living conditions, we cannot be satisfied by the appearance of activity. We must know whether results are being achieved.

The main obstacle to establishing a central social policy planning function is, again, the seriousness of our commitment to the objectives of anti-poverty and model cities programs. Where mayors and city councils are still wedded to the urban development goals of the recent past—improve the tax base, bring back the middle class—a city hall agency focusing on social policy planning will have little value. It may, in fact, be used as a way of sniping at neighborhood action programs or enmeshing them in reviews and delays. Thus the main prerequisite for establishing social policy planning as an on-going function of city government is a consistency of objectives at city hall and in the poverty areas. Neighborhood pressures from ghettos and poverty areas have helped reorient many programs toward helping the poor. When these pressures are accepted as a basis for city social policy, the time will be ripe for organizing social policy planning close to the mayor.

Where city hall is less committed to social action programs in poverty areas, a planning and technical advisory function should be lodged elsewhere. A city-wide anti-poverty board, for example, can supply planning support for neighborhood councils. Or a university may be the appropriate institution to undertake this function, drawing on its technical skills and its relative freedom of action to give direct help to citizen groups. Still another possibility is for national interest groups, such as civil rights organizations, to establish centers of social planning support and advice in the major cities.

If institutions are established for social policy planning on a continuing basis, the question still remains of what specific technical contributions planners can make to this process. The planning function that has already been organized for one area of social policy—health services—can serve as a useful illustration. In most large cities, some form of planning is under way for the health service system, sponsored by a hospital planning council, health and welfare council, public health department, or state or regional health planning organization. Fifty-five area-wide (county or multi-county) agencies are currently receiving federal grants for comprehensive health planning. When the health planning function is well established, it usually includes surveying existing health services, identifying unmet needs, projecting future needs, and proposing expansions or innovations to meet these needs. Some planning studies deal as well with environmental health, while others focus on specific plans for medical complexes or health services within low-income areas.

In an effort to learn how city planners might contribute to health planning, I recently reviewed the contents of some thirty health plans.[8] They indicated a number of topics of mutual concern to city planners and health planners, some neglected issues that city planners are reasonably well equipped to handle, and several ways in which city planners can contribute to the formulation of social policies dealing with health.

In order to project health service needs, most health plans make some use of information on existing and anticipated community characteristics: population growth and composition, housing conditions, and the economy. Yet a number of locational issues familiar to city planners receive little attention in these health plans: the spatial distribution of future population, changes in the transportation network, changes in travel and access patterns. These characteristics are important for forecasting localized needs for health services and for evaluating locations for health facilities. Further, many area-wide health plans give little consideration to the special characteristics and needs of neighborhood or sub-area populations. City planners can contribute to these aspects of health planning by drawing on their own skills in analzying locational issues, access and travel characteristics, and neighborhood population characteristics.

The same range of city planning methods would be useful for dealing with one of the more troublesome elements of health plans: the delineation of service areas for hospitals and other health facilities. The definition of service areas is important both for projecting bed needs of individual hospitals and for evaluating the access of people to health services. Studies of population distribution, travel patterns, and actual utilization of hos-

---

[8] This survey was conducted as part of a research project sponsored by the National Institutes of Health, "Relationships Between Health Service and Urban Planning," (project CH 00222–01–02) at the M.I.T.–Harvard Joint Center for Urban Studies. The author and William Nash were co-directors of the research project; James Peters was a research assistant working on the survey of health plans.

pitals—all within the scope of conventional city planning—can help to establish which population groups are served by individual hospitals.

City planning experience with the management of a planning process may well be applicable to components of health planning. There is a need for clearer statements of health goals, and for conversion of broad goals to operational targets toward which progress can be measured. There is a need to develop ways of involving citizen groups in health planning decisions. The implementation of health plans poses many problems, some of which are analogous to the implementation of urban development plans when individual development decisions are widely dispersed. In all these respects, recent city planning experience seems relevant to the issues confronting health planners, and there seems little doubt that city planners could contribute effectively as staff members of health planning organizations.

City planners can also support the work of health planning organizations by reorienting some of the work of urban planning agencies toward health issues. For example, health indicators might well be added to other characteristics used for neighborhood analyses, as a way of increasing sensitivity to health problems and helping to set priorities for health service programs. City planning organizations might well work jointly with health agencies to establish housing codes and inspection programs that will reflect special health considerations as well as usual environmental standards. Particular attention might be given, for example, to the elimination of conditions that cause home accidents.

City planners may be able to play a more central role in health service planning if they first become more expert in developing programs that mix environmental with social components. Increasingly, health planning is coming to see hospitals and medical facilities in relationship to communities, not as separate islands where medical care is given. There are significant experiments under way involving home care programs, half-way houses and other after-care facilities in residential neighborhoods, neighborhood clinics, and other programs that require a detailed understanding of the community and an ability to work closely with community groups. The problems are similar to those involved in planning neighborhood improvement and community action programs, and experience with these programs should provide a base for developing applicable planning methods.

Thus the example of health planning suggests that city planners have a background of technical skills and planning experience that will enable them to contribute to the development of social policy, when appropriate social policy planning institutions exist. Initially, city planners can draw on methods of analysis and plan development focusing on the physical environment. These methods will permit the city planner to play a useful but supplementary role in social policy planning. If city planners are to play major roles in these new institutions, they will also have to develop new skills more suited to joint social-environmental issues and to the special institutional context of social policy-making.

E. DAVID STOLOFF

Lecturer on City Planning at Hunter College Graduate School. Formerly planning and housing consultant. Director of Commission on Community Interrelations, American Jewish Congress; Consultant to the Harlem Anti-Poverty Agency; Assistant Director of Jersey City Planning Division. M.A., University of Chicago. Contributing author to recent book entitled *The Great Society Reader*.

Competence to Plan
Social Strategies

A COMMENT ON THE FRIEDEN PAPER

When Bernard Frieden suggests that planning cannot be done in poverty programs and model cities programs because of limited time horizons, politics, and agency opportunism, he implies that these conditions do not exist in other planning situations. Most planners would disagree. It is a constant struggle to get administrators to focus on long-range needs and priorities in physical planning, but it is the planners' clear professional responsibility to keep trying, rather than washing their hands of it as too difficult.

It is easy to read the 1968 Housing Act and conclude that at last the nation has decided to meet the housing needs of the poor. It looked that way in 1949, but it did not work out that way. I do not think things are different now. The Kerner Commission called for 6 million low- and moderate-income units over the next five years. The Housing Act spreads this out over ten years, and the rate of actual appropriations will spread it over a probable twenty-five to thirty years. Thus the real rate might be sufficient to replace the low-rent housing being destroyed by renewal and highway projects, but not much beyond that. There is an enormous gap between rhetoric and performance.

Frieden's paper is wrong in its assessment of the planner's role in social policy planning. Of all the helping professions, planners have the greatest potential for doing the social policy planning jobs of our society. The planners' approach to urban problem solving is essentially relevant and readily transferable to a wide range of issues and problems. However, if we do not recognize this potential and fail to project ourselves into policy planning positions, others who are less qualified and less planning-oriented will assume the responsibility.

Frieden seems to believe that planning skills are only tangentially relevant to the CAP and Model Cities programs, or that there is little planning to be done, and that planners are equipped to play only supplementary roles in social policy planning. He indicates that the practice of planning is too specialized in handling the physical environment to really make any fundamental contribution to social policy planning. If he is right and planners do not change quickly, the planning profession's survival is called into question.

There are only societal issues—not physical and social issues. It may be operationally useful to divide these issues and possible solutions into physical, social, economic, and other aspects. It is true that the planning profession is engrossed with the physical environment, and places too much credence on the assumption that bad environments cause social problems. Its basic methodology and electric approach to knowledge and problem solving, however, gives it special competence to plan the integrated strategies needed today. Comprehensive and integrative approaches are a unique quality of the planning profession.

It is clear that neither the housing specialist, nor the land-use specialist, nor the transportation specialist, nor the health specialist, nor the education specialist, can be considered urban planners in situations where a broad strategy involving some or all of these specialties is called for. There is such a thing as a conflict of interest within the helping professions. The specialist is bound to promote what he knows best and let others provide the countervailing arguments.

There are a number of social planning jobs to be done that professions less well equipped than planning are attempting to do. Planners would be abrogating professional responsibilities to let social policy decisions continue to be the result of the competition between the education, health, recreation, economic development, social work, and other functional specialists and special interests.

Inner city communities are beginning to understand that they cannot expect a suddenly conscience-stricken society to provide redress through an increase in community power and wealth. Communities want expert help in the identification of need and the ordering of priorities, and in the fight with bureaucracy and government for resources to carry out community programs. If planners are going to do that social planning job, they must become involved in a politics of planning. If they recognize that physical and social problems are essentially aspects of community problems, it is then clear that planners must engage in politics directed at community control for community clients. Planners must become advocates everywhere—in agencies at all levels—and activists when they can. If planners follow this advice, they may eventually be able to overcome the well earned distrust that communities have for planning experts.

There is a credibility gap between planners and poor communities. Too many poor and frequently black people have seen their homes replaced by civic or cultural centers, or high-rent housing, while they have been relocated to inferior housing deep inside the ghettos. Sometimes homeowning or middle-income Negroes benefit, but never the poor man.

We hear the anger, frustration, and exasperation of the youth and young men at the insensitiveness of not only the "Downtown Experts" but of the Negroes' the more middle-class-oriented brothers. They tell us that there are winos in the community—and they are people. There are junkies in the community—and they are people. There are crap shooters—and they are people. They are youths on the street, and they are people. Officials and planners pretend they do not *exist!* If we want the poor to believe that the Model Cities programs are real we must show how it will serve *them*.

If planners respond by denying competence to answer such questions, they will be guilty of evasion and will reinforce the communities' distrust. Planners must learn to look at and talk to the people of communities, and learn of the kinds of problems with which they are struggling. If planners have to become education or health or manpower experts to hear and respond, so be it. Planners must help the poor formulate programs that will speak directly to the needs of people; when these programs do not exist, they must invent them. When government does not have funds that can be directed of such innovations, planners must help dramatize needs and participate in strategies to change government response. At such times planning is politics and politics is planning.

This is the basic social planning job that needs to be done in our cities. It will not get done if planners keep functioning as they have been. There are some planners involved in fights for welfare rights, rent strikes, community control of schools—but not many. More must become involved in such ways and begin confronting the social issues facing urban communities.

In addition to becoming advocates and activists, planners must look for opportunities and assert their credentials for the general policy-making positions in human resources, anti-poverty, economic development, and similar programs. They must work with the other professions and social service programs in ways that Frieden outlines, for this not only will strengthen these programs, but add to planners' general knowledge and competence.

The training of planners must be revised so that they will be better equipped to serve as generalists and apply problem-solving skills to societal problems. Curricula need to be shifted in order that graduates view themselves as more than limited specialists and will seize the initiative in taking on more than physical problems.

Most important, planners must develop and extend their role with communities. If they sell their services short (as they have been doing in CAP and the Model Cities programs) and only help community efforts by projecting population and proposing various kinds of physical development programs, they will be doing themselves and the communities a disservice. Alternate plans or critiques of development proposals have their place, but are only a beginning. Planners must help communities evaluate social services—bringing in specialists when necessary—and work to develop strategies to solve community problems, both short- and long-range, involving specific problems as well as comprehensive social issues.

JEROME W. LUBIN

Chief of California Health Information for Planning Ser-
vice, Department of Public Health, State of California.
Formerly city planner for the Hospital Utilization Research
Project; Assistant Director, Syracuse City Planning Com-
mission; Planning Officer for Redevelopment Authority,
Allegheny County, Pittsburgh. B.S.S., City College of New
York; M.C.P., University of California.

Contributions to Social Policy Planning

A COMMENT ON THE FRIEDEN PAPER

The kinds of social factors that Bernard Frieden talks about have always
been a part of planning and the approach of most planners whom I know.
The "social factors" are what planners are trying to affect—even when
dealing with "physical factors." There should be little argument with most
of what Frieden suggests. Many planners feel they have been doing it all
along.

A perspective is required for a discussion of social planning today. We
live in a society that historically does little or no articulated social planning. It is, therefore, not surprising that planners are spending most of their
time on physical factors. This does not mean, however, that social factors
are absent. Local government does not generally have a recognized social
policy function, even as defined in Frieden's paper. Berkeley and San Francisco, which have established social policy planning positions, are the
exceptions.

If we attempt to bypass the city governments in establishing social policy
planning functions, are we not further delaying the time when social policy
planning becomes an on-going reality at the local level? It seems somewhat
unreal to bypass the city administration in establishing social policy planning and then expect that same administration to finance a planning agency
which supports the social policy planners, however indirectly.

299

However much one may disagree with a particular political administration within a community, the political orientation of the elected officials is the only workable guide that we have available. I prefer to trust elections rather than opinion polls or benevolent dictatorships.

Let us put the issue where it belongs. The problem is a general one of making large-scale local government more responsive. If we bypass the administration, we are aiding in avoiding the issue.

In framing programs, we are not studying but rather trying to translate studies into courses of action by the body politic. Frieden is calling for major changes in society and the role of government. Planners can play a role, but over-estimation of the planner's importance will only lead to more frustration, disappointment, and breast-beating within the profession. Political support is required for more effective planning, no matter how defined, and certainly for social planning.

It is common to identify social policy planning as oriented toward an easily identifiable disadvantaged poverty group. But social policy planning, to be generally accepted and effective, should deal explicitly with the needs of many groups within our society. To use the health field as an example, few families could readily afford to pay all of the costs associated either with the full course of treatment preceding and following major heart surgery, or a child born with a genetic defect who will require lifetime care. This is recognized by the distinction, within the health field, of the "medically" indigent as contrasted with the "indigent." In some medical circumstances, all but a small fraction of our population would be considered medically needy.

Frieden makes very valid points about the applicability of city planning techniques to health. There is a history of involvement of city planners in health planning. An outstanding early example is the work at Michael Reese Hospital in Chicago. I commend to your attention the report on the first five years of the program (August 1945 to July 1950) which is available in the *Town Planning Review* for January 1951. This same period of time saw the appearance of *Planning the Neighborhood,* under the sponsorship of the American Public Health Association, written by city planners. Both of the authors are still active in planning and health planning related activities today.

Planners who get involved in health planning should recognize that it is different from community public planning. There are some who feel that there is no consensus yet that there should be health planning. Indeed, some of the people who were involved with health planning during the

1940's have indicated that subsequent noninvolvement was not of their choosing.

Decision-making within the health field is of a decentralized nature. It takes place at the individual facility, at the individual practitioner level. Motivation of institutions and individuals is necessary if planning is going to be effective within the health field.

There are good reasons why physicians, in particular, have been conservative in their acceptance of health planning. Remember, it is an individual physician's signature at the bottom of the medical record. It is his patient who may live or die. He wants the best for his patient at the hospital at which he practices. Too often planning is presented as a means of stopping something rather than as a positive means of better meeting the needs of the physician as well as of the community.

A word about planning hospital service areas. They should be thought of as conveniences, as administrative devices. They are useful when trying to determine the spacing between particular kinds of services. As education theory has been revised in light of today's problems, we have moved from the neighborhood school to the educational park serving a base population in the range of 50,000 or more. The average patient goes to a particular hospital not because he lives near it, but because it is the hospital that his physician feels is best suited to the patient's needs and is available to the physician through admitting or referral privileges.

To be effective, we should decentralize planning. Planners should be in other agencies, both private and public whenever possible in the 314(b) agencies (the area-wide comprehensive health planning agencies). Whenever possible, encourage representation of planners on their governing boards.

If it is necessary to relieve guilt feelings about what some planners may term an "expediency strategy" approach, let us use the new jargon of a "systems approach." In the systems or Operation Research approach, we have the ultimate conceptual model with Mod 1, Mod 2, Mod 3, etc. This allows us to always have a goal at which we are shooting, but also have closer-range targets of something that makes sense and can be achieved within the operating milieu. It also allows us a systematic nonexpedient approach to revising Mod 1 and Mod 2 as change occurs, planned or unplanned.

Increased political support for social planning is needed. This support generally comes as a result of specific benefits for specific groups. Few people, other than planners, support planning per se.

ARCHIBALD C. ROGERS

Architect and Urban Planner, Baltimore, Maryland. Senior Partner, Rogers, Taliaferro, Kostritsky, Lamb. Recipient of Merit Awards from Housing and Home Finance Agency, American Institute of Architects, and National Institute of Homebuilders. Design Projects: Linear City, Brooklyn, N.Y.; Downtown Plan, Dayton, O.; Downtown Plan, Eugene, Ore.; Fountain Square Plaza, Cincinnati. B.A. and M.A. in Architecture, Princeton.

The Planner's Role on the Physical Design Team

The architect has traditionally thought of the design process as essentially artistic—the creation of art from the raw material of present problem and practical solution. The engineer has thought of it in terms of problem solving only—the well solved problem provides the most efficient system, structure, etc., for the least investment. To those outside the profession, the planner has seemed to think of the design process not as a process at all, but rather the natural by-product of the management of the economic, social, and political forces that produce our man-made environment—the design of a mechanism to manage these forces rather than the design of the physical end product of such a mechanism.

Design is all of these.

To design the mechanism that produces an increment of our physical environment is essential to the successful design of that increment; to solve the physical problem well is normally the first duty of the mechanism so designed; to go the final step and to make of the increment a work of art is essential to the fulfillment of the total process; otherwise it is aborted. The professional physical designer, by whatever label known, should encompass the whole process. This is, of course, impossible if one conceives of such a designer as a single individual in the circumstances of today's complex and large-scaled environmental increments.

Thus the evolution of the design team as the author or designer.

The team is not an extension of the traditional individual designer; it is

302

not staff for a flag rank "commander of decision-making"; it is not an hierarchical organization.

The design team, in fact, replaces these as the vehicle for the following:

1. understanding all of the influences that describe the problem to be solved, influences both internal and external;

2. designing and evaluating alternative mechanisms for organizing these influences to accomplish the solution;

3. designing and evaluating alternative solutions for adoption and implementation by this mechanism; and

4. translating the selected solution into the art of architecture.

From the above, it is clear that the design team is *ad hoc* and must be tailored (or designed) to fit the particular mission with which it is charged. Thus it cannot normally be found as a pre-existing entity, although there are many large multi-disciplined organizations who label themselves as design teams both in private practice and in government.

From this, it follows that there must first be a sophisticated *agent-provocateur* or initiator who describes the mission and designs the design team, at least in rough-sketch form. Such an initiator may be a local professional group (the AIA chapters in Baltimore and in San Juan), or a public official (the chairman of the City Planning Commission in New York), or simply a concerned and articulate citizen.

The design team will be large or small depending on the scale of mission. Scale may be thought of in terms of time, physical scope and complexity. A large but simple mission may require a smaller team than does a small but complex one. Its components will include the design disciplines if the mission deals with the physical environment. Also included, as required, are supporting disciplines in sociology, economics, functional programming, systems analysis, etc. While each discipline will describe the problem from its specialized viewpoint and will so evaluate alternative solutions, at the level of synthesis, the team functions as a peer group.

My personal experience in "teamsmanship" has convinced me that the design disciplines have no patent on creativity and that concepts described by mathematicians or economists or lay citizens are often uniquely valuable provided such a nondesigner has been invited to participate fully in the joys and pains of creative synthesis; permitted the time and resources to study the problem as a whole (in addition to his specialized facet); and educated or interpreted so that his description of concept can be truthfully translated to the others on his team.

Most architects and engineers assume the existence of a client as the source of decisions—a public agency, a building committee, an individual patron. It is perhaps the tragedy of the planner that he seems so often to have no client, or at least to have none who can render decisions.

Yet the planner's situation is probably more true to the real world than is that of the architect or engineer.

The architect of a federal building may belatedly discover that the agency signing his contract is not his real client; the real client may prove to be a Congressional sub-committee which controls the purse. The highway engineer may discover that the Bureau of Roads is not its real client as the interest groups affected by the highway render their decisions on his designs in the political or legal forum.

Thus the first step in the design process should be to identify, as part of the initial reconnaissance into the problem, the areas for action that involve specific public and private programs and resources.

When these have been identified, the design team should conduct a second reconnaissance into this spectrum of resources and propose to the initiator the design for a decision-making team to act as the client or sponsor of the work.

Thus the decision-making team is also *ad hoc* and specially tailored to the mission in hand. It may not even involve the iniating agency or the other party to the design team's contract.

The characteristics of those who constitute the decision-making team are the characteristics of power:

1. Authority over an area of action (a public program or a private institution) that can be used in the accomplishment of the mission;

2. Control over the resources within this area of action—not only financial but other resources as well, such as manpower, political support, etc.; and

3. A personal commitment to the mission in hand as an obvious condition precedent to his commitmnet of resources.

The members of the decision-making team, as in the case of the design team, will react to alternatives from their specialized areas of interest—but when all reactions are recorded and all alternatives thoroughly understood and evaluated. Then this team, too, must function as a peer group rendering a fully dimensioned or whole decision upon the whole design alternatives posed by the design team.

The design team must accept the probability that such decisions will represent compromises and must, at each rung of the decision-making ladder, from design objectives to construction, faithfully adhere to these decisions as givens for the next stage of design (even though each prior family of decisions must be re-evaluated as more detailed design alternatives are posed for decision).

The decision-making team must recognize that each decision represents a commitment to implement at some stage in the process.

Both the design and decision-making teams must have confidence that the decisions on which concept is based are, in fact, for real. The only way that this assurance can be given is the immediate ratification of decisions by the ultimate holders of power.[1]

This requires that public agency heads and private institutions, receiving recommendations from their representatives on the decision-making team, formally ratify these recommendations in whatever legal form is appropriate. This in turn requires that the agency head delegate real power to his representative on the team so that decisions are referred upward to the head for ratification—not for ex post facto review and amendment. This is the toughest stumbling block, due to the defensive and authoritarian nature of most governmental agencies—and some private institutions.

This also requires that the agency representative maintain continuing liaison with his superiors to be sure of his backing when he renders decisions, and to be sure that his superiors thoroughly understand the alternatives being considered.

There is, however, the ultimate ratifier behind such private or public officials—namely, the citizenry. And, therefore, decisions must also be ratified by the general public, within the area affected by the mission, at each step of the design process.

This is the most important, as well as the most difficult, aspect of the decision-making process. This public in most cities is now quite sophisticated; quite "anti-establishment;" and somewhat cynical. Its attitude is:

1. That of assuming it will be told what is proposed only after all decisions are taken and the design dinner cooked;

2. That the style of telling will be that of a public relations program to "sell" the decisions, perhaps seasoned with a public hearing or two announced in miniature legal notices buried in the local paper;

3. That public hearings themselves are quite pointless since the agency involved acts as convenor, judge, and promoter (no alternatives are re-

---

[1] In applying this concept to the downtown plan for Cincinnati, decisions taken by the Working Review Committee were immediately acted on by the City Plan Board and then by the City Council in the form of municipal ordinances.

viewed; opponents are argued down; all voters not present are recorded in favor); and

4. That the establishment (i.e., the holders of public and private powers) is the enemy and that "advocacy planning" is called for to defeat this enemy each time a positive proposal is advanced (and that is, therefore, "adversary planning").

To achieve ratification by such a public requires the following:

1. That the public be fully informed of all alternatives being considered and all decisions taken, from the beginning to the end of the process. This can be achieved by holding all presentations in public with anyone permitted to appear and be heard; by thoroughly educating the media as to the mission and the process; by the media publicly reporting all stages of the process; by a public relations program used as part of the education of media and of the public.

2. That the public be made aware of the fundamental alternatives which attend any mission involving an increment of the physical environment:

    a. Alternative (1) to abort the mission by public veto of official proposals, since the public can exercise its power negatively but cannot substitute positive action since this requires the power vested in the establishment;

    b. Alternative (2) to acquiesce in the mission as an alternative to veto; and

    c. Alternative (3) to participate positively in the mission so as to shape it to the best advantage and least disadvantage of the public community.

3. That, assuming Alternative (3), this public must be questioned at the very start as to its goals, problems, and opportunities. This requires a sympathetic group of inquirers on the design team and a sophisticated interpretation of the answers received, for the ostensible answer and the true answer are often different. The public must be questioned at each stage of the process as to its reaction to alternatives pending before the decision-making team. This again requires sympathy and interpretative expertise.

4. That the public must be directly involved—hopefully in a structured way—in the design and decision-making process. This involvement can be achieved by

    a. The self-design and establishment of a community team—to appoint such a team ex cathedra is generally fatal;

b. The requirement that the design team and decision-making team function from offices within the geographic area affected by the mission; and

c. That, at least in distressed inner city areas, the design team employ a significant number of local residents—not *qualified* local residents, for there are none—as apprentices for all disciplines involved on the team.

The above four-point program may work—although as an experiment it has hardly yet been tested—so that the decision-makers and designers are enlightened as to the true needs of the community involved; so that the community sees in the apprenticeship program benefits from the process itself, quite apart from the benefits assumed from the distant accomplishment of the mission; so that the community feels it has a stake in the mission and in its successful accomplishment since it has helped shape the mission through day-to-day contact with the design team and through formal dialogue with the decision-making team.

Experience does prove that an individual or group involved in decision-making becomes committed to the implementation of its decisions.

The above description requires the establishment of a three-legged development team—or team of teams—with each team playing its prescribed role.

The role of the design team is to understand the problem; to imagine its alternative solutions; to initiate proposals for action by the decision-making team.

The role of the decision-making team is to evaluate alternatives; to decide among alternatives; to implement its decisions.

The role of the community team is to understand its public constituency; to articulate the goals, problems, and opportunities of this constituency; to enlighten the designer's understanding and the decision-maker's evaluation.

The role of the total three-legged team is to use the design process—design that will produce a palpable artifact—to manage change. And this aspect of design is little understood by any of the design disciplines, with the exception of the planners.

Applied to the totality of our physical environment, a totality produced by the sensitive development of its increments, this mechanism and process holds out hope of producing a humane, adaptable, and relevant urban architecture.

Without such an approach, the prediction must be that planners will continue to "plan" relevant projects that will not be implemented; that engineers will continue to "engineer" functional artifacts doing perhaps more damage than is justified by their benefits; that architects will continue to "design" art works (or sculpture) disconnected from and irrelevant to the life that indwells these works.

And so, at last to the subject of this paper—the role of the planner in the design team.

Since the planner is a designer, as is the architect, engineer, and landscape architect, his primary role is to design—at all points in the process.

He may or may not head the team, and a head is necessary for administrative purposes. But leadership of the team will be assigned not by discipline but by quality of the individual, whether he be a designer or not. The fact that design teams have originated in connection with the Interstate Highway Program, for example, does not foreordain that an engineer will head the team, unless his individual characteristics justify this.

His primary role may well be that of the futurist or manager of change, a role which he now plays but which is generally insignificant because of the lack of a mechanism for implementing his concepts.

The three-legged development team provides him with such a mechanism.

Yet the end purpose of each incremental addition to our environment should be understood as art; and the architect, despite his training, is not the artist in the team. It is the team itself which is the artist.

And so we look to the mystery of art and try to understand this as our end objective.

There is a parable, going back a thousand years, attributable to Chuang-tzu, the Chinese philosopher. While I don't know what carpenters did in those days, apparently the carpenter in the court of the king made music stands. The king said that his stands were so beautiful that there must be something supernatural about the process—the *process,* mind you—through which they were produced. And the carpenter said, "No, my Lord, there is nothing supernatural about this. Being a good Taoist, I first fast for several days, then I spend several days in the proper pose examining my navel, and then I wander into the woods. And I talk to the trees, and the trees talk to me. And then a tree speaks to me as to the music stand which I have in my mind. I take that tree and I release from it the form which lies within it. You see, there is nothing supernatural about it." Of course, there is everything supernatural about it.

But this in capsule form is the nature of our calling. And so, as we look into the practical problem and strive for its practical solution, at some point it speaks to us; we at that point must be able to release the "art" which lies within it.

I believe that all art as a process is the same. Don Bragg, when he won the Gold Medal at the Rome Olympics, was asked a rather stupid question to which he gave a rather ungrammatical answer: "Mr. Bragg, how do you succeed in your chosen field as a pole vaulter?" He answered, "Well, each time before I jump, first I pray, then I think, than I 'guts it out.' " And this is a pretty clear statement, you see, of the artistic process. First you must pray, understand, contemplate your navel if you will; and into the exhaustion of mind and spirit that occurs if you really search, if you rally try to understand, comes often by intuition—the concept. Then, of course, comes the need to "guts it out"—to act, to execute, to initiate.

This holds true for the musician, for the architect, for the planner. It is unfortunate, in my own profession of architecture, that so many of us do not put this threesome together. There are many of us who want to be great designers. We are bored with trying to understand, so we short-circuit that part of the process and get right to the business of designing. Others are bored with executing. We are content with the pretty picture, and whether it is built or not is immaterial. And this short-circuiting is fatal if we speak of environmental design in its final physical form as a means of artistic communion.

Art is not icing on the cake; not something which, as an affluent society, we can finally afford. Art is a very essential and fundamental thing. It is a form of communion between eternity and time. Maritain speaks of the mysterious language of art, which he calls Poetry. And this language is certainly as true of architecture and planning, as it is of music and poetry.

Art then is the offspring of a wedding between time and eternity.

If this is so, one should see the characteristics of the parents in art. I do not suggest that this is a definition of good art versus bad art but rather the characteristics of art versus nonart. On the temporal side, one can identify four characteristics. First integrity, by which I do not mean honesty—merely that you cannot easily add to or subtract from the concept. Then power—power to move you, to move you to hate or to love. But power. Third is individuality. The art work is unique, even from the hand of the same artist. Finally the fourth characteristic, comprehendability. The human mind must be able to encompass the concept, the idea. And I believe a psychologist would say that these four characteristics describe the human animal, the healthy human animal. Because at rock bottom there is integrity, or he is fractured and in an asylum. There is power, clearly. There is uniqueness, since none of us is like any other who has been or is or will be. And we are comprehendable one to another.

But this describes only the vessel. Within this vessel flows the language of eternity—Poetry—the characteristic of the other parent.

If this really is art, it is a form of incarnation, a form of communion. It has a meaning and a purpose. The artist therefore is not properly a great hero, but an empty conduit and a servant, a listener and understander. And his work of art stands after him for the expression of this language. The result is communion between eternity and those who indwell that which we leave as our physical environment.

Art, thought of in this way, is all important; and of all the arts, those that deal with the physical environment are the most important. Because a book you can open or close, a library you can enter or pass by, but our environment is with us always, for better or for worse. As an optimist, I hope it will be for better.

Index

An alphabetical list of the titles of all papers in the Contents appears under the entry Articles and Comments.

This book was set on the linotype in Times Roman.
The display type is Optima.
The paper is Natural White Bookmark Offset.
Composition, printing, and binding is by
H. Wolff Book Manufacturing Company, Inc., New York City.
Designed by Jacqueline Schuman.